# Kettlebell
# Training

## Steve Cotter

**HUMAN KINETICS**

**Library of Congress Cataloging-in-Publication Data**

Cotter, Steve, 1970-
 Kettlebell training / Steve Cotter.
    pages cm
1.  Kettlebells. 2.  Weight training.  I. Title.
 GV547.5.C68 2013
 613.713--dc23
                              2013013814

ISBN-10: 1-4504-3011-2 (print)
ISBN-13: 978-1-4504-3011-1 (print)

This publication is written and published to provide accurate and authoritative information relevant to the subject matter presented. It is published and sold with the understanding that the author and publisher are not engaged in rendering legal, medical, or other professional services by reason of their authorship or publication of this work. If medical or other expert assistance is required, the services of a competent professional person should be sought.

The web addresses cited in this text were current as of August 2013, unless otherwise noted.

**Acquisitions Editor:** Tom Heine; **Developmental Editor:** Laura Pulliam; **Assistant Editor:** Elizabeth Evans; **Copyeditor:** Alisha Jeddeloh; **Graphic Designer:** Joe Buck; **Cover Designer:** Keith Blomberg; **Photograph (cover):** © Tono Balaguer/easyFotostock; **Photographs (interior):** © Human Kinetics; **Visual Production Assistant:** Joyce Brumfield; **Photo Production Manager:** Jason Allen; **Printer:** United Graphics

We thank Grinder Gym in San Diego, California, for assistance in providing the location for the photo shoot for this book.

Human Kinetics books are available at special discounts for bulk purchase. Special editions or book excerpts can also be created to specification. For details, contact the Special Sales Manager at Human Kinetics.

Printed in the United States of America     10 9 8 7 6 5 4 3 2 1

The paper in this book is certified under a sustainable forestry program.

**Human Kinetics**
Website: www.HumanKinetics.com

*United States:* Human Kinetics
P.O. Box 5076
Champaign, IL 61825-5076
800-747-4457
e-mail: humank@hkusa.com

*Canada:* Human Kinetics
475 Devonshire Road Unit 100
Windsor, ON N8Y 2L5
800-465-7301 (in Canada only)
e-mail: info@hkcanada.com

*Europe:* Human Kinetics
107 Bradford Road
Stanningley
Leeds LS28 6AT, United Kingdom
+44 (0) 113 255 5665
e-mail: hk@hkeurope.com

*Australia:* Human Kinetics
57A Price Avenue
Lower Mitcham, South Australia 5062
08 8372 0999
e-mail: info@hkaustralia.com

*New Zealand:* Human Kinetics
P.O. Box 80
Torrens Park, South Australia 5062
0800 222 062
e-mail: info@hknewzealand.com

E5718

This work is dedicated to my wife, Samantha, a most amazing and beautiful woman, the love of my life, and the person who drives me to be a better man in everything that I do; to my precious children, Rileigh, Elizabeth, and Daniel, who give me great pride for the wonderful people they have become; to my students, who inspire me to share my gifts and experience with the world; and to you, dear reader, without whom this work would have no purpose.

# Contents

# Foreword

The date was September 18, 2004. I was driving to my Brazilian jiujitsu (BJJ) school in Walled Lake, Michigan, to attend a kettlebell seminar with Steve Cotter. Earlier that week, I had seen a picture of Steve in a book doing a one-legged squat (pistol) with two 70-pound (32 kg) kettlebells. Crazy athleticism, world-class martial arts skills, and innovative views on fitness and coaching—I thought training with him would be awesome but somewhat of an impossibility due to him being in San Diego and me being in Michigan. Two days later, I noticed a flyer at our BJJ school that he was flying in to teach. Two days after that, I was training with him.

This stream of events changed my life and became a theme for my experiences with Steve. There are no impossibilities, and with the right thinking and attitude, you can manifest almost anything. Steve is much more than a great athlete. He transcends that by being a phenomenally gifted communicator, coach, and teacher. It's no surprise that since the afore-mentioned date, Steve has traveled all over the world teaching thousands of people and inspir-ing them in a similar fashion. I'm proud and honored to have him as a mentor, and I know countless others feel the same.

In this book, you have the rarity of a truly comprehensive reference source. Most fitness books and products tease with incomplete infor-mation so you will be locked into a never-ending purchasing loop of sequels, repeats, and so on. That is not the case here. Steve has taken a lot of time and effort in ensuring you get the whole picture and not just a snapshot of kettlebell lifting. You get the exercises, the progressions, the variations, the programming, and so much more.

Enjoy your journey! You have chosen an excel-lent navigator in Steve to take your knowledge, wellness, and performance to the next level!

*Ken Blackburn*
*IKFF international team leader, head master*
*trainer, and director of kettlebell competitions*

# Acknowledgments

I am a firm believer that there is a time to be a student and a time to be a teacher. There is a saying that when the student is ready, the teacher will appear. This principle has guided me in my own professional development over the years, sometimes as a student and sometimes as a teacher. In this fast-paced, instant-gratification world most of us operate in, it is easy to lose track of where we came from. The martial artist in me has always had a profound respect and appreciation for the traditional arts and their history. Behind every great student has been an effective teacher and behind every great athlete has been one or more effective coaches. One cannot truly understand all there is to learn without first understanding the work that came before us and that brings us to our current state of knowledge.

As such, it is an honor for me to thank the various kettlebell teachers I have learned from over the years of study, practice, and teaching of kettlebell lifting. In no specific order, I wish to acknowledge the following kettlebell instructors I have had the pleasure of interacting with and learning from in various stages of my development: Pavel Tsatsouline, Valery Fedorenko, Dmitri Sateav, Pantalei Filikidis, Oleh Ilica, Sergei Rudnev, Sergei Merkulin, Dr. Vladamir Tikhinov, Ken Blackburn, and Arsenij Zhernakov. In addition, before I ever picked up my first kettlebell, I was introduced to the Chinese martial arts and the art of teaching by my first physical training instructor, Sifu Mike Patterson, and later from the great Grandmaster Kao San Lun. In my life as a fitness professional, I would be remiss without mentioning my dear friend David Weck, inventor of the BOSU balance trainer and the WeckMethod, who has had a profound impact on my understanding of movement development and human potential. All of you, in one way or another, have taught me things of value and for that I am thankful.

Similarly and even more important to me is to acknowledge that behind every great work is a great team to support it and help nurture it along. My wife, Samantha, is my partner and whatever good I have accomplished is inspired by her love. Whatever I may achieve in life, nothing can ever make me prouder than being a father to my beautiful, talented, adventurous children, Rileigh, Elizabeth, and Daniel.

Special thanks to my friend Dave Depew, for making his excellent Grinder Gym in San Diego available for the photo shoot and to the outstanding models Alice Nguyen, John Parker and Cameron Yuen. There would be no finished work, without the professional guidance of the Human Kinetics team, editors Laura Pulliam and Tom Heine and our cameraman, Neil Bernstein.

Lastly, if an art form is to survive the generations of time, there must be a transmission of knowledge and experience from one generation to the next. In this spirit, I acknowledge the many students around the world with whom I have had the honor and pleasure of sharing my knowledge, experience, and method of kettlebell lifting.

# Introduction

In the last few years, there has been a significant increase in the popularity of kettlebells and kettlebell sport, a previously little-known fitness tool and ethnic sport originating from Russia. Athletes, coaches, personal trainers, fitness enthusiasts, and busy professionals looking to accomplish a lot of exercise in a short amount of time have all gravitated toward this remarkable all-in-one fitness method that seamlessly combines strength training, cardiorespiratory conditioning, core stabilization, coordination, and dynamic mobility into one intense workout. This rapid growth in interest and the associated emerging industry of professional kettlebell trainers that it has spawned necessitates a clear, concise book to explain the what, why, and how of kettlebells and to guide new users through safe and effective kettlebell training practice. This book, *Kettlebell Training*, provides the necessary information and technical expertise to lead you through this invigorating form of fitness training.

A fundamental component of kettlebell training is the use of this fitness tool to work the entire body as a functional unit. Unlike bodybuilding protocols that isolate muscle groups and train them independently, kettlebell training takes a more athletic approach and integrates the mind and body together. Most of the kettlebell exercises are performed while standing and train the movements along with the muscles. They work multiple joints in multiple planes of motion. As such, it is important to have a clear understanding of the training method and safe biomechanics of this dynamic movement system.

*Kettlebell Training* begins by introducing kettlebells as an ideal fitness solution in the busy modern world we live in. Instead of working individual components of fitness independently as is the traditional approach for gym-goers, with kettlebells you will combine such fitness goals as muscle toning, cardiorespiratory conditioning, muscular stamina, fat loss, and increased strength and power simultaneously due to the comprehensive, holistic nature of kettlebell training. Further, you will increase the general fitness attributes of agility, balance, coordination, strength, power, and endurance. If ever there were an all-in-one fitness program, kettlebell training is it!

Kettlebells have a unique design that makes them different in form and practice from the more widely known barbell and dumbbell. A brief explanation is given of the history of kettlebells, describing how they have come to take their place as a legitimate force in strength training methods alongside the other bells.

Before undertaking a serious training program, you need a thorough education regarding the main principles associated with this method of strength and conditioning training. This book looks at such variables as training frequency, load, volume, intensity, and duration; how to accomplish progressive resistance; ways to train the various energy systems of the body; and the general and specific skills involved in kettlebell lifting. Along with the training principles is a discussion of rest and recovery during your program and how to allow for this important factor.

Once you have a clear view of the benefits of kettlebell training, you are ready to start your program. The first step is to identify your personal fitness or sport goals, and you will receive guidance on how to set up a program in accordance with your goals. With your goals clarified, you are ready to go for it! Of course you want to accomplish your goals free of pain and injury, and therefore a discussion about injury prevention and safe practice is presented. A thorough section on warm-ups and cool-downs is included, because proper preparation and recovery are important components for reducing the likelihood of suffering injuries during intense physical exercise. Some common-sense tips about nutrition and hydration are also included in an appendix so that you can get the most out of your kettlebell training program.

The kettlebell exercises are organized under the main categories of basic, intermediate, and advanced. For each exercise, after an introduction is given, common errors are highlighted and key principles are reinforced. As you progress from basic exercises onward, this organization will help you to transition easily from one exercise to the next.

Armed with a virtual encyclopedia of kettlebell exercises, you will find the programming chapters in this book to be invaluable. Whether your specific goals are oriented more toward general fitness objectives such as fat loss and overall strength and endurance or you are a coach or athlete interested in kettlebell training for supplementary conditioning for your sport, you will find the programming guidance you need in these chapters.

If you are new to kettlebell training, welcome to the world of kettlebells! Get ready for a fun, intense way of moving and exercising. After beginning kettlebell training, you may well find that you have become fitter, stronger, and healthier than ever before. If you already have experience with kettlebells, this book will serve as a valuable resource to help you update your training and refine your understanding of kettlebell program design. Now let's begin your journey with *Kettlebell Training*!

# THE KETTLEBELL ADVANTAGE

What if I told you that you can reach all of your fitness goals by exercising just 30 minutes or less per day, 3 to 4 days per week, with only one inexpensive tool in the comfort of your own home or office? What if you could get the full benefits of an all-in-one exercise program without fancy equipment, awful-tasting and costly supplements, or expensive gym memberships? Well, you can, and this book will show you how. Welcome to *Kettlebell Training*, the book about the all-in-one, handheld gym called a *kettlebell*!

The fitness and strength and conditioning communities have come a long way in the last two decades. Not so long ago, our knowledge about fitness and training was limited to bodybuilding-based shaping programs, which often leave you feeling stiff and sore afterward; the long, slow, distance training methods such as jogging and cycling and other time-consuming aerobic-based conditioning programs that work the heart and lungs but do not strengthen the rest of your body; and the crowded, high-impact group exercise programs that are often tough on the knees, hips, and back and that can be frustrating for out-of-shape exercisers trying to keep up with the energetic instructor. To make matters even more difficult, most of these popular options for fitness training are one-dimensional, emphasizing strength, muscle toning, or cardiorespiratory fitness but rarely combining these important components into a comprehensive package. In addition, by focusing on one form over another, it is not possible to build a well-rounded athletic body. You wouldn't want a car that looks great but doesn't drive or that drives well but is an eyesore. You want a stylish, high-performance car that makes you feel good while driving it. The same is true for your body, and the time you invest in your fitness program should give you a body that performs as well as it looks and that makes you feel good!

In the last 10 years, a wave of new information has entered the fitness landscape, thanks in large part to the increase in globalization and information exchange among cultures. For example, if you are around 35 years of age, when you look back to the exercise culture of your teenage years, the fitness role models came from the bodybuilding culture symbolized by the great Arnold Schwarzenegger, the TV aerobics programs first popularized by Jane Fonda, and eventually the popular Tae Bo kickboxing series and the running craze initiated by the Cooper Institute and *The Complete Book of Running*, the successful book on running by Jim Fixx. We did not have a lot of information about how to train and how to reach our full physical and athletic potential. It was more about following the popular trends and hoping to find a program that you could stick with long enough to see results. Unless you were able to spend your days in the gym, the majority of people didn't have the time or knowledge to get into peak physical fitness.

But now we have access to the secrets of yoga from Indian culture, martial arts from East Asia, and strength and conditioning and athletic preparation from the former Soviet Union and Eastern Bloc countries. We can now use the best training information from around the world. Much of this information has been in practice for ages, yet we never had access to it. This recent influx of time-tested fitness tools and programs has created a new trend in how we approach exercise and fitness training.

## WHAT ARE KETTLEBELLS?

Ten years ago, no one outside of the former Soviet Union knew what a kettlebell was, let alone had ever seen or touched one. Now it seems almost every personal trainer is using kettlebells with his fitness classes and clients. What does the kettlebell training do so effectively that other training methods do not? To answer this, it is helpful to make a comparison between kettlebells and the other more recognizable bells, the dumbbell and the barbell (see figure 1.1).

Kettlebells have a unique design that sets them apart in form and practice from the more widely known barbell and dumbbell. *Kettlebell* comes from the Russian word *girya*, a cast-iron weight that resembles a cannonball with a handle. It is the configuration of the handle with the ball that makes kettlebell training unique. Though in the West the term *kettlebell* is used to describe this weight implement, a more precise translation would be *handleball*, and that is really what a kettlebell is, a ball with a handle.

Unlike traditional dumbbells, the center of mass of the kettlebell is extended beyond the hand.

This configuration allows ballistic, or fast, swinging motions that combine cardiorespiratory, strength, and flexibility training and that engage the entire musculature of the body all at once. In addition to being excellent for all-around fitness, these types of movements mimic functional activities such as shoveling snow or working in the garden.

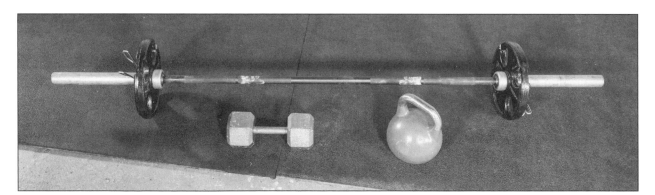

**Figure 1.1**  Comparison of a kettlebell, a dumbbell, and a barbell.

## KETTLEBELL HISTORY

Kettlebells have their origin in ancient Russia, where importance was placed on physical strength. The first recorded mention of the word *girya*, meaning a traditional Russian weight made of cast iron, was in a 1704 Russian dictionary. At that time kettlebells were used as counterweights in the local markets of farming villages. Russian farm workers discovered that the girya could be used as a fitness tool. As a pastime, contests were held in remote villages and nearby towns.

A 1913 article in the popular *Hercules* fitness magazine increased the recognition of kettlebells as a powerful tool for weight loss. By the 1940s, kettlebell lifting became the national sport of the Soviet Union. Powerlifters, Olympic athletes, and military personnel all benefited from lifting kettlebells. By the 1960s, kettlebell lifting had been introduced in schools and universities. In the 1970s, the sport became part of the United All State Sport Association of the USSR, but there were not yet any official rules or standards.

Finally, in 1985 a committee for the sport of kettlebell lifting was created, and kettlebell sport (also known as *girevoy sport*, the Russian name for kettlebell sport) was officially a formal sport with competitive rules and regulations. That year the first USSR national kettlebell championship was held in Russia. Today, kettlebells are used all over the world throughout all realms of athletics, martial arts, and general fitness training. There are no accurate statistics that show exactly how many people are using kettlebells in homes, gyms, and sport clubs around the world, but we do know that in the last few years the number has been increasing. For example, in the 2012 International Kettlebell and Fitness Federation (IKFF) National Kettlebell Championships, there were 175 registered competitors who lifted kettlebells.

# KETTLEBELLS FOR FUNCTIONAL FITNESS

In recent years, a new way of training our bodies has emerged, called *functional fitness* and *functional training*. Functional training combines both modern and ancient advances in physical conditioning with neuroscience in order to address the body as a functional whole rather than a collection of parts. In other words, these cutting-edge training programs no longer teach us to exercise individual muscles or even muscle groups, but rather they train the movements and motor patterns that give us effective movement. Instead of just being aesthetically based, like the popular bodybuilding programs of yore, today's functional fitness programs focus on performance. And by focusing on performance, they also build a healthy and beautiful body.

Your body can be accurately described as a kinetic, or movement, chain. Like a chain, the body consists of a series of interconnected links. These links form a system of levers composed of the joints and the muscles, bones, nerves, and connective tissues that work with the joints to produce effective movement. The functional fitness approach recognizes your body as an integrated whole, and its tools work your whole body and not just individual muscles.

It is an exciting time in fitness, and among the various tools and programs that are used in functional training programs, there is one tool that is leading the way. It shines the brightest as the single method that delivers the most bang for your buck—the kettlebell.

Kettlebell training has two primary uses or goals. First, there is kettlebell training to increase fitness and function by using a wide variety of movements along different planes, using varied repetitions, and working all body parts. Kettlebell training for fitness offers an almost unlimited variety of movements and programs to choose from, and the duration can be as short or long as you prefer. Second, there is training for kettlebell competition, which involves trying to perform as many repetitions as possible in a fixed time frame. Traditional competition lifts are the kettlebell jerk with one or two kettlebells, snatch with one kettlebell, and long cycle or clean and jerk with one or two kettlebells. Most competitions are 10 minutes long, but there are also 3- and 5-minute sprint competitions, marathons of continuous lifting for 1 hour or more, and team relays. Being competitive in kettlebell sport requires a high level of conditioning and well-rounded strength, aerobic capacity, and flexibility.

# WHY KETTLEBELLS?

When it comes to your fitness training, why should the kettlebell be your tool of choice among the myriad of options available to you? After all, your time is precious, and with so many options, how can you be sure that the kettlebell is the best answer to your fitness needs?

What makes the kettlebell so special, and why is kettlebell training the ideal solution for your fitness objectives?

## Practical

First of all, kettlebells are practical, because they work more than just one physical attribute, such as strength or cardiorespiratory fitness. Kettlebells combine the benefits of muscle toning, cardiorespiratory conditioning, and muscular endurance, leading to increased strength and power, improved flexibility and range of motion, fat loss, increased lean muscle mass, reduced stress, and increased confidence! No other tool does so many things simultaneously.

## Versatile

The versatility of the kettlebell as a strength and conditioning tool is without parallel. The deep eccentric loading that occurs when you swing the kettlebell between your legs develops a powerful hip thrust extension that is fundamental to all kinds of athletic movements, including running, jumping, squatting, lunging, and kicking, and it strengthens and shapes the gluteal muscles, developing a healthy lower back and giving your posterior a nice, rounded shape. Its offset center of gravity maximizes shoulder strength and flexibility. Its rounded handle and dynamic movement patterns develop remarkable hand, grip, and forearm strength. A strong back is a healthy back, and the kettlebell works every conceivable angle of your back both statically and dynamically. The handle shape and position allow you to pass the kettlebell from hand to hand in virtually unlimited juggling patterns, something no other type of bell allows.

## Unique

As mentioned earlier, kettlebells are unique. They are not the same shape and do not have the same properties as the more widely known barbells or dumbbells, which are also fantastic exercise tools but are not as versatile as kettlebells. The kettlebell design of a ball with a handle allows the user to do not only traditional weightlifting maneuvers, such as the press, clean and jerk, snatch, and squat, but also unorthodox skills, such as kettlebell juggling. Because the load of the ball is in front of the handle, unlike in a dumbbell, where the load is in line with the handle, even the most basic kettlebell movements cause you to work through a larger range of motion, increasing the flexibility and mobility demands of the exercise. For example, you cannot swing a barbell between your legs, but you can do so with a kettlebell. This swinging extensively increases the range of motion that you can exercise your hips through, increasing flexibility and recruiting muscle fibers you didn't even know you had.

## Inexpensive

Fortunately, it is easy to get started with kettlebell training. Kettlebells are inexpensive, do not require a lot of space to use, and are convenient.

A single kettlebell costs less than $100, and with a few hundred dollars you can outfit your entire home gym with enough kettlebells to progress in your fitness goals for many years. Because they are made of steel or cast iron, you will never have to replace them—they will last a lifetime. Kettlebells are an all-in-one handheld gym, and because they are portable, training can take place indoors or outdoors; in your home, office, or garage; or if you prefer, the gym or local park. There is almost no limit to where you can train with kettlebells.

## Fun

Kettlebell training is fun, and not just because you get results quickly. Usually when people use a kettlebell for the first time, once they catch their breath, the first words out of their mouth exclaim how different kettlebell training is from anything they have ever done before. Kettlebells demand full engagement of the body and mind!

## Efficient

Kettlebell training is efficient. If an effective tool is one that gets the job done, an efficient tool is one that gets the job done in less time, and that is what kettlebell training is all about. Because kettlebell training combines the benefits of strength training, anaerobic and aerobic cardio-respiratory training, and flexibility and mobility, you will never again have to spend hours each week moving from weight training to aerobic training to stretching. With kettlebell training, you do it all at the same time, which means you have more time to spend with your loved ones and in other important aspects of your life.

## Athletic

Finally, kettlebell training is athletic. It is not just a way to build your body but also a way to build your skills. Even if you do not feel you are an athlete, with kettlebell training you will learn to move like one. Kettlebell training will help you to develop all the major athletic attributes, including strength, power, mobility, balance, agility, coordination, endurance, and stamina, which are integrated using this simple but highly effective training system.

Kettlebell training is one of the most exciting exercise methods ever to be used in fitness and sport conditioning. If you are serious about improving your health, fitness, and physical performance by losing fat and building a lean, functional body, kettlebell training is for you!

This book will be your practical guide for effective exercise with kettlebells by arming you with the knowledge you need to progress safely. Basic, intermediate, and advanced exercises and sample kettlebell training programs will provide you with the education necessary to help you develop all-around strength, flexibility, conditioning, and mobility. With this book, you have all the knowledge you need to make serious changes in your fitness. No more excuses, no more limitations. Now you are ready to get started with the kettlebell advantage!

# GETTING STARTED WITH KETTLEBELLS

Kettlebell training has captivated fitness enthusiasts around the world because it incorporates so many important physical characteristics into a single workout with a single tool. Strength, power, endurance, and mobility are all challenged with kettlebell training. Before starting your own kettlebell training program, it's necessary for you to have a complete introduction to the tool and method of training. You need to know what types of kettlebells are available and what is the best choice for you, how to purchase kettlebells, what to wear during training, and where you can train. This chapter provides the information you need to begin your kettlebell training with confidence.

## TYPES OF KETTLEBELLS

There are two common types of kettlebells: the cast-iron classic, or fitness kettlebell and the steel competition, or sport kettlebell. In spite of their names, the competition kettlebell can be used for fitness goals and the classic bell can be used for competition.

### Cast-Iron Classic Kettlebell

The cast-iron classic, or fitness, kettlebell, as shown in figure 2.1, is a less expensive type of kettlebell because it is easier to make. The material is solid and will last for years or even a lifetime. Classic kettlebells are great for general fitness because unless you are very advanced, you will not be doing hundreds of repetitions without stopping, so the precision of the kettlebell is not as important as it is for the competitive lifter. Cast-iron kettlebells are made using molds of various sizes. The heavier the kettlebell, the larger it is. For example, an 8-kilogram (18 lb) classic kettlebell will have a small ball or body and a thin handle. A 32-kilogram (71 lb) kettlebell, on the other hand, will be similar in dimensions to a competition kettlebell. When training with kettlebells for general fitness, kettlebell dimensions do not matter as much as they do in competitions, which you will learn about in the next section. For a competitive kettlebell athlete, these varying sizes are not ideal because every time you use a kettlebell of a different size, the position of the kettlebell in your hand and against your body will be slightly different, making it harder to build consistent technique. But for general fitness, this difference will not be as noticeable as you will be starting with 10, 15, 20, or 30 reps at a time, not 50, 80, or 100 reps. Another advantage of the cast-iron kettlebells is that they are a bit less expensive than competition kettlebells and are still plenty sturdy, so they are a good investment considering cost, quality, and performance.

**Figure 2.1** Cast-iron classic kettlebells.

## Competition Kettlebell

The competition, or sport, kettlebell, as shown in figure 2.2, is also the international standard of measurement and design for kettlebell training and sport. Though kettlebell lifting is only about 10 years old in most of the Western world and Asia, in Eastern Europe and particularly in Russia, kettlebell training has evolved into a high-level competitive sport. As with all sports, there are standardized equipment and rules. Kettlebell experts looked at design and performance and came up with measurements that are best suited for performance. All competitive kettlebell lifters train and compete with standardized kettlebells.

The competition kettlebell is made of steel and is hollow. Aside from being made from steel and thus more expensive than types made from less expensive materials, the competition kettlebell has a universal design and measurement:

- Height—228 millimeters (8.5 in.)
- Diameter—210 millimeters (8.25 in.)
- Handle diameter—35 millimeters (1.4 in.)

The dimensions of the kettlebell do not change regardless of the weight. For example, an 8-kilogram (18 lb) competition kettlebell will be the same exact dimensions (within a specified standard margin of error) as a 16-kilogram (35 lb), 32-kilogram (71 lb), or even a 48-kilogram (106 lb) kettlebell. The size of the kettlebell does not change no matter how heavy or light the kettlebell is. This is made possible by using a mold that is hollow on the inside. A light kettlebell such as 8 kilograms will be made from aluminum and will be hollow inside. As the kettlebell becomes heavier, heavier metals are used and the inside is filled to equal the desired weight of the kettlebell. So the difference between an 8-kilogram and a 48-kilogram kettlebell is that an 8-kilogram kettlebell will be completely hollow inside and a 48-kilogram kettlebell will be made of steel filled with solid lead on the inside. Weights heavier than 48 kilograms can also be specially made for advanced lifters, but in order to keep the standard dimensions, a very heavy metal has to be used and the cost becomes high. Because the different weights are all the same size, a color code is used so that athletes can quickly recognize what weight each kettlebell is instead of having to glance at the number.

The universal dimensions are important because it is necessary to have a standard size in order to develop precise technique. In kettlebell sport an athlete may lift the kettlebell 100 or even 150 times or more without stopping, so every repetition has to be precise. Uniform equipment allows for uniform practice. Because of this attention to detail, paying a little extra for the competition-style kettlebell is usually a worthwhile investment. If something is worth doing, it is worth doing well!

**Figure 2.2** Competition kettlebells.

You may not want to invest the extra expense for competition kettlebells. If your goal is to use kettlebells to increase general strength and conditioning, the cast-iron kettlebell will still get the job done effectively. If you can afford it and prefer the highest quality, invest in competition kettlebells. To use a car analogy, competition kettlebells are like the Mercedes or Porsche of kettlebells—worth the extra if you can afford it. However, there are also other good cars, and if you only need to drive to the corner office and not in the Grand Prix, a Ford or Chevy may be the better choice for you. The main advantages of the competition kettlebell are quality and performance.

## IMPORTANT KETTLEBELL QUALITIES

There are number of qualities to keep in mind when testing and deciding which kettlebell to purchase. Once you have determined whether your goals are fitness or sport oriented, there are several other differences to consider among the various kettlebell options before deciding which type to purchase.

### Load

There are two types of load for kettlebells: fixed load and adjustable load. Fixed-load kettlebells (see figure 2.3) always stays the same, so you'll need a variety of light, medium, and heavy kettlebells as part of a complete kettlebell training program. Fixed-load kettlebells are more common and convenient because it is time consuming to have to change the load every time you want to move up or down in weight. Fixed-load kettlebells are one continuous piece; there is no space or break between the handle and the bell or body. This is the preferred type of kettlebell for serious lifters because no time is wasted in changing the loads—you just change kettlebells. Because you need multiple kettlebells in order to develop a complete training program, fixed-load kettlebells cost more than adjustable-load kettlebells.

In contrast to fixed-load kettlebells are adjustable-load kettlebells. In this case you only need one kettlebell (or two if you are going to perform double kettlebell exercises). There are several versions of adjustable-load kettlebells, including plate loaded and shot loaded.

**Figure 2.3** Fixed-load kettlebell.

### Plate-Loaded Adjustable Kettlebells

There are three types of plate-loaded adjustable kettlebells (see figure 2.4). One is not really a kettlebell at all but is still classified as such. It's actually a handle that is attached to weight plates with screws and bolts. One brand of kettlebell handle is the Kettlestack. Another type of plate-loaded kettlebell is made from hard plastic and has a casing that screws apart. When you open this kind of adjustable kettlebell, there are several slices or pieces of plastic. Some are hollow and some are solid. Depending upon how many hollow or solid pieces you insert, you can vary the weight of the kettlebell, typically ranging from 16 kilograms (35 lb) at the lightest up to 32 kilograms (71 lb) at the heaviest. There are also smaller versions that use lighter weight ranges. Once you select the combination of pieces to make the desired weight, you screw the handle and ball together with a bolt and a washer that runs from the base all the way through the body of the kettlebell. Yet another kind of adjustable kettlebell combines the plates with the solid outer casing. This type of adjustable kettlebell is made of steel and you screw the handle away from the ball. Inside is a rod that you can stack weight plates on. More weight plates will make a heavier kettlebell and fewer will make a lighter one.

The main advantage of adjustable kettlebells is that you have to buy fewer kettlebells, so they are less expensive. Another advantage is that one or two adjustable kettlebells take up less space in your training area compared with having a kettlebell for each weight you want to train with. The drawback of adjustable kettlebells is that they are not of the standard dimensions for kettlebell sport, so they cannot be used for competition training.

### Shot-Loaded Adjustable Kettlebells

Shot-loaded kettlebells are not so common, but in the early part of the 20th century, they were more popular. They were typically made

**Figure 2.4** Plate-loaded adjustable kettlebells.

of metal with a hole and a plug on one side or the bottom (see figure 2.5), and they were filled with sand, water, lead, or even mercury! Mercury is a heavy metal and was used in order to fit more density (weight) into a kettlebell. These were the kettlebells used by circus strongmen such as the famous Arthur Saxon and Eugen Sandow. An advantage of shot-loaded adjustable kettlebells is that the user still gets the feel of real steel in the hands but is able to do so with only one or two kettlebells since the load can be adjusted. A disadvantage is the inconvenience of having to change the load as well as the mess and labor involved in adding or subtracting materials into or out of the kettlebells. Also, it is not easy to find heavy metals, and mercury is a highly toxic substance.

One additional feature that is unique to shot-loaded adjustable kettlebells is that if the kettlebell is not completely filled, the shot inside will shift around during movement of the kettlebell, giving an added training effect as the body adjusts to the shifting loads. An inexpensive form of steel shot is BBs, which can be found in many sporting goods stores that carry hunting equipment. This is an interesting feature but is not significant enough to overshadow the benefits and convenience of modern fixed-load kettlebells.

## Handle Style

The handle is the first and primary part of the kettlebell that you will be in contact with. You want a handle that feels right in your hand: the right size and thickness, the right amount of spacing between the handle and the bell, and the right texture, not too smooth (slippery) and not too rough (tearing the hands). You want the handle just right so that it almost floats in your hand when you are using it. The handles may differ in shape and diameter and may be a single piece or multipiece, as shown in figure 2.6.

## Handle Thickness

Depending upon where you get your kettlebell and what kind it is, there can be great variation in handle thickness. There are kettlebells with very thin handles and kettlebells with handles so thick you cannot even fit your hand around them! Most kettlebells have a handle thickness that corresponds closely to the international standard for competition kettlebells, which is approximately 35 millimeters (1.4 in.). For most women, a 33-millimeter (1.3 in.) handle,

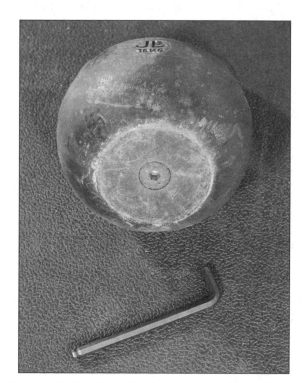

**Figure 2.5** Shot-loaded adjustable kettlebell.

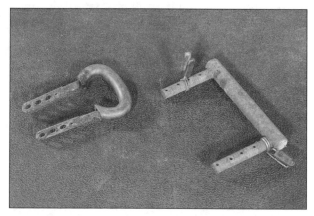

**Figure 2.6** Kettlebell handle: single piece and multipiece.

**Figure 2.7** Kettlebell handle thickness: 33 millimeters and 35 millimeters.

**Figure 2.8** A standard kettlebell will have sufficient space for you to fully insert your hand into the handle.

as shown in figure 2.7, is best because it is thick enough to strengthen the hands, wrists, forearms, and fingers but thin enough to get your fingers around the handle. For men, a 35-millimeter handle, as shown in figure 2.7, will challenge your grip but is not too thick to prevent you from being able to do the exercises. I suggest not going with a handle thicker than 35 millimeters for general kettlebell training. Thicker handles are great for hand and grip training, but they are too thick to be able to get the full benefits of high-repetition kettlebell lifting for fitness. Though there are differences in handle diameter among the various types of kettlebells available, most kettlebells of 45 pounds (20 kg) and heavier have a handle between 33 and 35 millimeters. Smaller kettlebells typically have thinner handles. Among the types of kettlebells, only competition kettlebells have a uniform handle diameter, ball diameter, and height.

## Spacing, Height, and Length of Handle

You also have to look at the spacing between the handle and the ball. If the space is too narrow, it will be difficult or impossible to put your hand deeply into the handle, which is important for many of the core kettlebell exercises, such as the clean, press, snatch, and

so on. If there is too much space between the handle and the ball, you will not have a close fit with the kettlebell secured against your forearm, which means the hand will be too loose and there will be less stability in your movements. So you want the right amount of space that allows you to fit your hand into the handle with the sides of the handle next to both sides of your wrist. The standard spacing for a good kettlebell is 55 millimeters (2.2 in.) from the bottom of the handle to the top of the ball (height of handle) and 186 millimeters (7.3 in.) from one side of the handle to the other (length of the handle). See figure 2.8 for a standard kettlebell handle.

## Handle Surface

The surface of the handle can be smooth to varying degrees. Many kettlebell brands come with either a painted or powder-coated handle. At low reps, such as sets of 20 or fewer, these smooth coatings make the kettlebell move smoothly in the hands and may prevent excessive blisters and hand tears. However, they make it harder to grip the kettlebell later on in your session and during high-repetition sets when you begin to get sweaty.

For these reasons, I recommend a smooth steel-polished handle for serious kettlebell lifters. These handles have no paint and are polished to provide a smooth, bare-metal handle. They offer more friction during lower reps, but once you begin to get sweaty, they make for a better grip. The smooth steel handles hold chalk much better, which becomes increasingly important when higher and higher repetitions are performed. Sweaty hands decrease the ability to hold the kettlebell, and if you can't hold the kettlebell, you cannot swing, clean, or press a kettlebell and burn all those calories! So, the grip and how it feels in your hand is an important part of your lifting.

Most people thus want a smooth handle—but not too smooth! Too smooth is just as bad or even worse than too rough. Some of the worst tears come from painted or otherwise too-smooth handles. Of course, a handle that is too rough will cut your hands and be uncomfortable. Although the manufacturing and distribution of kettlebells is getting better every year thanks to their explosion in popularity, there are still a lot of poor-quality kettlebells. If you get a kettlebell that is too rough, you may need to use a metal file to work out the rough spots. Some people even use a handheld electric router to smooth out the rough patches on the handle, but if you use a router, be careful not to overdo it.

You will also need some sandpaper. Sandpaper is used for finishing touches to make the handles exactly as you like them to feel. If they are too rough, you can smooth them. If they are too smooth, you can rough them up a bit so you can find a better grip. If a handle is not holding chalk, sanding it by hand will make it hold chalk better. In short, as a kettlebell lifter, your personal kettlebell is like a baseball player's bat or glove—you have to work it into the perfect feel for your body and hands. It all comes down to performance, and to perform at your best, you have to feel at your best and the tool has to float in your hands. This rhythm is an important component of kettlebell training that we will discuss more in the chapters on technique. Figure 2.9 shows some examples of kettlebell surfaces.

## Diameter and Shape

The kettlebell has a unique design. Some of the key exercises cannot be done with other weight training implements, or at least not in the same

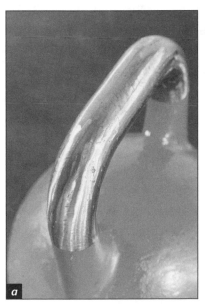 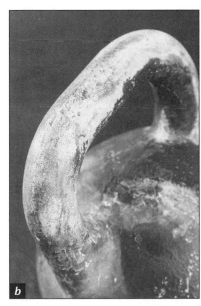 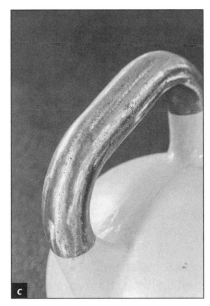

**Figure 2.9** Kettlebell surfaces: *(a)* a too-smooth handle, *(b)* a too-rough handle, and *(c)* a well-prepared handle that is smooth with a bit of roughness.

way. For example, there are many important distinctions between the standard barbell or dumbbell clean and the kettlebell clean (which we'll learn about later). This is due to the shape of the kettlebell and the distance between the handle and the weight ball. The center of mass of the ball extends well beyond the hand, whereas with a dumbbell, the weight is in the hand. The spacing between the center of load and the kettlebell handle allows for swinging movements and movements that release and catch the kettlebell. The design also allows the kettlebell to sit against the arm or body in almost every exercise. This gives greater leverage to the loads, with more parts of the body in contact with the kettlebell. The position of the handle allows the grip, wrist, arm, shoulder, legs, and core to strengthen all in one line. Because you can insert your hand deeply into the handle, there is no cramping or bending of the wrist when you hold the kettlebell. The hand and forearm can be in neutral alignment. This gives your arm much greater endurance compared with holding a dumbbell, where the hand and wrist are crooked backward, putting great strain on the forearm muscles. If your forearms and grip give out early, then you can't hold it. If you can't hold it, you can't swing it!

## Durability

Kettlebells can last a lifetime. The steel versions are the strongest and last the longest. They are virtually indestructible. Using them outdoors and in damp climates will lead to rust on the handles, so you will need to keep some sandpaper handy to keep the rust off. Some steel kettlebells come with an antirust finish; however, serious kettlebell lifters remove this finish with paint remover or other removal agents. For good training, nothing beats the touch and feel of pure steel in the hands! Cast-iron kettlebells are generally strong, and although they are not as strong as steel, they will last almost forever if you do not drop them on a hard surface. Plastic and vinyl kettlebells will wear out from filling and emptying and if used or kept outdoors.

You will eventually need to replace the screws that connect the handle to the plates on the traditional adjustable kettlebells. The plastic versions available today will last for some years, but of course they are not as resilient as the steel or cast-iron single-unit pieces. If you drop the kettlebells frequently, such as will happen during kettlebell juggling, or if you treat them roughly, the finish will come off faster, and the kettlebells will have scratches and marks on them. This will not affect performance, only appearance.

## Weight

Kettlebells typically range from 8 kilograms (18 lb) up to 48 kilograms (106 lb), but they can actually range from as light as 2 kilograms (4 lb) up to almost 90 kilograms (200 lb). They come in a variety of shapes and sizes. Some people even weld two kettlebells together to make a heavier kettlebell! The traditional Russian unit of measurement, *pood*, refers to weight; a pood is approximately 16 kilograms (35 lb). In kettlebell terminology, a 16-kilogram (35 lb) kettlebell is a 1-pood kettlebell, a 32-kilogram (71 lb) kettlebell is a 2-pood kettlebell, and so on.

There is no foolproof guide for determining the perfect kettlebell weight for you, but you can follow these basic considerations: Are you a kettlebell expert or a beginner? Are you in great shape already or are you starting out on your way to wellness and strength? Are you a heavy or large-boned person or are you light and thin? These factors and more will influence the load selection. In time, serious kettlebell lifters will gather an assortment of weights, which is important for adaptation and progressive overload.

Most men can start with a 16-kilogram (35 lb) kettlebell. To benefit from double kettlebell training, I suggest getting a pair of 16-kilogram bells. If you are 130 pounds (61 kg) or less or have no background in strength training, a 12-kilogram (26 lb) kettlebell might be a better starting weight. If you are unsure, you can always start lighter and graduate to heavier kettlebells as you progress. This is a good thing to keep in mind for long-term success. Women typically begin training with an 8-kilogram (18 lb) kettlebell. Very athletic or strong women can start with 12 kilograms (26 lb), but again, when unsure it is better to start lighter and move to heavier weights than the other way around.

## Finish

In some cases, cast-iron kettlebells are covered with a rubber coating or have a rubber base on the bottom so that the kettlebell doesn't scratch the floor if you set it down. However, they tend to be unwieldy and bounce when dropped, which is an annoyance and potentially dangerous if the kettlebell were to bounce back into you. These rubber-coated kettlebells are only advantageous if you will be setting them down on hardwood floors.

## Comfort

It is important to select a kettlebell that is a good match for your body size and fitness level. The weight of the kettlebell has to be appropriate for your current level of strength and conditioning. As you become stronger and fitter, you will want to progress to heavier kettlebells to emphasize strength and use lighter kettlebells to emphasize cardiorespiratory conditioning. Another consideration is how the kettlebell feels in your hand. For example, for an average-sized man, a thick handle may not provide enough grip work, but for a woman with small hands, a thinner handle might be more appropriate because a thick handle would be difficult to hold onto.

## Price

Steel kettlebells are the highest quality and most expensive. Vinyl and plastic kettlebells are the least expensive and lowest quality; they are a waste of money and should not rightly be considered kettlebells. Adjustable kettlebells are a bit more expensive per piece, but you will not require as many pieces since you can change the weight as needed. Cast-iron kettlebells are a

---

### BEWARE OF VINYL AND PLASTIC KETTLEBELLS

Vinyl and plastic kettlebells can be found in many sporting goods stores. They are typically the least expensive versions, but they are really only kettlebells in name. They do not perform like a kettlebell, and the shape and design do not allow for proper mechanics of kettlebell training. In most cases the space between the handle and the ball is so narrow that a person could not fit her hand through it. These kettlebells have a plug on the top or side of the ball that can be removed so that water or sand can be added for greater resistance. The only advantages are that they are very cheap and if you drop them there is no damage to the floor or yourself. This type of kettlebell may be a nice introduction to kettlebells for children while they learn the basics of safe practice, but aside from that, it is the least effective type and is not recommended.

---

good combination of quality and price—they're less expensive than steel and slightly less durable. I suggest investing in either steel or cast-iron kettlebells only. For example, a good 16-kilogram (35 lb) cast-iron kettlebell should cost $60 to $100, depending on the company and quality. A comparable steel kettlebell will typically be $5 to $10 more.

## THE KETTLEBELL DIFFERENCE

Experienced weight trainers who are veterans in the weight room but unfamiliar with kettlebells often make the statement that you can use a dumbbell or any other weight in place of the kettlebell to do the common kettlebell exercises, such as the swing, press, or snatch. However, this is an erroneous assumption—there are some significant differences between kettlebells and any other form of load by the nature of the kettlebell design.

## How Kettlebells Differ From Dumbbells

Some of the key kettlebell exercises in this book cannot be done with other weight training implements. For example, as mentioned previously, a barbell or dumbbell clean is different from the kettlebell clean in many important ways because of the shape of the kettlebell and the distance between the handle and the weight ball. As mentioned earlier, the center of mass of the weight ball extends well beyond the hand, whereas with a dumbbell, the weight is in the hand, not in front. This spacing between the center of load and the kettlebell handle allows for swinging movements and movements that release and catch the kettlebell.

The design also allows the kettlebell to sit against the arm or body in almost every exercise. This gives greater leverage to the loads, with more parts of the body in contact with the kettlebell. The position of the handle allows the grip, wrist, arm, shoulder, legs, and core to strengthen all in one line. Because you can insert your hand deeply into the handle, there is no cramping or bending of the wrist when you hold the kettlebell, and the hand and forearm can be in neutral alignment. This gives your arm much greater endurance compared with holding a dumbbell, where the hand and wrist are crooked backward, putting great strain on the forearm muscles. Remember, if your forearms and grip give out early, then you can't hold it, and if you can't hold it, you can't swing it!

When it comes to progressively higher repetitions, in particular with the ballistic or fast lifts, the ability to keep your wrist, hand, forearm, and fingers neutral and relaxed opens up the possibility of being able to work until systemic exhaustion. This is a key distinction between doing any lift with a dumbbell versus a kettlebell. If you look at movements such as the swing, snatch, clean and jerk, press, push press, or squat, you can see a big difference in the alignment of the hand and grip when holding dumbbells and when holding a kettlebell. For any of these exercises, a person with equal training in technique will be able to do far more repetitions with a kettlebell compared with the same load in a dumbbell.

The dumbbell necessitates a cramped wrist. No matter how strong and conditioned you are, you will reach a point where your forearm, wrist, and hand will fatigue and you will not be able to hold onto the dumbbell any longer. Doing the same exercise with a kettlebell of an equal load, you can insert your hand deep into the handle, and the center of the bell is lower on your forearm (instead of in the hand as with a dumbbell), which means the load is closer to your center of mass. This closer relationship between your center of mass and that of the kettlebell gives you greater control over the kettlebell. With enough practice you can keep your hand relaxed and neutral, which means your arm will not fatigue as quickly, allowing you to work to the full extent of your cardiorespiratory and muscular stamina. In other words, the grip will not give out first, so you can work longer. This seemingly simple concept makes a world of difference in the number of calories you can burn in a single workout. The shape and design thus are an important part of the kettlebell difference.

## How Kettlebells Differ From Barbells

The best way to describe the difference between a kettlebell and a barbell is to note that you cannot swing a barbell between your legs. Think about it. Just think about it—don't try it! If you try it, you are most likely going to smash the barbell into your shins when trying to swing it between your legs. In other words, you can't swing a barbell between your legs. However, you can swing a kettlebell between your legs!

This is one of the most important qualities of a kettlebell, making it unique in both design and function. Because you can swing a kettlebell between your legs, you can activate and exercise to great effect what in athletics is called the *posterior chain*. This consists of the all-important muscles, joints, and fasciae (chain) of the backside of your body (posterior). In simple terms, the main areas of the posterior chain are your lower-back muscles, glutes, hamstrings, and calves. A lot of attention is currently given to developing the posterior chain in athletic conditioning programs, and this trend has also influenced modern fitness programs.

Kettlebell exercises, especially those that use the swinging motion of the pendulum, such as the swing, clean, and snatch and all their variations, work the posterior chain. When you swing the kettlebell behind you between your legs, it puts a fast (ballistic) and heavy load on these strong muscles. The swinging motion behaves like a pendulum, which means it relies upon inertia and momentum. Every time you load the posterior chain (the backward portion of the swing), it stretches the muscles on the rear side of the body. The muscles, joints, and tissue behave like a spring when under load. When you load a spring mechanism, it naturally is ready to unload, and it is this unloading phase (when the kettlebell is swinging in front of you) where the speed and power are expressed. So the simple act of the most basic kettlebell lift, the swing, works a whole new world of muscles you may never have felt before. When swinging a kettlebell for the first time, most people comment on how they can feel it in the butt and the legs. There may be no single exercise that lifts and tones the rear end more than a kettlebell swing (and snatch).

So far I have spoken only of the unique advantages of the kettlebell when compared with the barbell and dumbbell. Kettlebells are used most effectively to develop strength endurance, not pure or limit or maximal strength. This is because a kettlebell is a fixed weight. Once you can lift a given weight one time, in order to progress you will have to either find a heavier load or lift the same load more times. If the weight is fixed, the only way to keep progressing is to increase the volume through increased repetitions. So, even with heavy kettlebells, the goal is almost always to do more reps as you become fitter.

If your goal is to build absolute strength or mass, beyond a certain point a barbell becomes better suited for your task. If you are a strong athlete, at some point you will want to use a barbell for core movements. An advantage of a barbell is that you can load it very heavily. When you adapt to a given load, you can add more weight to the bar and try to keep getting stronger. Of course barbells and dumbbells are also great; they are just different than kettlebells. A well-constructed program may incorporate barbells, dumbbells, and kettlebells along with other tools as well.

## KETTLEBELL LIFTING ENVIRONMENTS

Once you have decided to begin training with kettlebells and have purchased one or more to train with, the next thing to decide is where you will do your training. A popular benefit of kettlebells is their portability. Kettlebell training is all the rave in outdoor boot camps, fitness classes, and individual training sessions. Each person can grasp a kettlebell or one in each hand (the real training maniacs might even grab two in each hand!) and head out to the yard, parking lot, or local park or field. Have handle, will travel—you can carry it. In short, a kettlebell is a handheld gym that makes exercising in a comfortable environment much easier compared with bulky equipment.

Of course, you may prefer to train in a traditional gym. Bodybuilding gyms, CrossFit gyms, powerlifting gyms, hard-core functional training gyms, strongman gyms, athletic gyms, and commercial gyms all make great settings for kettlebell training. All you need is the right equipment, the know-how, and the desire and you can train anywhere.

### Training at Home

Many busy professionals or heads of households prefer the luxury and convenience of kettlebell training at home. You can train in a special exercise room, in your garage, or on carpet, wood, or cement. You just need a space that's about 10 by

10 feet (3 by 3 m), and you can get in a full-body kettlebell workout in the comfort of your own home. The space should be well ventilated and with enough light to see clearly, and there should be no obstructions in the training space that can be tripped over or otherwise pose a safety hazard. Common sense should always be in full effect when selecting an appropriate setting for kettlebell training. You may need to move your pet, kids, or valuables out of the training space.

## Training at Work

Some dedicated people bring a kettlebell to work and keep it under their desk or in the closet or break room. If you are a busy professional in a fast-paced life, you probably do not have time to drive back and forth to a gym. If you are working long hours, you may value the benefits of short kettlebell breaks to charge you up, tone your muscles, and burn some calories. You can keep it moderate intensity so as not to sweat in your work clothes, or if you have the facility, you can do an intense 20- to 30-minute workout on your lunch break and still have time for a shower and bite to eat before going back to the grind. Where there is a will, there is a way, and with the portability of kettlebells, there are no excuses or limitations for those who want to train.

## Training With a Trainer

While some people are highly motivated self-starters, others prefer the guidance, supervision, and knowledge of a certified kettlebell trainer. If you choose to work with a fitness professional, look for one who has a specialized degree or certification in kettlebells. Several national and international kettlebell organizations provide professional certifications. Look for an IKFF-certified kettlebell trainer (CKT) at www.ikff.com. The IKFF holds a high standard for certification, ensuring standards of practice; however, it is possible you won't have access to an IKFF-certified trainer and may need to look elsewhere. Here are some useful guidelines to help you in selecting a good kettlebell trainer.

### Technical Experience

Because kettlebells have technical specificity, only a trainer who has spent time practicing the basic lifts can understand the differences between good and bad form. Demonstration of good form is the first step in teaching kettlebells.

### Clear Communication

There are individual differences in how each person learns. Some learn through visual instruction, others through tactile (touching) instruction, and still others through verbal instruction. The trainer's experience is only as helpful as her ability to get you, the student, to understand and replicate the lesson.

### People Person

Some people may prefer a nice-guy atmosphere and others may respond better to a drill-sergeant atmosphere. The personality the trainer brings to your sessions is a personal preference. No matter whether you have a loud and bossy trainer or a polite and soft-spoken trainer, what is important is that he is genuinely interested in not only your progress but first and foremost your health and well-being.

### Atmosphere

Whether you prefer a Spartan-like gym or a posh, country-club environment, indoors or outdoors, the training environment should be conducive to learning and not a distraction. Everyone is different, some prefer a dungeon-like atmosphere and others put higher importance on the cleanliness of the equipment and training space. Some like to have music while training, and others value the silence. Some exercisers are demonstrative when training, grunting and screaming at times during the lifts, and others show no emotion—cool, calm and collected. The important things is to create an environment that best enables you to concentrate and focus on the training before you.

### Cost

There can be great variance in what a kettlebell trainer charges, depending upon the city or region, the experience of the trainer, and the overhead costs involved (e.g., fancy gym, garage, outdoors, YMCA). You might pay anywhere from $25 for a typical trainer to well over $100 an hour for an experienced or highly recognized trainer from New York or Los Angeles. If you don't have a budget for personal training, look for qualified trainers who offer group or semi-private classes where the cost is shared among several participants.

## Training With a Partner

If you have a good friend or someone you like to work out with, kettlebell training is a great way to challenge and push each other to give that extra effort. If you do not train with a partner, consider doing so. It could be just the spark you need to stay focused and committed. If you tend to skip workouts, once you have a schedule with another person expecting you, it is less likely that you will skip training. Whomever you select as your training partner, make sure it is someone who is supportive and attentive. Kettlebell lifting is fun, but it is also serious business and you can get hurt if you do not pay close attention to form, load, and environment.

## Training Alone

You may prefer the inner focus and tranquility of training alone. Many accomplished kettlebell lifters do most of their training alone at home, in a gym, or even outside. The important thing to keep in mind is to have a clear training space that is as free of distractions as possible. Try to turn off your phone and tablet and concentrate on the work for your kettlebell session. You will get a more productive workout as a result.

# KETTLEBELL LIFTING ATTIRE

Some mention should be given to what to wear during kettlebell training. The clothes you work out in should enable free, unrestricted movement and should in no way interfere with your training.

There is no specific clothing that must be worn and you will see people lifting in both loose and tight clothing. There are, however, a few points to keep in mind in order to optimize your kettlebell training sessions.

## Gloves

Wearing gloves is more common among less experienced lifters. You will rarely if ever see an experienced or advanced lifter using gloves, because gloves reduce the feel of your hand on the kettlebell. The gloves can bunch up and get caught in the spinning handle, and certain gloves also add thickness to the hand, making it more difficult to adequately insert your hand into the handle. This can adversely affect the mechanics of the lifts, especially during high-repetition sets.

However, at least in the early days of your training while you are still trying to master the movements, you may complain about the grip and your hands. The best solution is to learn good technique! If you have good technique, you will be able to move your hand back and forth between the handle and ball without catching or tearing the skin. You will learn to toss and catch the moving kettlebell from the fingers to the base of the palm, completely avoiding the handle spinning in your palm and the resulting blisters and tears. But it will take some time before your technique becomes smooth, so in the beginning stages you may want to use gloves. My advice is to start with no gloves and as your hands begin to get tender, slip the gloves on to finish the workout with no tears. With more training, you will need to use the gloves less and less.

Advanced competitive kettlebell lifters perform exercises such as the gloved snatch, but in this case the gloves are workman gloves used to make the grip harder and to make the kettlebell more difficult to hold onto.

## Shoes

There are a variety of shoes that you can wear while training. Serious lifters and competitive athletes usually wear Olympic weightlifting shoes. These are leather shoes with a hard, raised, wooden heel, often with a thin strip of rubber on the bottom. The heels elevate the lifter's hips a few inches, making positions like the clean and overhead lockout (e.g., jerks) more stable. They also provide stability to the ankle and heel, making it easier to transfer power from the ground.

Many kettlebell lifters who train for fitness wear Vibram FiveFinger shoes because of the barefoot feel. They are a great alternative to traditional shoes. Some people also like to go completely barefoot, and this is also fine. Just be careful to move your feet if you ever drop the kettlebell. Quick feet are happy feet! Another option is a flat-soled shoe such as Converse All Stars.

What I caution against is wearing overly cushioned shoes such as running shoes. Running shoes tend to have too much cushion and are very soft, making it more difficult to push off the ground. Hard and flat shoes are a better choice for kettlebell lifting. If you are training at a gym or combining running with your kettlebell workouts, you may decide to bring a second pair of shoes for kettlebell lifting.

## Wristbands or Wrist Wraps

Wristbands or wrist wraps are optional, but you may want to put some on at least in the early stages of kettlebell training. Wristbands should not be too thick, because thick ones will impede the ability to fully insert your hand into the handle. An elastic bandage wrapped around each wrist works well. There are also thin canvas wraps that can be fastened with Velcro strips.

Wrist wraps offer some cushion while you are learning how to flip the kettlebell over your hand, or more correctly, slip your hand into the handle. There is a learning curve, so in the beginning of practice you may bang your wrist and forearm a bit from time to time. With more practice, you will learn to slide your hand effortlessly through the handle, eliminating the banging almost entirely. Still, the wraps or bands will cushion the impact just enough to avoid discomfort. If your forearms sweat a lot, the wraps or bands will also help keep the kettlebell in proper alignment on your arm and hand and will reduce the amount of sweat dripping to your hands and therefore the kettlebell itself. Again, if you do use wraps or bands, do not use thick ones. If they are too thick, they will prevent you from inserting your hand deep enough into the handle because the wrap will get caught while you are inserting your hand.

## Weight Belts

Weight belts are used by serious kettlebell lifters. They are similar to powerlifting belts but are not as thick. Weight belts used for kettlebell lifting are thin and are not worn tightly over the abdomen; instead, the belt is worn low at the top of your pelvis so that you can gently place your elbows in between the top of the belt and your belly. This allows you to relax your shoulders more by resting your elbows on your ilia (see figure 2.10). This is a method used specifically for the jerk and the clean and jerk, in which an athlete lifts two kettlebells overhead as many times as possible in 10 minutes. The belt helps the athlete relax and regenerate when the kettlebells are on the chest so that she can do a greater volume of work. It is a higher-level skill and concept. For general fitness training, a weight belt is not needed.

**Figure 2.10**  The lifting belt is worn loose and low on the hips below the waist so that the lifter can place the elbows between the body and the inside of the belt.

## Tops and Bottoms

As far as specific clothing goes, the main things to avoid are T-shirts that are too slick, including those that are made of synthetic fibers or that have large logos. If the T-shirt is made of a slick material or has a slick logo, once you start to sweat, it becomes difficult to hold your arms and forearms against your torso because the slick shirt makes your arms slide out to the sides. When you are tired and have kettlebells in your hands, slick shirts just make it harder, and if you cannot keep your arms against your body in certain lifts, you are at a mechanical and performance disadvantage. This is not as important for the swing and snatch, because the kettlebell and arm do not stay against the body for a long time. But for other lifts such as the clean, squat, press, or jerk, it is necessary to be able to hold your arms against your body. So wear a simple cotton shirt that will stick to your body and arms when you are tired and sweaty.

Pants can be whatever is comfortable, short or long. However, they should not be too baggy. The shorts or pants should fit well in the crotch because when you swing the kettlebell back between your legs, such as during the drop from the snatch, the thumb, fingers, or kettlebell itself can get caught in the baggy part of the crotch and interfere with your lifting mechanics. Form-fitting shorts or even tights or cycling shorts are great for kettlebell lifting.

# ADDITIONAL EQUIPMENT AND CONSIDERATIONS

Once you have picked out your kettlebells and training environment, you will need a few other small items to round out your training equipment. These will make your program more organized and efficient. There is nothing worse than starting a workout and then realizing you can't complete it because you are missing some small but important tool. Here are the members of the supporting cast that will make the star of the show, the kettlebells, shine brighter.

## Timer

Programs and methods for training with kettlebells revolve around using repetitions, time, or a combination of both as the determining factor. Repetition, time, load, and speed or rate of movement are factors that are frequently manipulated to alter training process and effect.

For example, your program may focus on reps, such as doing the one-arm press with 16 kg (35 lb) kettlebells for 3 sets of 10 reps with each arm. Or, it may call for you to do the one-arm press with 16 kg for 2 minutes per arm. It may tell you to self-pace or to follow a specific pace, such as 12 reps per minute for 2 minutes with each hand or 15 reps per minute for 3 minutes with each hand. If you are using a time-based method, you will need either a clock with a second hand that you can watch or some kind of timer that beeps. A popular timer among kettlebell lifters is the Gymboss, which allows you to set intervals and beeps at the completion of each preprogrammed interval. This tool is very helpful for building programs around time.

## Stretching Mat

Stretching after kettlebell training is part of a complete and well-rounded program. Kettlebell training puts the body under load, so naturally some compression occurs in the joints of the body. Stretching for a few minutes after training is important for elongating the body and helping to decompress after the vigorous strength training. If you do not have a padded area to stretch in, you may want to pick up a portable stretching mat.

## Chalk

Chalk is an important part of a kettlebell lifter's arsenal. If you tend to sweat a lot, kettlebells will bring it out of you. When you get sweat on your hands and on the handle, it becomes difficult to hold the kettlebell. If you can't hold it, you will drop it or have to place it down, and that effectively ends your training set. To progress in kettlebell training, you want to be able to work for longer and longer periods of time or otherwise to do more volume per unit of time, so you need chalk to ebb the flow of sweat. The most common chalk is powdered magnesium, which can be found in most outdoor or adventure stores that cater to rock climbers or wherever you can find gymnastic equipment. You can buy chalk in individual blocks, in bags, or in bulk. Chalk is inexpensive.

The flip side is that chalk is messy and can get everywhere. Few commercial gyms allow chalk because it leaves a trail wherever it is used. Cleanliness and hygiene are a concern and the reality is that chalk is hard to contain. You can put the chalk powder into bowls and buckets to mostly contain it, but it will be in the air and whatever you touch. Find a chalk-friendly gym to train in, or if possible, dedicate a room or area of the garage to training to keep the chalk from mixing with the nontraining areas.

Chalk also dries your hands faster because it absorbs moisture. If you are lifting kettlebells but still want to keep healthy, soft hands, you will have to take time to care for your hands by filing, moisturizing, and sometimes even

## KETTLEBELL SAFETY TIPS

Be mindful of the training environment as well as the equipment you are using. Here are some general safety guidelines:

- Have a clear floor space with no obstacles on the floor to trip over, including people, pets, and furniture and other objects.
- Make sure the ceiling is high enough that you will not hit it with your hand or the kettlebell. Stay clear of walls and mirrors or anything else that can be broken if you lose control of the kettlebells or need to drop a bad rep to the side.
- Never try to save a bad rep. If you start to lose control of the kettlebell during a lift, move out of the way quickly and push the kettlebell away from you as you step away. It is a good idea to do your training in an area where a dropped kettlebell will not damage the environment (e.g., rubber flooring or outdoors). Keep in mind that quick feet are happy feet—if you drop a kettlebell, move your feet out of the way.
- Chalk is excellent for preventing slipping. When doing high-repetition movements such as the swing, clean, or snatch, chalk is helpful in allowing you to train longer without dropping the kettlebell or letting it slip out of your hand.
- Eliminate distractions and don't watch TV, read the paper, or text or talk on the phone. Devote your kettlebell training time to the training and try to put off other activities until your workout is finished. Kettlebell training requires strong concentration and any distractions will not only make the workout less productive but will also increase the risk of injuries.
- Have a towel available to remove excess sweat.
- If outside, do not stare directly into the sun during overhead lifts.
- Have some drinking water available and stay hydrated.
- If the kettlebell bangs your wrists or causes pain in the beginning, you can wear wrist wraps or wristbands to provide some cushion. In time your technique will improve and you will no longer hurt your forearms or wrists.
- Wear shoes with hard soles shoes or at least flat soles. Bare feet are also OK. Running shoes are not good for kettlebell training because they are too soft and do not provide enough foundation to push from.
- Do not wear baggy shorts. You might catch your thumb in them on the backswing in swings, cleans, or snatches. Wear close-fitting shorts or tights.
- The set is not over until the kettlebell is on the ground. Don't place the kettlebell down sloppily and risk straining your lower back.

shaving raised callouses. Kettlebell lifting is not great for manicured hands, but it sure is wonderful for the rest of your body!

If your training environment does not allow powdered chalk, the next best option is to use liquid chalk, which is easier to contain to your hands and the kettlebell handles. It dries fast and only gets on the handle of the kettlebell and your hands. As long as you don't touch other things, you will be able to confine the chalk to your hands and kettlebells. It is certainly a better option than no chalk at all. You can find liquid chalk online.

## Towel

Keep a small towel handy to wipe sweat off yourself and the kettlebell handle. Because kettlebell training is high-intensity exercise, you are going to be sweating a lot. The sweat can adversely affect your performance by making your hands and the kettlebell slippery, and as a result it can become a safety hazard. All it takes is one wayward kettlebell flying out of your hand during snatches to appreciate the importance of keeping the sweat under control.

## Water

Have some drinking water available, especially for longer or super-intense kettlebell training sessions. You will sweat a lot and need to replace your fluids. Dehydration can greatly reduce performance, particularly during the end of a long, grueling training session. It is also a health hazard and can cause weakness, nausea, dizziness, cramping, and lightheadedness.

## Sandpaper

As mentioned previously, a fine-grit sandpaper (appropriate for steel) should be kept on hand to periodically smooth out rough spots and remove old, caked-on chalk from the handle. In place of sandpaper you can also use steel wool.

Now you have all your options for equipment and training environments listed clearly. You have the equipment and training space and you are ready to go. In the next chapter we take a look at foundational exercise principles so you can understand more about the science behind kettlebell training.

# EXERCISE PRINCIPLES

Now that you have learned what a kettlebell is and why it might be an ideal tool and training method for helping you to achieve your fitness goals, you are almost ready to begin learning the basic exercises. But before doing so, it will be helpful for you to understand some of the underlying exercise principles involved in kettlebell lifting so that you have a firm grasp of what is and what is not likely to occur during the various stages of training. This will help you in setting clear, specific goals and increasing your likelihood of achieving them.

The kettlebell has a unique design and offers some unique applications for fitness, but it is not magical and you are subject to certain anatomical and physiological laws whether you are using a kettlebell, barbell, dumbbell, or any other exercise implement. This chapter discusses these important exercise guidelines so that you have a detailed road map of the strengths and limitations of this remarkable tool. First, it outlines the physiological principles of exercise science, and it explains how to use these important fundamentals in order to intelligently structure your kettlebell training sessions. Then, it introduces the various physical skills involved in kettlebell training and explains how to develop them.

Some basic governing principles relate to all types of exercise and physical activities, including kettlebell lifting. It will be helpful for you to be aware of these basic concepts in order to fully realize the benefits of your kettlebell training program. You should keep these principles in mind while designing your individual program so that you can most effectively accomplish your fitness goals by setting up and manipulating the various components of your kettlebell workouts.

## FITT PRINCIPLE

*FITT* is an acronym that describes some of the key exercise principles associated with kettlebell training and all other kinds of exercise. The elements of this handy acronym offer guidelines for structuring your training program. *FITT* stands for frequency, intensity, time, and type. It is a convenient way to remember the exercise variables you can manipulate to keep things constantly varied, to help stave off the boredom of a never-changing program, and to keep your body continually challenged.

### Frequency

*Frequency* describes how often you exercise. It can reflect the number of kettlebell workouts per week or month, the number of exercises per workout, the number of sets per exercise, or the number of repetitions per set. For example, if you exercise once a day for 4 days per week, your frequency is four workouts per week. If you exercise twice a day for 3 days per week, your frequency is six times per week.

In order to maintain a healthy body and to become fitter, a general recommendation is to exercise at least 4 days of the week. Keep in mind that there is an inverse relationship between frequency and intensity, which is the *I* in FITT.

Collectively, frequency and intensity will equal the total volume of exercise, which is the total amount of exercise performed per unit of time (e.g., day, week, month). The more frequently you exercise, the less intense the workouts can be. Conversely, the more intense the workouts are, the less frequently you can exercise. This has to do with the effect of total volume of exercise on your body's ability to recover, which is the subject of this chapter's sidebar.

## Intensity

*Intensity* refers to how vigorously you perform your kettlebell exercises. It can also describe the amount of energy or effort needed to execute a particular exercise or exercise session. The intensity of exercise can be expressed in several ways.

Kettlebell lifting combines cardiorespiratory training with resistance training. The intensity of your kettlebell workout can be measured as a function of cardiorespiratory intensity or resistance intensity. One simple way to measure the intensity of your workout routine is to wear a heart rate monitor, which measures intensity as a function of your heart rate. This method of determining intensity relates to the cardiorespiratory component of kettlebell training. In this case intensity is expressed as a percentage of maximal heart rate and is shown in heart beats per minute (BPM). A more intense kettlebell workout will produce a higher (faster) heart rate, and a less intense workout will produce a lower heart rate. To be able to use and understand the readings of a heart rate monitor, you need to know a few keys points about the heart rate and optimal heart rate training zones for various levels and fitness and training goals.

A widely accepted formula for determining your maximal heart rate (MHR) is to subtract your age from 220 for men and 226 for women. This number gives you a close approximation of your MHR. For example, a 40-year-old man would have an MHR of 180 bpm (220 – 40 = 180), and a 40-year-old woman would have an MHR of 186 (226 – 40 = 186). Various percentages of your MHR will give you the various training zones.

You will need to know how to quickly and easily find your heart rate. Immediately upon completing your training set, find your pulse by placing your index and middle fingers at your neck just to the side and slightly above your Adam's apple (see figure 3.1*a*). Alternatively, you can find your pulse on the lower portion of your wrist just above the palm (see figure 3.1*b*). You will feel your heart beating in either of these two locations. Count how many beats

 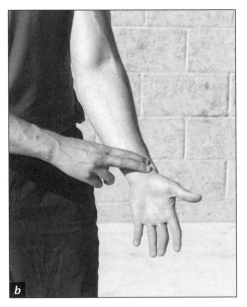

**Figure 3.1**  Finding your pulse: *(a)* at the neck or *(b)* at the wrist.

occur in 15 seconds and multiply that number by 4 to give your beats per minute (BPM). For example, if you count 40 beats in 15 seconds, your heart rate is 160 BPM.

### Warm-Up Training Zone or Healthy Heart Zone (50-60 Percent of MHR)

This is the zone that is best for beginners who are just starting a fitness program. It is also the best zone for warming up before a more intense workout. This zone is associated with reducing body fat, lowering blood pressure and cholesterol, and decreasing degenerative heart conditions. It is relatively safe due to its mild intensity. In this healthy heart zone, up to 85 percent of the calories burned are fat, 10 percent are carbohydrate, and 5 percent are protein.

### Fitness or Fat-Burning Zone (60-70 Percent of MHR)

This zone provides the same health benefits as the healthy heart zone; however, it is more intense and will burn more total calories. It is appropriate for more experienced exercisers who still wish to emphasize fat-burning properties. It burns up to 85 percent of calories as fat, 10 percent as carbohydrate, and 5 percent as protein.

### Endurance or Aerobic Training Zone (70-80 percent of MHR)

This training zone improves cardiorespiratory function and can actually increase the size and strength of your heart. It is the optimal zone for endurance training, and it is the right zone for a more experienced lifter who has a good foundation of kettlebell technique and is in good health and physical fitness. More total calories are burned in this zone than in the previous zones, with about 50 percent of total calories burned as fat, 50 percent as carbohydrate, and less than 1 percent as protein.

### Performance or Anaerobic Training Zone (80-90 Percent of MHR)

This is the zone that improves $VO_2max$, which is the maximal amount of oxygen that the body can consume during exercise. The anaerobic training zone improves the function of the cardiorespiratory system and the body's ability to tolerate higher levels of lactate, which means you will be able to better withstand fatigue during intense exercise. This zone is high intensity and burns more calories than the previous zones, with about 15 percent of total calories burned as fat, 85 percent as carbohydrate, and less than 1 percent as protein.

### Maximal Effort Zone (90-100 Percent of MHR)

This is the all-out zone, sometimes referred to as the *red line*. This zone burns the highest number of calories; however, it is very intense and most people cannot sustain exercise in this zone for more than a few minutes. This zone is best used by highly conditioned athletes and typically during interval training in which short, high-intensity bouts alternate with longer, moderate-intensity bouts. This zone burns about 10 percent of total calories as fat, 90 percent as carbohydrate, and less than 1 percent as protein.

For beginners to kettlebell fitness, the majority of your workouts will be in the healthy heart zone, so you can gradually develop your aerobic fitness at manageable intensities. After some weeks of training when you have improved your fitness, you can begin to incorporate more workouts in the fitness zone. Experienced kettlebell users will stay in the fitness and endurance training zones for most of their workouts. Advanced exercisers and the highly fit will incorporate more workouts in the performance zone with periodic training sessions in the maximal training zone. All exercisers of any level should incorporate a warm-up in the healthy heart zone.

Intensity can also refer to the amount of stress an exercise or exercise session puts on your body. One such measure of intensity is the heaviness of the load you are using. Lifting a 32-kilogram (71 lb) kettlebell will be far more intense than lifting a 12-kilogram (26 lb) kettlebell for the same exercise. Here intensity refers to a percentage of your repetition maximum (RM), which is the maximum amount of weight that you can lift during a specific exercise and a specific number of repetitions. For example, 1RM is the maximal weight of a kettlebell you can lift for 1 rep, and 10RM is the heaviest kettlebell you can use to complete 10 repetitions. In either case, lifting a heavier kettlebell will be more intense than lifting a lighter kettlebell.

For general health and fitness, most kettlebell workouts should be of moderate intensity. Beginners are advised to use lighter weights at

## MONITOR INTENSITY WITH RPE

A useful subjective guide you can use to monitor intensity is called the *rating of perceived exertion*, or RPE. The RPE is typically a subjective scale from 1 to 10, with 1 being very easy, 5 being moderately intense, and 10 being maximally intense. If you are planning a moderately intense kettlebell workout, you should maintain an RPE between 4 and 6 during your workout. If you are planning an easy workout, your RPE should be in in the range of 2 to 3.

The intensity of your kettlebell workouts can be strenuous, moderate, or mild. What is mild to one person may be quite intense to another, and the intensity and associated RPE of a particular exercise or session will depend upon such variables as your age, your level of stress, how much rest you had, the altitude of your location, and of course your current level of fitness. For example, a professional or high-level amateur athlete may be able to easily run a mile in under 6 minutes. However, an office worker may struggle to run the same mile in under 10 minutes. In this case the intensity levels are very different for each person.

Even what you have eaten or not eaten can affect your RPE. For example, if you drank too much coffee, or if you ate a heavy meal just before your workout, your RPE might be higher than if you were training on an empty or only slightly full stomach. It bears repeating that the more intense the exercise or exercise session, the less intense the frequency and volume.

higher repetitions for safety. In other words, use a lower-intensity effort for longer duration of time. A more highly conditioned athlete will work at higher intensities than a beginning exerciser by using progressively heavier kettlebells. In a structured program, kettlebell users of all levels use some form of varying intensity, which means some workouts will be moderate, some intense, and some mild. This topic is discussed in detail in chapter 9, Creating a Customized Fitness Program.

## Time (Duration)

*Time* or *duration* is the length of time you are active in any one kettlebell lifting session. The term *time* is used interchangeably with the term *duration*. Time is usually expressed in minutes. However, in kettlebell lifting, there is another important facet of time, referred to as *tempo*, *speed*, or *pace*, that has an effect on the total volume of work performed in a given set of an exercise.

The total time of a workout is one component—time or duration can be used to represent the length of a single resistance training session. For example, the duration from start to finish of your kettlebell workout may be 30 to 45 minutes. The time of an individual set is another measure. For example, doing 1 set of 30 repetitions may take you 1 minute.

In addition, during some lifts, the time and tempo are both calculated. Let's say, for example, that you are to do a one-arm press for 2 minutes, equaling 1 minute per hand. Suppose you are using a 16-kilogram (35 lb) kettlebell for the press. If you press one time (1 repetition) every 4 seconds, you are going to do 15 repetitions per minute, totaling 30 repetitions over 2 minutes. This will give you a pressing volume of 476 kilograms (1,050 lb) of resistance during that 2-minute set. However, if you press at a tempo of 1 repetition every 5 seconds, you will get a total of 12 reps per minute or 24 total reps in the 2 minutes. This would give you a pressing volume of only 380 kilograms (840 lb) of resistance during the same 2-minute variation. If you are moving faster, say 1 repetition every 3 seconds, you will get 20 reps per minute for a total of 40 reps over 2 minutes and 635 kilograms (1,400 lb) of pressing resistance in the same 2 minutes. You will become very familiar with this concept of tempo during your kettlebell workouts.

Take a look at table 3.1. In this table, there are four different kettlebell lifters, each selecting a different load to train with. The numbers illustrate the work load for a single exercise set. Notice by changing the variables of load, tempo, repetitions and duration, we get workloads that are all within the same range of total volume.

Also note that for general health and fitness goals, it is recommended that kettlebell workouts last 30 minutes to 1 hour for at least 4 training days per week. This may seem like a lot, but consider that initially you will be working at mild to moderate intensities. It is important for beginning exercisers to gradually build up the frequency, intensity, and duration of kettlebell training in order to stay injury free, to allow for adequate recovery between workouts, and to build confidence through setting and achieving manageable fitness goals.

## Type

*Type* refers to the type of exercise you're doing (e.g., running, walking, kettlebell lifting). Our focus here is on lifting kettlebells, which is a form of exercise that combines cardiorespiratory conditioning, resistance training, and mobility or range of motion. Because kettlebell training combines multiple facets of exercise, it is a time-efficient method for developing all-around fitness. Though kettlebells emphasize a combination of training goals, it is also possible to use them in a way that focuses on one quality over the others. For example, if your goal is to increase maximal strength, you can structure your program to use heavier kettlebells for lower repetitions. On the other hand, if you want to emphasize cardiorespiratory endurance, you can program higher repetitions with light kettlebells to improve aerobic fitness. If your aim is muscle sculpting or hypertrophy (increasing the size of certain muscles), such as in bodybuilding, moderate-weight kettlebells for moderate repetitions are an effective way to accomplish that. For all-around physical fitness, however, programs use a combination of light, moderate, and heavy kettlebells in repetition schemes ranging from high to moderate to low.

We are emphasizing the efficacy of kettlebells as a stand-alone fitness tool, and you can certainly achieve great improvement in your fitness goals if you choose to use only kettlebells in your programs. However, kettlebells also can be combined effectively with other methods, including barbells, dumbbells, yoga, running, and other favorite activities.

## PUTTING THE FITT PRINCIPLE TO WORK

When you exercise at sufficient frequency, intensity, and time and you select an appropriate type of exercise that keeps your interest and motivates you to stick with the program, your fitness will improve and you'll start to see changes in your appearance, body weight, body-fat percentage, cardiorespiratory endurance, muscular strength and stamina, and mobility. These physiological improvements that occur as a result of sticking with a program are known as the training effect.

**Table 3.1   Kettlebell Training Volume Comparison**

|  | Load | Tempo | Reps | Duration | Total volume (kg) |
|---|---|---|---|---|---|
| Lifter A | 12 kg | 24 RPM | 96 | 4 min | 1,152 kg |
| Lifter B | 16 kg | 18 RPM | 72 | 4 min | 1,152 kg |
| Lifter C | 20 kg | 20 RPM | 60 | 3 min | 1,200 kg |
| Lifter D | 8 kg | 25 RPM | 150 | 6 min | 1,200 kg |

Your muscles will adapt to your current fitness level through the principles of overload, specificity, reversibility, and individual differences. If you appropriately stress your system through a progressive kettlebell program, your body will adapt and improve its function.

If the stress is not intense or frequent enough to appropriately overload the body, then no adaptation will occur. If the stress is too intense or excessive in volume, injury or overtraining will result. The best improvements in performance will occur when the optimal stresses are introduced into your kettlebell program.

As positive adaptation occurs, it will be time to change one or more of the FITT variables so that you can continue to progress into your next training phase. For example, if you've been training with kettlebells 3 days a week for 30 minutes and your progress has stalled, you could modify your program by adjusting one or more of these variables:

- *Frequency*—Add one more day of kettlebell training.
- *Intensity*—Use a kettlebell that is 2 to 4 kilograms (5-10 lb) heavier.
- *Time*—Increase your workout time by 10 to 15 minutes.
- *Type*—Change your focus from low-intensity aerobic training to more anaerobic training, doing multiple high-intensity sets with shorter rest periods in between.

An overriding objective for the progress-minded exerciser is to avoid training plateaus and successfully navigate plateaus when they occur. A plateau occurs when your body has returned to homeostasis, which is the physiological process the body uses to maintain a stable internal environment. Beginners may go as long as 6 months of training before a plateau occurs, with dramatic strength gains often occurring in the first few months of training. Soon, however, these gains begin to level off, or plateau. At this stage, you need to adjust your training techniques in order to continue to progress. You can use the following techniques to break out of your plateau.

### Increase Intensity

One way to move out of a plateau is by making your muscles work harder. At this point in training you can change the program from low weight and high reps to high weight and low reps. For example, change from 3 sets of 20 reps to 3 sets of 5 reps with a heavier load.

### Vary the Exercises

If you have been doing mostly vertical lifts, such as the snatch and press, switch to more horizontal lifts, such as renegade rows and bottoms-up push-ups. Changing the exercises and motor patterns stresses your muscles in a new way and allows overworked areas to rest and recover.

### Change the Order of Exercises

Sometimes you move past a plateau by modifying the order in which you perform the lifts. When your body fatigues in an unexpected order, your muscles will adapt differently.

### Add or Subtract Exercises

In time and with experience, you will remove some exercises from your program and add others. In general, look to do more with fewer movements by selecting compound exercises. For example, the clean and press combines a vertical pull and a vertical press into a single exercise.

### Get Adequate Rest

Rest and recovery via adequate sleep are critical for health as well as performance both in and out of the gym. Training plateaus are sure to occur if you are chronically tired. It is also likely that you will develop injuries if you are overly tired from lack of sleep. At certain phases throughout the year, you should take a 1- or 2-week break from training in order to give the body a full and complete rest.

### Analyze Your Nutrition

Are you getting sufficient protein and the right amounts and types of carbohydrate and fat? Are you digesting your foods well, or do you often experience bloating, excessive gas, indigestion, or heartburn? Are you eating quality foods and adequately hydrating throughout the day? Do you need supplementation because you are missing vital nutrients through diet alone? It is important to assess your nutrition as it relates to health and performance, and this is an ongoing and individual process.

A few words about a popular theory of training called *muscle confusion*: This concept says that in order to avoid or break out of training plateaus, you must constantly vary exercises, sets, reps, and weight. The tactics described previously are ways to modify a set program, and they work well when you are in a training plateau but are not a good general training strategy. Too much variation or changing things around will distract from the larger goal of building a solid foundation, which is built from progressive overload of the basics.

Ultimately, increased volume of exercise (total tonnage) is what results in increased fitness. Always record your load, reps, and sets to determine your total volume. When you see that your volume has maxed out or is decreasing, you have reached a plateau and one of the muscle-confusion techniques described earlier can help you to get past that sticking point and may also provide some new motivation by breaking the monotony of a strict program. Of all the factors discussed, rest and nutrition should be prioritized. In addition, adjusting one or more of the FITT variables every 4 to 6 weeks will enable you to continue making progress over the long term.

Understanding what the FIIT principle is and how to control the variables of frequency, intensity, type, and time enables you to structure ongoing progress within an exercise program. The next step is to match this knowledge with a realistic assessment of your current fitness level and set goals to create a practical and motivational kettlebell training practice.

# SETTING GOALS, ASSESSING FITNESS, AND TRAINING SAFELY

In chapter 5 you will learn how to warm up, and in chapter 6 you will begin learning the basic exercises of kettlebell training. I am firm believer that if something is worth doing, it is worth doing well. Before you can do something well, you need to have a clear idea about what you want to accomplish. In other words, you have to have a plan, and before you can have a plan, you have to have a goal. Goal setting is crucial to success in any worthwhile endeavor that you put your time and effort into, and kettlebell training is no different.

This chapter discusses how to set goals and the process for organizing your goals so that you have the best chance of accomplishing them. Further, to help with setting realistic goals, it's important to be aware of your current fitness level and what is a realistic goal for you. Toward that aim it is valuable to do a general assessment of your current level, and this chapter provides some safe assessment exercises you can do to check your physical readiness for kettlebell training and to allow for safe passage into the basic exercises that you will be learning. Finally, the chapter closes with a discussion of the best practices for kettlebell training, taking into account quality over quantity and the creation of a safe training environment. Before embarking on your kettlebell training program, it is advisable to get a checkup from a physician to make sure you have a clean bill of health.

## SETTING GOALS

Goal setting is a key component for success in kettlebell training. It is a powerful way of motivating yourself to take action and follow through to accomplishment. A ship would never set sail without a definite destination; otherwise it would just wander the oceans endlessly. Goals work like the ship's compass—they define a destination for all your hard work and effort and help you to set up the right map or plan for your success. Without goals, there is no plan and no purpose for your hard work. You would just be navigating the sea of kettlebell exercises without any realistic chance of arriving at your destination. Why leave things to chance when a bit of time spent identifying and committing to some tangible goals will get your there faster and more reliably? All of us have ideas about what we want to do, have, or become. "I want to lose weight" or "I want to look good in my bikini" are ideas about something, but they are not goals. There is no commitment, no plan, just thoughts about what might be appealing to you. A goal is more than an idea. A goal starts as an idea and then goes through steps to take it from the world of ideas into the world of results. Aiming toward a goal also provides motivation to actually achieve the goal.

So, how do set your goals? A helpful acronym to consider when creating goals is *SMART*, which stands for **s**pecific, **m**easurable, **a**ttainable, **r**elevant, and **t**imely. These five words tell us about the nature of goals and how to create and then realize them in your kettlebell training programs. There is some variance in how these SMART goals can be stated. There is not a consensus about exactly what the five keywords mean or what they are in any given circumstance. For example, the A in SMART, can also be stated as "achievable" or the R, can also be stated as "realistic."

## Specific

This first word in the acronym emphasizes the need for a specific goal. The goal has to be clear and unambiguous, without the vagueness of noncommittal statements. Specific goals offer more clarity and are much more likely to be accomplished than general goals because specificity gives substance and accuracy to your vision. Clear goals are also measurable (see the following section). When your goal is clear and specific, with a definite time set for accomplishing it, you will know what is expected, and you can use the specific result as motivation. When a goal is vague, or when it's expressed as a general statement, such as "to lose weight," it has little motivational value. To increase your chances of success, set clear goals that have specific and measurable guidelines. "I will train with kettlebells 3 days each week for 30 minutes per session and lose 20 pounds (9 kg) by the first of June" is an example of a clear, specific goal. In setting specific goals, you have to be able to answer the W questions:

- *Who* is involved? Are you training alone or with a partner? Does your goal involve other people in any way?
- *What* is your objective, that is, what do you want to attain? Losing weight or decreasing clothing sizes are aesthetic-oriented goals; running faster or lifting heavier loads are performance-oriented goals. What are the requirements and limitations? What do you need to give up in order to prioritize the accomplishment of your goal? Goals must be realistic and choices have to be made. Staying up late partying and waking up early to work out are in opposition. Be willing and able to give up certain comforts or destructive habits if the goal is important to you.

- *Where* will the goal be realized? Will you train at home or in a gym? Knowing and being comfortable in the environment gives more confidence.

- *When* will you accomplish your goal? Don't leave things to chance—have a target date in mind for accomplishing the current goal.

- *Why* are you doing this? What are the reasons or benefits of reaching your goal? The underlying motivation may be internal or external, but having a clear purpose for setting the goal is crucial.

## Measurable

The second word in SMART, *measurable*, points out the necessity of establishing definite criteria for measuring the progress toward each goal you set. If your goal cannot be measured, you have no way of knowing if you are making progress toward its successful completion. When you measure your progress, it helps you to stay on track, reach your target dates, and experience the excitement of accomplishments that motivate you to make the sustained effort necessary to reach your final goal. A measurable goal will answer questions such as "How much?", "How many?", and "How will I know when it is accomplished—what do I look for?"

For example, in the previously stated goal of "I will train 3 days per week for 30 minutes per session and lose 20 pounds (9 kg) by the first of June," you answer how much (3 days per week), how many (20 pounds), and how you will know when it is accomplished (by the first of June). You may decide to weigh yourself once per week and lose an average of 4 pounds (1.8 kg) per month over 5 months. All of these processes can be clearly measured.

## Attainable

The third word in the acronym focuses on goals that are *attainable*. They have to be likely to achieve. An attainable goal may challenge you to push yourself in order to achieve it; however, the goal is not extreme or out of reach for your current level. A goal that once seemed too far out of reach will start moving closer. With some dedicated and consistent effort, you can accomplish it. Goals should not be too far-fetched or too easy to accomplish. A goal that is too difficult makes it unlikely for you to be successful. At the same time, a goal that is too easy or does not require much effort will not be meaningful to you. There is a relationship between the difficulty of a goal and performance of a task. Specific and challenging goals lead to better performance than unclear or easy goals do. Having a goal that is too easy is not motivating. Difficult goals are more motivating than easy goals because there is a greater sense of accomplishment when you achieve something you had to work hard for.

By listing your goals, you build self-esteem and the confidence needed to achieve them. Once you determine which goals are most important to you, you will start to find ways to bring them to life. You will begin to see yourself as worthy of owning these goals and you'll acquire the successful traits to allow you to achieve them. A goal that is attainable will often cause you to identify previously overlooked possibilities and bring you closer to the realization of your goals. You will be able to attain almost any goal you set for yourself if you plan your steps well and establish a time frame that enables you to accomplish each step along the way. A goal that is attainable will answer the question, "How can the goal be accomplished?"

## Relevant

The fourth word in the acronym states the need for making your goals *relevant*. Relevant goals focus on objectives that you are willing and able to work toward. The goal can be lofty as long as you have a strong belief that it is possible for you to reach it. If you believe that the goal can be accomplished, then it is relevant for you. Perhaps you have accomplished something similar to your current goal in the past, and if so, you can be sure that your current goal is also relevant. Ask yourself what conditions would need to be present in order for you to accomplish your goal. An important facet of your goal is its level of challenge. We are all motivated by achievement. You will place value on your goal according to the significance of what you expect to accomplish. If you know that you will be well rewarded by your efforts, you will be highly motivated to follow the program until you realize the goal.

For a goal to be relevant, it also has to be realistic. If you truly believe you can accomplish it, then it is realistic for you. For example, if it currently takes you 12 minutes to run 1 mile (1.6 km), it is not realistic to set a 5-minute mile as an immediate goal. But a goal of running a mile in 10 minutes is certainly within your reach if you put in the work over the next several months. Once you accomplish that, you may set a new realistic goal of running the mile in 8 minutes and then 7 minutes and then 6 minutes. If you can run a mile in 6 minutes, then setting a goal of a 5-minute mile may be realistic. Try to always keep your goals in the context of where you are now. A relevant goal will answer an important question: "Does this seem worthwhile?"

If the goal does not seem worthwhile, you are not likely to stick with it and put in the work required to get there. But if it is worthwhile to you, you will keep at it in measured steps and you will reach the finish line. When setting your goal, make it a challenge. If it is too easy and you don't expect the achievement of the goal to be significant, your effort is not likely to be meaningful either. Just keep in mind that you have to strike a balance in setting a goal that is challenging but still realistic. If you set a goal that is too difficult to achieve, you will fail, and failing may be even more demotivating than setting a goal that is too easy. Human beings have an innate need for success and achievement and are motivated by goals that are challenging but realistic. Make sure your challenging goals are realistic and attainable for you.

## Timely

The fifth word in the acronym, *timely*, emphasizes the need to qualify your goal to be accomplished within a specific time frame by giving a date of completion. A commitment to a deadline helps you to focus your energy on the completion of the goal by that date. This aspect of SMART goals serves the purpose of preventing your goal from being overrun by the occasional dramas that can sometimes arise in life. A timely goal imposes a sense of priority and urgency. With no time frame tied to the goal, there's no sense of urgency. If you want to lose 20 pounds (9 kg), when do you want to lose it by? "Someday" is not nearly specific enough, and that ambiguous approach will not get you to the finish line. But if you commit to accomplishing the goal within a given time frame, such as "by the first of June," you've then programmed your unconscious mind to begin working on the goal. Commitment is a key component to success. The harder the goal, the more commitment is required.

Timely goals also have to be tangible, meaning you can experience them with one of the senses, such as taste, sight, touch, hearing, or smell. A tangible goal is also more likely to be specific and measurable and therefore achievable. A timely goal answers these questions: "When?", "What can I do today?", and "What can I do 6 weeks, 6 months, or 1 year from now?"

Setting specific, measurable, attainable, relevant, and timely goals is an important first step on your path to a stronger, fitter, more energetic body and will serve to guide the progress of your kettlebell training. The goal of goal setting is to be successful, and you need to set goals to be successful. Create clear, challenging goals and commit to accomplishing them.

## ASSESSING FITNESS

Kettlebell training is dynamic and requires a certain base level of physical readiness. You do not have to be fit or athletic to begin kettlebell training. However, you do have to have some control over your body to ensure that you can begin your kettlebell training safely and free of injury. For that reason, before you pick up the kettlebell for your first training, it is recommended that you do a few simple tests to check your readiness. The following movements test your core stability (midsection), shoulder stability, and hip and trunk mobility. If you pass these tests, then you can be reasonably certain that you have the base-level readiness to begin your kettlebell training program with confidence.

## ASSESSMENT EXERCISE 1: KETTLEBELL DEADLIFT

**Figure 4.1**   Kettlebell deadlift.

With the kettlebell on the ground, stand with your feet shoulder-width apart with the kettlebell just in front of you (see figure 4.1*a*). Keep your chest lifted as you sit back with your hips until your hands can reach the handle (see figure 4.1*b*). Grab the handle with both hands and stand up by pressing your feet into the ground until your body is fully upright (see figure 4.1*c*). Repeat by sitting back to lightly touch the kettlebell to the ground. Do 10 controlled reps with a light weight, and then repeat with a more challenging weight. For example, women might start with 8 kilograms (18 lb) for 10 reps and then use 12 kilograms (26 lb) for 10 reps, and men might start with 16 kilograms (35 lb) for 10 reps and then use 24 kilograms (53 lb) for 10 reps. This basic exercise teaches you to keep your center of gravity aligned vertically over your base of support. It is important to have control over your center of mass because kettlebell training involves such dynamic movements. A strong and stable base will keep you safe when swinging the kettlebell. Note that this assessment exercise can be modified if necessary to make it easier to perform correctly by placing the kettlebell on a short box or step to reduce the range of motion.

## ASSESSMENT EXERCISE 2: SQUAT

**Figure 4.2** Squat.

Stand with your feet shoulder-width apart or slightly wider (see figure 4.2*a*). Each person has to find the appropriate stance for his body. It may be shoulder-width for you but 1.5 times shoulder-width for someone else. The distance between your feet will vary according to flexibility, height, limb length, and leg strength. If you are not very flexible yet, you will probably not feel stable with a narrow stance and will feel more comfortable with feet wider than shoulder-width. Sit the hips back and down, as if you are sitting in a chair, and keep your chest lifted and trunk arched as much as possible (see figure 4.2*b*). Press the heels of the feet firmly into the ground; do not let the heels rise or weight shift onto toes. In the ideal squat, you should aim to sit all the way down to full range of motion in the flexed (bottom) position. It may take you some time to develop this flexibility and that's OK; work at your range and aim to improve it over time. From the bottom position, stand up by pressing your feet firmly into the ground. Repeat for 10 repetitions.

Squats are a basic function and a basic exercise for developing leg strength and endurance. Strong legs are a by-product of kettlebell training, and you will need to pay close attention to your legs and feet because they are your connection to the ground and the foundation from which strength, power, and endurance are developed using kettlebells. This assessment exercise can be modified if necessary to make it easier to perform correctly by squatting onto a chair or box to reduce range of motion.

## ASSESSMENT EXERCISE 3: ONE-ARM PRESS

**Figure 4.3**   One-arm press.

The one-arm press tests your core stability and the stability and mobility of the shoulder girdle and upper back. Stand with your feet shoulder-width apart (see figure 4.3a). Use two hands to pick up a kettlebell and position it in the hand (see figure 4.3b). Keep your legs straight and midsection firm (tight but not tense). Inhale deeply and as you push the kettlebell directly up over your shoulder, exhale. Press until your arm is straight, with no bend in the elbow, and the kettlebell is directly over your feet, or base of support (see figure 4.3c). Inhale again while the kettlebell is locked out overhead, and as you exhale let the kettlebell drop to your chest again (see figure 4.3d). Do 3 repetitions with each arm. This assessment exercise can be modified if necessary to make it easier to perform correctly by selecting a lighter kettlebell or using a light dumbbell or weight plate.

## ASSESSMENT EXERCISE 4: PLANK

**Figure 4.4** Plank.

The plank is a movement to test the stability of your hips, shoulders, and midsection. Starting in a facedown position on the floor, make tight fists with both hands and bend your elbows so that you form a right angle with each arm between the forearm and upper arm. Keep your abdominal muscles tight and hips pressed forward (in line with the spine), and stay balanced on the balls of your feet (see figure 4.4). Balance yourself on your forearms and toes with nothing else touching the ground. Hold this position for 30 seconds and work up to 1 minute. This assessment exercise can be modified if necessary to make it easier to perform correctly by elevating the upper body to decrease difficulty.

These four assessment exercises will give you a baseline to gauge your readiness for kettlebell training. Although it is not a requirement to pass these assessments, they can give you the confidence that you have adequate strength and control to take on the more vigorous kettlebell training that lies ahead. If you can pass the four assessments, your basic fitness is sufficient that you can safely begin kettlebell training, keeping in mind gradual progress and a conservative start. On the other hand, if you struggle to perform any of the assessment tests, you should commit 2 weeks to practice the four exercises to develop more strength and confidence.

## TRAINING SAFELY

In order to have good results, you need to set SMART goals, as we learned about earlier in this chapter, and achieve them. You also need to take the proper approach to training so that you can find better results compared with results achieved in ignorance of these guidelines. The following best practices for kettlebell training are important standards to keep in mind throughout your kettlebell journey to better fitness.

**Remember Quality Over Quantity**

Each movement has to have your full attention. A program may ask for a certain number of reps; however, the quality of the reps is more important than the quantity. If the set calls for 10 reps and your form starts to fall apart on rep 6, you should stop, take a short break, and finish the last 4 reps with precise form. The way you practice is the way you will perform. Demand excellence of yourself and you will become excellent!

**Monitor Your Exertion**

You will have good days and not-so-good days. Sometimes you will feel energetic and other times you will feel tired. The same exact workout, performed on different days, may feel very different and produce a different training effect in your body. There are a lot of factors that influence your workout and how you feel. Remember the RPE (rating of perceived exertion) discussed in chapter 3? RPE is a subjective way to gauge your intensity. You want to be able to recover between sets, and RPE is a convenient and effective way to monitor your workout intensity and recovery periods and to focus on quality repetitions.

Listen to your body and pay attention to the signs and internal dialogue your body has with you. Do not ignore yourself! Some days are better than others. You should challenge yourself but not overdo it. Again, use RPE as a way to monitor your intensity and push yourself, but do not push too hard, too soon. Don't be afraid to take an occasional day off if your body is telling you that you need the extra rest. Also, get plenty of sleep between your kettlebell workouts so you can fully recover from one workout and be ready to go after it again the next time.

### Don't Skip the Warm-Up and Cool-Down

Take the time to prepare with a thorough warm-up before vigorous exercise. A good warm-up takes 5 to 10 minutes. Also take time to stretch and cool down following vigorous exercise. Allow 5 to 10 minutes after your kettlebell training to decompress, stretch out, and reduce the excitation of your nervous system. The cool-down is every bit as important to your long-term progress as the workout itself. The warm-up and cool-down will be explained thoroughly in the next chapter.

### Take Your Time

When working out with kettlebells, progress conservatively and do not rush! Refrain from moving too fast and doing too much volume or progressing too quickly in load. Developing skill and fitness with kettlebells takes time and practice. But there is no hurry; it is worth doing well and staying injury free. You can always do more next time, but if you do too much, too soon, you will most likely pay a big price and may not bounce back so quickly. If you're unsure, be conservative. The main cause of injuries is selecting a kettlebell that is too heavy or doing too much volume of training with poor form (emphasizing quantity over quality).

## INJURY PREVENTION

There is a saying associated with sport, weightlifting, and gyms that connotes a macho, win-at-all-costs mentality: "No pain, no gain." Many young athletes have grown up hearing this from coaches, friends, and teammates. But is it really good advice? Is it necessary to achieve pain in order to see benefits or feel accomplished? In fact, "No pain, no gain" is bad advice, and heeding that advice is a sure recipe for injury, burnout, and poor results in training. Pushing yourself in training is important to go beyond your current level of strength and fitness, but you have to be smart about how hard and how often to push. Do not ignore your body's warning signs. If you feel burning, weakness, or extreme fatigue (RPE over 8), the smart thing is to stop, rest, and maybe call it a day. "Live to fight another day" is probably a better mantra to follow when it comes to long-term success in your kettlebell program.

Be careful not to strain. As you become more experienced, you will be able to push your body further in your training, but you have to be patient. Stop short of straining. Go a bit further each time, but it is not worth it to push too soon. Leave a little something in the tank, so to speak.

Also, think long term. Your progress should continue over time, so do not try to accomplish all of your fitness goals in a day or a week or a month. Remember that Rome was not built in a day, and be willing to invest in your long-term progress by being consistent with gradual improvements from week to week and month to month. Before you know it, you will look back and see all your progress.

After assessing your current level of readiness and ensuring that you have a safe training environment to work in, you can develop SMART goals. These goals will have you focused and ready to achieve increased strength and fitness through a well-planned kettlebell training program.

# WARMING UP AND COOLING DOWN

Starting a new exercise program is motivating and exhilarating. Having made your decision to begin kettlebell training, the goal orientation inspires you to jump in and get going. Before doing so, consider that a workout should not just include working out but also warming up beforehand to prepare your body for the vigorous workout and cooling down afterward to allow the body to settle down and unwind before going on with your day.

A well-designed kettlebell workout consists of three phases:

1. Preparation phase, or the warm-up

2. Main phase, or the workout

3. Final phase, or the cool-down

The main phase is what people are usually referring to when they say they are working out or training (you will find the kettlebell techniques for the main phase in chapters 6, 7, and 8). The main phase involves acquiring skills (learning), mastering the kettlebell exercises, and practicing and progressing in those exercises. This part of the workout makes you breathe heavily and really work. However, a common mistake is to do just the main phase and nothing else. A well-rounded and well-structured workout also contains a preparation warm-up phase and a final cool-down phase. The warm-up gradually prepares your muscles and heart to move from inactivity to moderate or heavy activity and prepares your mind for the hard training ahead. The cool-down reverses the process, gradually reducing your heart rate and preparing your muscles for the next training session. The hard training in the main phase does not in itself provide a complete or well-rounded kettlebell training session. By taking time to warm up before and cool down after each kettlebell training session, you will help prevent unnecessary injuries and reduce muscle soreness.

## PREPARATION PHASE: WARM-UP

Before you jump into the main phase of your kettlebell training, it is important to prepare your mind and body for the hard work to follow. The preparatory warm-up involves performing exercises to prepare for the kettlebell lifts that follow in the main phase of the workout. Being prepared mentally and physically before the main phase can make the difference between a successful and an unsuccessful workout. You will not be able to perform optimally until you are warmed up, and a proper warm-up provides numerous physiological and psychological benefits (see table 5.1).

There is also a safety component to be mindful of in any sensible kettlebell program.

**Table 5.1** Physiological and Psychological Benefits of a Warm-Up

| Physiological benefits | <ul><li>Increases blood flow to the muscles used</li><li>Increases heart rate and circulation</li><li>Increases muscle temperature and raises core body temperature, making the muscles more pliable</li><li>Increases delivery of oxygen and nutrients to the muscles, with an associated increase in cardiorespiratory performance preventing you from getting out of breath early or too easily</li><li>Prepares the nerve-to-muscle pathways for exercise</li><li>Decreases muscle stiffness, preparing the muscles for stretching, which may help you avoid injuries such as muscle tears and pulls</li><li>Increases production of synovial fluid, which reduces friction between the joints</li><li>Activates a full and free range of motion in muscles and joints</li><li>Increases adrenaline</li><li>Improves efficient cooling (sweating) by activating heat-dissipation mechanisms in the body and may help to prevent overheating during the main phase</li><li>Improves coordination and reaction times</li></ul> |
|---|---|
| Psychological benefits | <ul><li>Increases arousal</li><li>Provides stronger focus of your attention to the task</li><li>Gives time to clear your mind</li><li>Gives time to review your goals and skills</li><li>Creates the correct mind-set for a successful training session</li><li>Engages the body and the mind together and prepares them for learning</li></ul> |

A proper warm-up can save a lot of unnecessary wear and tear on your body over years of physical training with kettlebells or any other vigorous activity. If you just jump into the kettlebell lifting and don't take time to warm up, the blood vessels that supply the heart and working muscles don't have enough time to properly dilate. This can result in a sudden rise in pressure in the blood vessels. Not only is this not good for healthy people, it can be dangerous for someone who already has high blood pressure at rest. In addition, because the blood flow is restricted, there is an inadequate supply of oxygen to the muscles that need it, including the heart. Chest pain, heart damage, or muscle pain can be a result. Further, moving straight into intense exercise without a preparatory warm-up can cause arrhythmia (abnormal heart rhythms), early fatigue, muscle strains (cold muscles are more prone to injury than muscles that have been warmed up), and joint injury (the synovial fluid that lubricates the joints circulates more freely when the body temperature is slightly increased).

It is not uncommon for many people, even those with a lot of experience, to deemphasize or skip altogether the preparation phase and not include any warm-ups in their program or at best do only a few sets of the lift with a light weight because they are in a hurry to get to the meat of the workout. They view warm-ups and cool-downs as less important or a waste of precious time. If you think that warm-ups and cool-downs are time-wasters, think again. Warming up before kettlebell training and cooling down afterward are more important than you may realize. In fact, they are paramount in making sure that your kettlebell training is safe and effective.

The degree and duration of the warm-up and cool-down depend on a few factors, including age, fitness level and training experience, injuries and health history, weather, and the type and intensity of the main phase to follow. It also most likely will vary from one workout to the next. Generally speaking, a thorough preparation phase consists of anywhere from 5 to 30 minutes of low-intensity movement. The older and more unfit the exercise participant, the longer the warm-up should be. Also, the more intense the workout, the longer the warm-up should be. A quick 20-or 30-minute main phase may require only a 5-minute warm-up, but a serious athlete training for 2 hours may need an extensive warm-up taking up to 30 minutes to complete. In any case, the warm-up should be intense enough to raise your body temperature but not intense enough to fatigue you. Use good awareness of how you are feeling in addition to sound judgment and technique.

Each person will have her own method of warming up. For example, it will take longer to warm up on colder days or in cooler climates. Make sure that the warm-up remains relevant to your age, experience, and abilities and to the intensity and duration of the kettlebell workout you will do in the main part of the training. With more experience, you will develop a good intuition for the appropriate warm-up for a given training session and you can just feel your way through it. Developing the perfect warm-up is an individualized process that comes with practice, experimentation, and experience. Find what works best for you by trying various movements, combinations, and durations to determine the right amount of preparation to get your body and mind primed for the main phase ahead.

Be sure you do not warm up too early. The benefits of the warm-up will be lost after about 30 minutes, so do not take too long to move from the preparation phase to the main phase.

A well-constructed warm-up consists of up to four separate stages, each one preparing for the next stage. You may include each stage in your warm-up or select only one or two stages suitable for the workout to follow. Understanding the various stages gives you a great deal of freedom and adaptability when creating warm-ups. The four stages of a warm-up are as follows:

1. General warm-up
2. Dynamic mobility warm-up
3. Sport-specific warm-up
4. Static stretching warm-up

Note that if you are short on time, such as if you have only 30 minutes to train and cannot commit 10 or 15 minutes to the warm-up, you should do a minimum of a sport-specific warm-up before beginning any kettlebell workout.

## General Warm-Up

The overall approach to the general warm-up is to focus on warming the large muscle groups of the body such as the quadriceps, calves, hamstrings, hip flexors, shoulders, and so on. The general warm-up is divided into two parts: aerobic activity (pulse-raiser) and joint mobility exercises (rotations).

### Aerobic Activity

Aerobic activity to raise the pulse can consist of any number of aerobic movements that circulate blood and oxygen to supply the muscles with more energy. The most common aerobic activity is an easy jog of 5 to 10 minutes. In place of jogging you can select any of these light aerobic activities:

- Brisk walking
- Marching in place
- Skipping forward and backward
- Lateral shuffling
- Low-intensity agility drills, such as two-legged hopping in all directions, speed ladders, or cone drills
- Body-weight squats or other simple calisthenics
- Shadowboxing, which is throwing loose, easy punches while bouncing and shuffling around like a boxer
- Skipping rope
- Other light-intensity cyclical aerobic movements

In most cases, the selected movements should use only your body. For example, jogging on the ground is preferred to jogging on a treadmill because on a treadmill you only need to lift your foot and let the belt pass, whereas you have to propel yourself forward when running on the ground. As another example, riding a bicycle requires a degree of balance and core stability that a stationary bike cannot offer. Mastering your own body weight in basic movements is the fundamental athletic use of your body that all sports and other activities, including kettlebell lifting, are built upon. In some cases, such as for convenience or in poor weather, you might use an aerobics machine such as a treadmill, stationary bike, or elliptical trainer. However, when possible, natural movement is preferred to the machine-based alternative. The focus of the pulse-raiser is simply to raise your core temperature, gradually increase your heart rate, and increase your cardiovascular output (get your blood pumping). Increased blood flow in the muscles improves performance and flexibility and reduces the likelihood of injury.

## Joint Mobility Exercises

Upon completion of the gentle pulse-raiser, you will move directly into joint mobility rotations, which help your joints to feel loose and lubricated so that they move smoothly and with relative ease. Joint rotations lubricate the entire joint with synovial fluid and permit your joints to function more easily when called upon to lift the kettlebells.

Perform joint rotations by gently moving the joints in circular motions both clockwise and counterclockwise. Work from top to bottom or vice versa, or you can begin at your center (waist, hips, and low back) and then move to the extremities. For most joint mobility exercises, do 10 to 20 repetitions or as many as needed for the joints to feel stretched and warmed. Be sure to mobilize all the major joint structures of your body, which include the following:

| | |
|---|---|
| Fingers and knuckles | Neck |
| Wrists | Hips |
| Elbows | Spine |
| Shoulders and shoulder girdles | Ribs |
| Trunk | Knees |
| | Ankles |
| | Toes |

The following are some joint mobility exercises that I use and recommend, and they collectively represent the major joints of the body. This list of exercises is by no means exhaustive and only introduces the study of joint mobility, representing movements that are relatively simple. The study of mobility is as unlimited as life, and movement training as a study has a rich culture in such art forms as dancing, yoga, martial arts, and many other movement-based systems.

## FINGER FLEXION AND EXTENSION

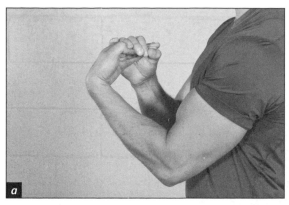 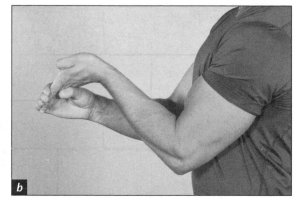

**Figure 5.1** Finger (a) flexion and (b) extension.

With your palm facing up, use the opposite hand to alternately pull your fingers toward you (see figure 5.1a) and push them away from you (see figure 5.1b). Hold each end position for 1 second. Switch hands and repeat.

## INTERLOCKED WRIST ROLLS

**Figure 5.2** Interlocked wrist rolls.

Interlace your fingers with your palms facing each other (see figure 5.2a). Circle your wrists in a clockwise direction for 10 to 20 seconds (see figure 5.2b) and then repeat in a counterclockwise direction.

## ELBOW CIRCLES

**Figure 5.3** Elbow circles.

Make a relaxed fist with both hands (see figure 5.3a). Rotate your arms at the elbow joint so that the right arm circles in a clockwise direction and the left arm circles in a counterclockwise direction for 20 to 30 seconds (see figure 5.3b). Reverse directions.

## FOREARM EXTENSION AND FLEXION

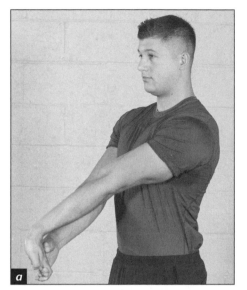 

**Figure 5.4**  Forearm *(a)* extension and *(b)* flexion.

With your palm up, extend your elbow straight and point your fingers toward the ground so that the palm is facing forward. Using the opposite hand, push the fingers toward you while pushing the palm farther away from you for 2 seconds (see figure 5.4*a*). You will feel the stretch in the top of the forearm. Next, grab the back of the hand and push the palm back toward you for 2 seconds (see figure 5.4*b*). You will feel the stretch on the backside of the forearm. Repeat with the other hand.

## SHOULDER ROLLS

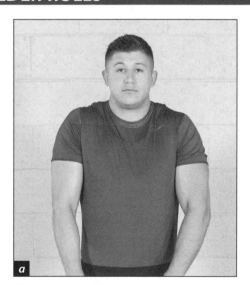 

**Figure 5.5**  Shoulder rolls: forward with *(a)* both shoulders and forward with *(b)* one shoulder.

Make big circles while shrugging your shoulders as if you are trying to scratch your earlobes with the top of your shoulder. Move both shoulders at the same time forward (see figure 5.5*a*) and then backward. Then, alternate moving one shoulder at a time forward (see figure 5.5*b*) and backward.

## NECK TILTS

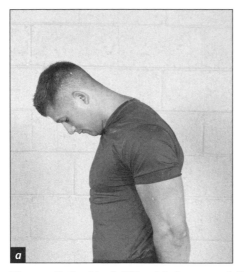
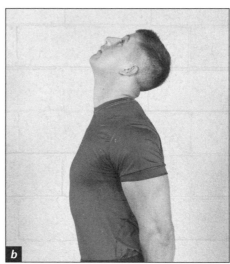

**Figure 5.6**  Neck tilts: *(a)* down and *(b)* up.

Look forward and drop your chin to your chest for 2 seconds (see figure 5.6*a*). Then, lift your chin and look up, lifting the chin to the ceiling for 2 seconds (see figure 5.6*b*). Repeat this up and down and gradually increase the range of motion as your neck relaxes.

## NECK ROTATIONS

**Figure 5.7**  Neck rotation.

Look forward (see figure 5.7*a*). Leading with your eyes, turn your head to the left while keeping your shoulders still and only turning your head (see figure 5.7*b*). Then, turn your head to the right. Repeat this side-to-side motion and gradually increase the range of motion, holding the end position for 2 seconds on each side.

## NECK CIRCLES

**Figure 5.8**   Neck circles.

Let your head be heavy and relaxed (see figure 5.8*a*) and move the entire head in large circle in a clockwise direction (see figure 5.8*b*). Then, repeat the movement in a counterclockwise direction. To control the movement, take 2 to 3 seconds per rotation.

## HIP CIRCLES

**Figure 5.9**   Hip circles.

Place your hands on your hips (see figure 5.9*a*) and make a big circling movement in a clockwise direction with your hips as if you were using a hula hoop (see figure 5.9*b*). Repeat the circle 10 to 15 times and then move in a counterclockwise direction. Maintain a steady cadence of about 2 seconds per rotation.

## TRUNK TWISTS

**Figure 5.10**  Trunk twists.

Stand with arms out to your sides and relax (see figure 5.10a). Twist your body to one side as you shift your weight to the side you are twisting, and at the same time, raise the opposite foot while you pivot (see figure 5.10b). Repeat the twist back and forth from one side to the other. Gradually increase the range of motion as you get warmer.

## LATERAL BENDS

**Figure 5.11**  Lateral bends.

Stand upright and drop your hands relaxed to your sides (see figure 5.11a). Tilt your body to one side and allow that hand to slide down along the side of your body (see figure 5.11b). To help maintain alignment, lift your opposite elbow up as you bend. Do not bend forward; try to stay as upright as possible so the stretch is along the side of your body. Then, tilt the other direction, repeating back and forth. Use a cadence of 2 seconds per side.

## WAIST BENDS

**Figure 5.12** Waist bends.

Place your hands on your hips and keep your legs straight (see figure 5.12*a*). Fold forward at the waist as you look down to the floor (see figure 5.12*b*). Raise yourself with the hips and look up as you do a gentle backbend (see figure 5.12*c*). Repeat continuously, 2 seconds in each direction.

## FIGURE-EIGHT WAIST CIRCLES

**Figure 5.13** Figure-eight waist circles.

Place hands on your hips (see figure 5.13*a*). Fold forward at the waist as you exhale (see figure 5.13*b*), and as you inhale, circle your trunk up (see figure 5.13*c*) and back into a gentle back bend. Exhale and fold forward again, then inhale and circle up and back in the opposite direction. Repeat in each direction continuously, 2 seconds in each direction.

## SPINAL ROLLS

**Figure 5.14** Spinal rolls.

Stand upright and relax completely (see figure 5.14a). Exhale as you fold forward at the waist, dropping your upper body toward the floor (see figure 5.14b). Inhale and slowly roll back up to the upright position, moving one vertebra at a time from the lower spine up to the upper spine (see figure 5.14, c and d).

## LATERAL RIB OPENERS

**Figure 5.15**  Lateral rib openers.

Interlace your fingers and press your arms overhead with palms facing up (see figure 5.15*a*). Inhale in this position, and then exhale as you reach up and over to the side, stretching the side of your opposite rib cage (see figure 5.15*b*). Inhale, return to start position, and exhale as you stretch the ribs on the other side. Repeat continuously, taking 3 seconds to stretch to the side and back to the top.

## KNEE CIRCLES

**Figure 5.16**  Knee circles.

With your feet together, place your hands on your kneecaps (see figure 5.16*a*). Gently bend the knees into a partial squat with heels flat on the floor and circle them clockwise until they are straight again (see figure 5.16, *b-d*). Repeat in a counterclockwise direction.

## ANKLE BOUNCES

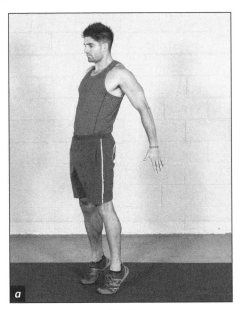 

**Figure 5.17** Ankle bounces.

Rise onto your toes as high as you can (see figure 5.17a), and then lift your toes as you rock back onto your heels (see figure 5.17b). Repeat this toe–heel movement back and forth. Use your hands to counterbalance your lower-body motion so you can maintain balance.

## Dynamic Mobility Exercises

You are warming up for a workout that is going to involve a lot of dynamic activity, so it makes sense to perform some dynamic exercises to increase your dynamic flexibility. During the warm-up, you can do dynamic stretching along with a minimal amount of static stretching. This will prepare your body for the dynamic and explosive kettlebell lifts during the main phase of the training. Dynamic mobility is accomplished by performing movements in all directions while gently increasing range of motion and speed. Do as many sets as necessary to reach your maximum range of motion in any given direction, but do not work your muscles to the point of fatigue. Remember, this is just a warm-up; the real workout comes afterward. A word of caution—this type of dynamic stretching can cause injury if overdone or performed improperly, so you have to be meticulous when performing it. Sets of these movements should be in the range of 10 to 15 repetitions, and 1 to 3 sets of each movement should be enough.

## ARM TWIRLS

**Figure 5.18**   Arm twirls.

Stand tall with your elbow straight (see figure 5.18a) and circle your arm up with fingers pointing to the sky (see figure 5.18b). Your biceps should brush your ear with each pass. You may not yet have the flexibility to touch your biceps to your ear, but work toward it over time. Continue to circle your arm down (see figure 5.18c) and let your palm brush your thigh. Continue this twirling movement, gradually going faster and faster, and then move the arm in the opposite direction. Repeat in both directions with the other arm. You may also perform this exercise by moving both arms simultaneously, repeating in both directions.

## CHEST HOLLOW AND EXPAND

**Figure 5.19**  Chest hollow and expand.

Stand tall and exhale while hollowing your chest and crossing one arm over the other with palms down (see figure 5.19a). Inhale and separate the arms with palms up as you expand your chest forward (see figure 5.19b). You may also perform this exercise by separating the arms diagonally with one high and one low and repeating in opposite directions.

## VERTICAL CHEST OPENER

**Figure 5.20**  Vertical chest opener.

Stand tall and inhale as you swing both arms overhead and open the chest (see figure 5.20a). Exhale and swing both arms down and back (see figure 5.20b).

## DYNAMIC CLAPPING

**Figure 5.21**   Dynamic clapping.

Clap your hands in front of you with your arms straight (see figure 5.21*a*). Swing both arms back and clap the palms together behind you, keeping the arms straight (see figure 5.21*b*). Try to keep your hands up high and not drop them too much as they move behind you. You will feel this dynamic stretch in the chest, shoulders, and upper-back muscles.

## BOOTSTRAPPERS

**Figure 5.22**   Bootstrappers.

With feet together, fold forward and place your fingers or palms on the floor. Squat down onto the balls of your feet, keeping your hands on the floor (see figure 5.22*a*), and push your knees back until they are straight (see figure 5.23*b*). Repeat this bending and extending of the knees and gradually increase speed as you get warmer. You should feel this stretch in the backs of your legs.

## LEG SWINGS

**Figure 5.23**  Leg swings.

Balance yourself by gently holding a wall, sturdy chair, or stretching bar and put all your weight on the leg closest to the wall or chair (see figure 5.23*a*). With the other leg, pull your toes toward you (dorsiflex the foot), and keeping your trunk as upright as possible, swing the leg forward and back (see figure 5.23, *b* and *c*), going slightly higher on each rep until you are eventually warm enough to reach maximal height in both directions.

## Sport-Specific Warm-Up

Sport-specific warm-ups involve exercises and drills that mimic the main activity to follow but are performed at a low intensity. The sport-specific warm-up can start with a low-intensity version of the kettlebell lifts to be performed in the main phase and can be viewed as the transition between the warm-up and main phase. For example, if the main phase of your workout calls for you to press with 16 kilograms (35 lb), you may do a few sets of presses for low reps with 8 kilograms (18 lb), 10 kilograms (22 lb), and 12 kilograms (26 lb) as part of your sport-specific warm-up.

You may prefer to start your sport-specific warm-up with general kettlebell exercises such as around-the-body passes and halos, then progress into light, low-rep sets of core lifts such as the swing, clean, or press. Move from light to progressively heavier kettlebell lifts that you will be doing in the main training, only lighter and with lower volume.

## Static Stretching Warm-Up

Stretching is not warming up in itself; however, it is part of the warm-up. Following your aerobic activity, joint rotations, dynamic mobility exercises, and sport-specific exercises, you should engage in some slow, relaxed, gentle static stretching as the final part of your preparation phase. This is the most individualized portion of your workout because you will choose stretches to meet your preparation needs. Static stretches can be used in order to stretch specific problem muscles. This is personal and may be dictated by past or current injuries and also the particular techniques to be performed in the main part of the training session. For example, if your session will have a lot of pressing movements, you may need to spend some extra time doing static stretches for your shoulder girdle, chest, and back muscles. Or, if you have a tight neck one day, you may want to spend a few extra minutes performing some light neck stretching before you move into the main part of the training.

Static stretching increases the range of motion in the joints that will be used in the main phase of the kettlebell workout. You should perform these warm-up static stretches only at the end of the warm-up phase when your muscle are thoroughly warmed and thus more elastic, reducing the likelihood of injury. Any static stretches during the warm-up should be held for only 5 to 10 seconds per stretch. Remember that stretching muscles when they are cold may lead to a tear. Stretches should not be forced or done at a speed that may stretch the joint, muscles, and tendons beyond their normal length. The static stretches during the warm-up should be short and at a gentle intensity. The majority of static stretching should take place at the end of your training as part of your cool-down. To get noticeable benefits from your stretching, perform the stretches a minimum of three times per week for at least 10 minutes, preferably upon completion of your kettlebell training or other intense exercise. Following are some common static stretches that you can use.

## BEHIND-THE-BACK SHOULDER STRETCH

**Figure 5.24** Behind-the-back shoulder stretch.

Stand upright and interlock your fingers behind back (see figure 5.24*a*). Pull your hands upward until you reach your maximum range and hold the position for a few seconds (see figure 5.24*b*). Relax your arms down again and repeat for 3 to 5 more reps.

## SHOULDER STRETCH

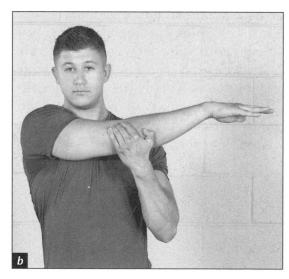

**Figure 5.25** Shoulder stretch.

With your elbow extended and palm facing down, reach your arm across the opposite side of your body (see figure 5.25*a*). With your other hand, reach across and grab your triceps or elbow, and without twisting your trunk, pull firmly on the triceps or elbow until you feel the stretch in the rear part of your shoulder (see figure 5.25*b*). Hold for 10 to 20 seconds and then repeat with the other arm.

## TRICEPS PULLS

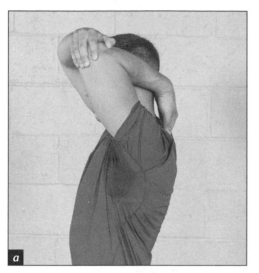
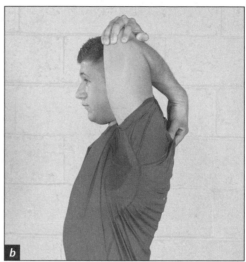

**Figure 5.26** Triceps pulls.

Reach one arm overhead and bend the elbow so that the hand and wrist drop behind your back, the elbow is pointing up to the ceiling, and the fingers are pointing down to the floor. Reach behind your head with your opposite hand and push down on the elbow (see figure 5.26 *a* and *b*). Keep your chest lifted and push back with your head against your arm. Hold this position for 10 to 20 seconds, and then repeat with the other arm.

## NECK FLEXION STRETCH

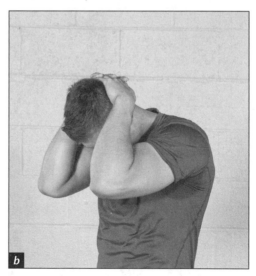

**Figure 5.27** Neck flexion stretch.

Interlace your fingers and place your hands behind your head (see figure 5.27*a*). Without bending your trunk, pull down on your head and press your chin to your chest (see figure 5.27*b*). Feel the stretch in the back of your neck and hold the position for 5 to 10 breaths.

## LATERAL NECK STRETCH

**Figure 5.28** Lateral neck stretch.

Look forward and reach with your hand up and over to the opposite side of your head (see figure 5.28a), gently pulling your head to the side and bringing your ear closer to the top of your shoulder (see figure 5.28b). Be careful to elongate the side of the neck you are pulling rather than compressing the side moving closer to your shoulder. Hold for 10 seconds and then repeat on the other side.

## STANDING KNEE-TO-CHEST STRETCH

**Figure 5.29** Standing knee-to-chest stretch.

Stand upright and lift one knee as high as you can without leaning back (see figure 5.29a). Keep your supporting leg straight, and with interlaced fingers, place your palms on your shin just below knee level and pull your knee to your body (see figure 5.29b). Keep your abdominal muscles tight so that you stay upright and do not lean back. Hold with firm pressure for five breaths and then repeat with the other leg.

## STANDING QUADRICEPS STRETCH

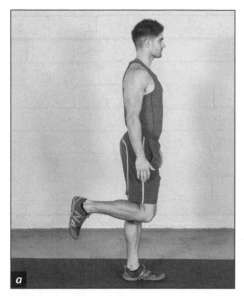

**Figure 5.30** Standing quadriceps stretch.

Stand upright and bend the right leg behind you (see figure 5.30*a*). Reach behind to grab your foot or ankle with your right hand and stretch the other arm overhead. Stretch the quadriceps by pulling in firmly and folding forward slightly at the waist (see figure 5.30*b*). Keep the knee of the stretched leg pointing down to the floor and touching or close to the other leg. The knee on the support leg stays straight. Hold for 10 to 15 seconds and then repeat with the other leg.

## STANDING HAMSTRINGS STRETCH

**Figure 5.31** Standing hamstrings stretch: *(a)* grabbing the calves if you're less flexible and *(b)* grabbing the ankles if you're more flexible.

With your legs about hip-width apart, fold forward at the waist while keeping your spine long and not rounded. To keep the spine extended, reach your chin forward while you push your buttocks back. Keep as much distance as you can between your chin and your backside. Keep your knees straight and fold as far forward and down as you can. If you are less flexible, grab the backs of your legs at the calves (see figure 5.31*a*); if you are more flexible, grab the backs of your ankles (see figure 5.31*b*). Hold this position for 5 to 10 breaths, pulling firmly with your arms and feeling the stretch in the backs of your legs.

## CALF STRETCH

**Figure 5.32**   Calf stretch.

Place your hands against the wall with one foot forward and the other foot back and the toes of both feet pointing forward (see figure 5.32*a*). Shift your weight to the front leg by bending the front knee until the rear knee is extended straight (see figure 5.32*b*). Feel the stretch in the back of your rear leg. Stretch deeper by pressing the rear heel firmly into the floor and shifting more weight onto the front leg. You will have to play with the distance between your feet until you find the distance that gives you the best stretch. Hold for 15 to 20 seconds and repeat with the other leg.

## SPINAL FLEXION

**Figure 5.33**   Spinal flexion.

Place your hands and feet on the floor with your knees straight and hips pushing up and back (see figure 5.33*a*). Use firm pressure from your palms to continue pushing your hips as far back as possible and drop your head so that you are looking down and between your feet (see figure 5.33*b*). If your knees are bent, come up onto the balls of your feet and press your knees back until your legs are straight. Over time as you become more flexible in this position, drop your heels to the floor while keep your legs extended. Hold this position for 5 to 10 breath cycles.

## SPINAL EXTENSION

**Figure 5.34** Spinal extension.

Lie on your belly with your palms flat on the floor slightly wider than shoulder-width apart and your feet together (see figure 5.34a). Press your feet away from you, trying to make your lower spine as long as possible. Inhale and look up, and while pressing into the floor with your palms, lift your upper body off the floor while keeping your hips pressed into the floor (see figure 5.34b). Your chest is lifted and your shoulders are pressed down, *not* shrugged. Hold this position for five breath cycles (a cycle is one inhalation and one exhalation). You will feel the stretch along both sides of your spine. You can also perform this exercise with a twist: At the top of the stretch, twist your upper body to one side and hold that position for three breath cycles, and then twist the other direction. Repeat to the right and left another two or three times.

## KNEE-TO-CHEST STRETCH

**Figure 5.35** Knee-to-chest stretch.

Lie on your back with both legs extended (see figure 5.35a). Bend one leg, and with interlaced fingers, grab just below your knee and pull the knee firmly to your chest (see figure 5.35b). Hold that position for 5 to 10 seconds and then extend the leg back to the floor and repeat the stretch with the other leg. You should feel this stretch somewhat in your hips but primarily in your lower back. Repeat with both legs another three or four times.

## CHILD'S POSE

**Figure 5.36** Child's pose.

Begin on your hands and knees (see figure 5.36a). Press your hands and fingers firmly into the floor and use strength from your hands to push your hips back as far as you can while dropping your hips to just above or onto your ankles (see figure 5.36b). Drop your head to the floor and try to elongate your spine as much as you can (see figure 5.36c). Hold this position for 10 breath cycles.

Remember that the warm-up should cause mild sweating, but it shouldn't leave you fatigued, because fatigue will likely decrease performance. Upon completion of the warm-up, you should be sweating lightly and have an increased heart rate and core temperature. Now you are ready to move into the main phase of your training session, which is covered in chapters 6, 7, and 8. Additionally, sample workouts are found in chapters 9 and 10.

# FINAL PHASE: COOL-DOWN

Just as it is important to warm up for your kettlebell training, you also need to allow time to return your body and mind to their normal state by way of a gentle cool-down, the final phase of a complete kettlebell training session. The cool-down does the following:

- Allows the heart rate and body temperature to gradually decrease and circulate blood and oxygen to muscles, restoring them to the condition they were in before exercise.

- Reduces the risk of blood pooling by maintaining muscle action and heart rate to pump blood back to the heart.

- Reduces the risk of muscle soreness and reduces waste products from the muscles, such as lactic acid, which can build up during vigorous activity.

- Gradually returns breathing to resting levels.

- Helps avoid fainting or dizziness, which can result from blood pooling in the large muscles of the legs when vigorous activity suddenly stops.

- Helps to decompress the joints after the kettlebell weight training compresses them.

- Elongates and prepares the muscles for the next exercise session, whether it's the next day or in a few days.

- Transfers excess heat from the muscles to the environment in relatively cool conditions, and returns the body to a normal functioning state.

- Reduces excitation of the nervous system caused by the increase in adrenaline from the training.

The cool-down is often neglected despite its vital role in an effective training program. It is especially important after high-intensity exercise such as kettlebell training. The cool-down should occur immediately after the main part as a component of the recovery process, while you are still warm. During exercise, your heart and legs act as cooperative pumps working to keep your blood flowing efficiently between your upper and lower body. When you contract your leg muscles, the veins in your legs are squeezed and the blood is pushed up to the heart. When you stop exercising, the heart continues to beat at a much faster rate than normal. If you stop suddenly, the muscles will not be able to pump the blood back at the required speed, which can cause the blood to pool in the veins. Your brain will be denied the oxygen it needs and you might faint. Therefore, continuous rhythmic movement in the legs right after exercise is critical in order to prevent the blood from pooling. In addition, without a cool-down, metabolic waste materials such as lactic acid will not be removed, resulting in postexercise stiffness and soreness. Low-intensity movement with your legs allows for a safe, gradual reduction in heart rate and blood pressure until they reach normal resting levels.

A proper cool-down consists of 5 to 15 minutes of low-intensity movement. Older and deconditioned people may need a longer cool-down. Wait until your heart rate has gone down to 120 BPM or lower before sitting or lying down. Also note that because body temperature stays elevated for some time after exercise, after the cool-down is an appropriate and effective time to increase flexibility by performing sustained static stretching.

A thorough cool-down consists of three parts. It has the reverse goal of the warm-up, this time moving from more to less dynamic movements. Here are the three parts of the cool-down:

1. Sport-specific activity
2. Dynamic stretching
3. Static stretching

## Sport-Specific Activity

Sport-specific activity in the cool-down gradually reduces your heart rate and blood flow as well as removes metabolic by-products. Perform at least 5 minutes of sport-specific activity after the main part of training has been completed. A serious kettlebell athlete will typically run for 20 to 30 minutes or more at an easy to moderate intensity after kettlebell lifting. This may seem like a lot, but with more experience and improved conditioning, your volume of kettlebell training increases. Relative to kettlebell training, which is high intensity, jogging is low intensity and thus serves as a good cool-down after the main phase of training. However, if you like to run, you should jog on non-kettlebell-lifting days and add jogging as part of your cool-down only once you become accustomed to the intensity and energy output of kettlebell training. Don't try to do too much, too soon! In place of running you can do any low-intensity movements or even a few light sets of the lifts you were training in the main phase.

## Dynamic and Static Stretching

Flexibility is an often misunderstood component of kettlebell training. It is not essential for a kettlebell lifter to be able to do the splits, but it is important to have full range of motion in all joints and major muscle groups used in the kettlebell exercises. Therefore, stretching is an important part of cooling down after a kettlebell workout. It is performed during the final phase of your cool-down, when your muscles are warm and prepared to lengthen and there is a lower risk of injury. Stretching will help relax your muscles and improve flexibility, which is the range of movement about your joints. Stretching also relieves tightness and soreness in fatigued muscles and helps you to feel more recovered from the strenuous kettlebell training.

Make the stretches in your cool-down more thorough than your warm-up stretches, holding each position for a longer duration and moving deeper into the stretch. Stretch all the major muscle groups that you have used during your

---

### COMMON MISTAKES TO AVOID WHEN STRETCHING

Consistent stretching is an important part of a well-rounded kettlebell training program and will go a long way toward improving flexibility and ease of movements. However, improper technique or harmful habits can create injury. Be aware of the some of the common pitfalls to avoid while stretching.

**Inadequate or Insufficient Warm-Up**

We stretch most effectively when the body is warm. Increased body temperature increases circulation and the movement of fluids. Stretching while cold or stiff is less productive and more likely to cause discomfort or injury.

**Insufficient Rest Between Workouts**

Stretching while tired or sleepy is generally not a good idea. Your focus is less sharp and you are more likely to lack the concentration needed to ensure good positioning and mechanics.

**Overstretching**

While stretching, you will feel some tension in your muscle, but if you feel sharp pain, it might mean that you have caused tissue damage, which may cause pain and soreness. If you stretch properly, you will not be sore the day after. If you are sore, it may be an indication that you are overstretching and that you need to go easier on your muscles by reducing the intensity of the stretches you perform. The easiest way to overstretch is to stretch cold muscles without a proper warm-up.

---

exercise, especially the hamstrings, quadriceps, trunk (spinal) extensors, calves, shoulders, and forearms, which are the muscle groups that do most of the work in kettlebell training.

When done properly, stretching can do more than just increase flexibility. The benefits of stretching include the following:

- Improves physical fitness.
- Ensures full range of movement.

- Optimizes the learning, practice, and performance of skilled movements.
- Increases mental and physical relaxation and promotes development of body awareness.
- Reduces risk of injury to joints, muscles, and tendons and reduces muscular tension and soreness.
- Increases suppleness due to stimulation of the chemicals that lubricate connective tissues.

There are two main styles of stretching, dynamic and static, which will be covered in this section. Start with some light dynamic stretches until your heart rate slows down to its normal rate, and then move into static stretching.

## Dynamic Stretching

Dynamic flexibility is the ability to attain a large range of motion at a joint with accompanying movement and consists of simple movements that require large ranges of motion. Revisit the Dynamic Mobility Exercises section earlier in this chapter and select two to four dynamic exercises that work the areas of your body that feel tight after the main workout. The difference between the dynamic mobility exercises done during the warm-up and the dynamic stretching done during cool-down is the intensity. You will be gentler during the warm-up and more vigorous during the cool-down since you are already thoroughly warm.

## Static Stretching

Static stretching improves overall flexibility and is a great tool to promote relaxation, improve recovery time, and increase blood flow. A cool-down that includes static stretches will prevent the negative effects of an abrupt stop in activity while promoting improved recovery time, relaxation, stress reduction, and flexibility. Static stretching involves stretching to the furthest tolerable position of the muscle length without pain and holding that position for 10 seconds up to 3 minutes. You can hold

the stretches longer for any areas that are extra stiff or tight. After a short rest (as the muscle relaxes), move further into the stretch. There should be no pain, bouncing, or jerking movements during the stretching. Gentle static stretches are helpful during the warm-up but should be used primarily in the cool-down while the muscles are warmer and better able to lengthen, because stretching a cold muscle can increase the risk of injury from pulls and tears. Perform some or all of the same static stretches that you did during the warm-up, only move deeper into each stretch and hold each posture for a longer duration, trying to increase your range of motion.

Following are a few guidelines for static stretching:

- Stretch in both directions (if you stretch to the left, stretch also to the right).
- Stretch slowly and smoothly so that you avoid fast, jerky movements and do not bounce.
- Stretch to a point where you feel a mild but not painful stretch on the muscles, and stretch no further than the muscles will go without pain.
- When you repeat the stretch, you should be able to stretch a little further without pain. Don't try to increase flexibility too quickly by forcing a stretch.
- Hold each stretch for 10 to 30 seconds (or more).
- Breathe slowly in and out and do not hold your breath (see the sidebar, Breathing While Stretching, for more information on breathing).
- Stretch often—every day, if possible.

It takes your body approximately 3 minutes before it realizes that it doesn't need to keep pumping all the blood to your muscles that is needed during exercise. A cool-down should last a minimum of 3 minutes, and preferably 5 to 15 minutes. If you are still sore the day after your kettlebell workout, a light warm-up or

## BREATHING WHILE STRETCHING

On a moment-to-moment basis, breathing is the single most health- and life-giving activity that we can do under our conscious control. Just as training allows the body to move fast or slow in long or short movements, so too can the breath be guided into varying lengths, depths, and speeds. In fact, there are entire systems of breath study, such as the Chinese qigong arts (literally meaning "breathing skill") and various yoga practices. All these forms of breath training combine movement with breath. Stretching is no different, and just as you should never hold your breath while lifting kettlebells, proper breathing is equally important to safe and effective stretching. The most significant benefits of breathing correctly while stretching are the increase in oxygen supplied to the blood and the increased fluidity of motion that occurs while the muscles elongate at the moment of the exhalation.

Take slow, relaxed breaths as you stretch, exhaling as the muscle is lengthening. Inhale slowly through the nose, expanding the abdomen (not the chest); hold the breath a moment; and exhale slowly through the nose or mouth. Do not force the breath; let it be smooth and even.

cool-down is a good way to reduce any lingering muscle tightness and soreness, and it can be performed by itself even on non-kettlebell-training days. Other helpful options for a cool-down might include yoga, meditation, qigong, massage, a steam room or sauna, or a brisk walk. Any of these options can be suitable ways to relax the body after hard training and help you recover better while bring the body back to a steady state.

The preparation and final phases of your workout consist of a warm-up and cool-down and are basic components of a well-structured kettlebell routine. They both play important roles in preparing you for the main phase of the training session and optimizing the recovery process after your kettlebell training, and a training session is not complete without these phases. Your ideal warm-up and cool-down will vary somewhat from day to day, and with more familiarity you will be able to design your own routines based on your experience and such factors as the weather, how loose or tight you feel, and how intense your main workout will be. As long as you understand the general approach, you can substitute any number of movements for similar movements.

# BASIC EXERCISES

You've learned about the benefits of kettlebell training, selected the right kettlebells for your training needs, learned the basic concepts of exercise physiology, set some SMART goals for yourself, and learned how to warm up and prepare for your kettlebell training and how to cool down afterward. Now it is time to pick up your kettlebell and get started! This chapter explains the basic exercises using a single kettlebell, points out the key training principles, makes you aware of common errors and how to avoid them, and provides corrective exercises to aid you in the learning the exercises correctly. Before getting into the actual kettlebell exercises, we need to cover some important information about lifting technique and breathing technique, which are necessary to set the right conditions for productive training.

## KETTLEBELL LIFTING TECHNIQUE

The body working together as a cooperative unit is a fundamental objective for all athletic movements, and kettlebell lifting is athletic. Proper technique begins with your first contact with the kettlebell: your grip. As soon as you touch the kettlebell, you have set your body in motion, and the movement of the rest of the body will follow the lead of that first point of contact.

## Gripping the Kettlebell

The key design feature of the kettlebell is the handle and its relationship with the bell. The design of the tool determines the gripping techniques. The majority of kettlebell exercises involve either a finger-hook grip or a hand-insertion grip, and thus correct technique in these two positions is important to learn at the start of your kettlebell education. Inefficient grips cause decreased circulation to the forearms, wrists, hands, and fingers, leading to premature fatigue. You cannot reach your anaerobic and aerobic thresholds if you have to put the kettlebell down before reaching maximum effort.

To properly grip the kettlebell, with your palm up, insert your middle finger through the middle of the kettlebell (see figure 6.1a). This creates even weight distribution among all the fingers. From there, create a hook grip by placing the index finger under the thumb (see figure 6.1b). This describes the optimal grip and best combination of grip stability and mobility. In some cases you may not be able to grip the kettlebell in this manner because your hand and fingers cannot make a complete loop—your fingers are too short or the handle is too thick. If this is the case, use an alternative grip with the fingers gripping the handle and the thumb placed on the outside of the handle to secure it (see figure 6.2).

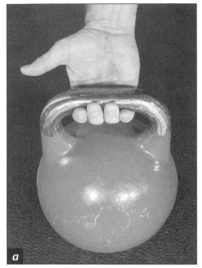
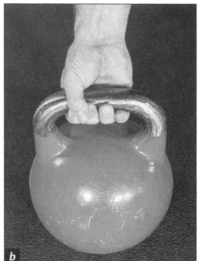

**Figure 6.1** Proper kettlebell grip.

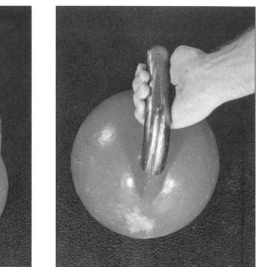

**Figure 6.2** Alternative kettlebell grip where the thumb is outside the handle.

You should be aware of common incorrect grips so that you can avoid them:

- Crushing the handle by squeezing your palm, as shown in figure 6.3a. Here the hand is not inserted fully into the handle and there is too much tension and pressure from the hand. Note the forearm muscles already pumping with this grip.

- Holding too loosely and not securing the handle with the thumb, as shown in figure 6.3b. The kettlebell will move around too much with this grip and can slip out of your hand during training.

- Holding with only the fingertips, as shown in figure 6.3c. In an effort to decrease the painful dry skin in the folds of the fingers, the lifter may let the kettlebell slide to the fingertips. The handle is not secured with this grip, and it should be avoided.

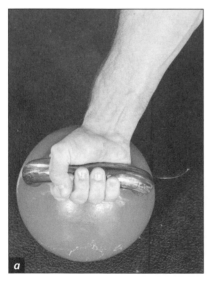
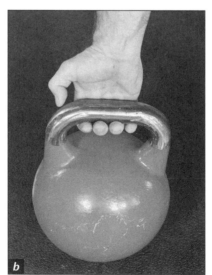
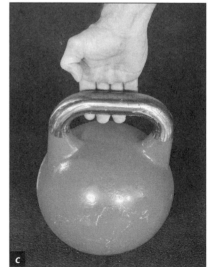

**Figure 6.3** Incorrect kettlebell grips: *(a)* squeezing the palm, *(b)* holding too loosely, and *(c)* holding with only the fingertips.

## Chalking the Kettlebell

In chapter 2, we learned about the importance of using chalk to prevent sweat from getting on your hands while lifting kettlebells. Here, you'll learn how to properly apply chalk to the kettlebell handle.

Ideally, you want to be able to hold onto the kettlebell as long as possible during your working sets, and usually chalk helps prevent slippage. You will have to experiment with chalk and determine whether it gives you better results. If your hands respond positively to chalk, it creates an enhanced grip. For some people, the chalk can dry the hands too much and cause blisters. Your reaction to chalk will also vary depending upon the climate.

Following are the steps for properly applying chalk to your kettlebell:

1. Sand the kettlebell handle using a fine sandpaper (see figure 6.4a). This creates the slightly rough surface needed for the chalk to bind to the bell.

2. Mist the kettlebell lightly with water from a spray bottle (see figure 6.4b).

3. Massage the chalk onto the handle (see figure 6.4c). If done correctly, these steps will cause the chalk to bind to the handle.

Note that if the chalk morphs into a paste, too much water was used. If none of the chalk binds to the handle and it falls off, the handle may be too smooth or the chalk too fine.

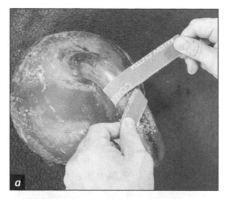

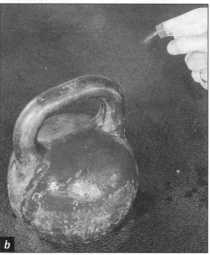

**Figure 6.4** Applying chalk to the handle of a kettlebell: (a) sanding, (b) misting, and (c) massaging.

## Breathing Technique

You will use two common breathing techniques with kettlebell training: paradoxical breathing and anatomical breathing. The use of one over the other is determined by your effort. In general, brief, high-intensity sets with a heavy load use the paradoxical breathing technique. Longer sets with a lighter load generally use the anatomical breathing technique.

### Paradoxical Breathing

This method of breathing is similar to what you might have learned in gym class. With this type of breathing, you inhale on compression and exhale on extension. For example, for a squat, you would inhale as you descend and then exhale as you stand up. This way of breathing is ideal for heavy loads and for deconditioned people due to the thoracic pressure and spinal stability it provides.

### Anatomical Breathing

This method of breathing is also called *matching breathing* because it's congruent with the natural movement patterns of the body. With this type of breathing, you exhale on compression and inhale on extension. For example, in a squat you would exhale as you drop down and inhale as you stand up. This way of breathing is ideal for endurance and work capacity because it helps you better manage your heart rate. It is used by kettlebell sport lifters to achieve world-class results.

For the following exercises, we will focus on the anatomical breathing technique. These movements are all rhythmical, and matching your breath with the motion of the body will enable you to maintain a steady breathing rate and thus heart rate as you gradually increase the duration of the sets.

## BASIC KETTLEBELL EXERCISES

Now the basic kettlebell exercises will be introduced, one by one. These exercises are the key skills and techniques that you will build your programs around, as you will see later in the book.

Follow a progression of light to heavy when learning the kettlebell lifts and during workouts. Remember, proper technique always surpasses load in terms of importance, safety, and results. Thus, avoid the common mistake of going too heavy, too soon. Also, you should follow a progression from neurologically simple to neurologically complex. Thus, for a beginner, start with the exercises in the Introductory Kettlebell Moves section. From there, move into the classical lifts and then the more advanced variations. Failure to follow this logical progression can result in improper learning and injury.

In addition, although maximal tension is applicable to lifting very heavy kettlebells and certainly barbells, it's not applicable to developing work capacity and endurance (the primary goal of kettlebell training). Thus, it's important to focus your alignment, posture, and mentality toward achieving maximal relaxation in all the exercises. This will keep your heart rate down and a steady flow of oxygen and nutrients to the muscles. This type of relaxed, rhythmic, submaximal resistance training enables a higher volume of training and thus leads to increased fitness. Be mindful to smooth out every rep of every exercise such that it would appear effortless to someone watching (even though it certainly is not!).

## Introductory Kettlebell Moves

Before swinging, cleaning, or pressing your kettlebell, you'll want to get comfortable handling it and moving it from one hand to another in order to develop confidence and control. The following movements are a safe and simple introduction to the tool as well as a helpful, low-intensity warm-up before the more vigorous kettlebell exercises. The idea is to get comfortable handling your kettlebell, including picking it up, placing it down, and moving it around the body and from hand to hand, all skills you will use in the exercises to follow.

# AROUND-THE-BODY PASS

**Figure 6.5**  Around-the-body pass.

The around-the-body pass serves as an excellent warm-up, especially for the arms, core, and grip. To perform this exercise, maintain good posture and alignment as you pass the kettlebell around the body while your hips remain facing forward throughout (see figure 6.5). Breathe normally throughout the exercise. Vary the tempo of the movement and reverse directions several times.

### Key Principles

- Keep your eyes forward to maintain good posture and develop kinesthetic awareness.
- Ensure the kettlebell is close to the body but not so close as to create collision and injury.

| Common error | Error correction |
|---|---|
| Allowing the momentum of the kettlebell to rotate your hips as you pass from hand to hand | Keep the abdominal muscles firm. Check your form in a mirror and watch your movement. Make sure there is no twisting of the hips and that they start forward. |
| Dropping the kettlebell onto a delicate floor as you pass it around the body | Place a thick rubber mat underneath you if you don't want to damage the floor. Also, remember that quick feet are happy feet and your instinct knows best. In case of a drop, move quickly and let the kettlebell hit the mat. |

## HALO

**Figure 6.6**  Halo.

The halo is a phenomenal exercise for shoulder and cervical mobility. Many people love the way it makes the shoulders feel and incorporate it in their warm-up and for rehabilitation and prerehabilitation purposes. To perform this exercise, hold a light kettlebell by the horns, or sides of the handle, in front of your face using both hands (see figure 6.6a). Circle over and across the top of the head and continue the circle all the way around (see figure 6.6, b and c). The kettlebell drops lower as it comes behind you and rises again as it moves back up in front. Breathe normally throughout the exercise. Work in both directions.

### Key Principles

- As the name suggests, keep the path of the kettlebell comparable to a halo around the top of your forehead.
- Relax the elbows and allow them to articulate freely.
- Ensure the kettlebell is close to the head, but use caution to avoid accidental contact with the upper extremities.

| Common error | Error correction |
|---|---|
| Dropping the head and looking down, flexing the neck | Pick a spot on the wall in front of you and keep your eyes focused on this spot throughout the exercise. |
| Using a load that is too heavy | Realize that this exercise is for improving mobility, not strength. Select a light load and increase repetitions. Never overdo this exercise. |

## FIGURE-EIGHT BETWEEN-THE-LEGS PASS

**Figure 6.7** Figure-eight between-the-legs pass.

This is a gentle warm-up and a surprisingly good conditioning movement for the legs and core. It involves elements of coordination and body awareness, which makes it challenging and engaging. To perform this exercise, pick up the kettlebell and hold it in front of you with either hand with feet shoulder-width apart and a slight bend in the knees (see figure 6.7a). Pass the kettlebell from the left hand to the right through your legs from front to back (see figure 6.7b). Continue the momentum to circle back in front of the body and pass to the other hand (see figure 6.7c). Exhale as you switch hands. This will automatically create an inhalation at the other movement points. Continue this continuous figure-eight pattern. Change direction and pass from back to front.

### Key Principles

- As you pass the kettlebell between the legs, maintain a neutral spine position and crease in the hips.
- Keep the kettlebell close to the body, being careful not to hit yourself with it.

| Common error | Error correction |
|---|---|
| Colliding the kettlebell into your leg | Select a light weight that you can easily control. Also ensure that your feet are shoulder-width apart and watch the path of the kettlebell to guide it smoothly from hand to hand. |
| Letting the kettlebell slip out of your hand | Use plenty of chalk on your hands and the handle to prevent slips. |

## BOX SQUAT

**Figure 6.8**  Box squat.

The box squat helps you become familiar with proper squat mechanics while simultaneously providing a degree of safety and structural support in the bottom position. This version of the box squat is used to teach proper hip action in the squat, teaching you how to sit back and load your hips while keeping tension in the hips. To perform this exercise, stand in front of a sturdy box or chair with feet shoulder-width apart or slightly wider (see figure 6.8a). Lower to touch your buttocks and upper hamstrings to the top of the box without actually sitting on the box, keeping your weight on your heels and keeping full control of your body (see figure 6.8b). Inhale as you descend and exhale as you stand up. When done correctly, you will properly engage your hips and make your squat less of a knee-dominant movement.

### Key Principles

- Do not collapse on the box; it is only a focal point to reach for.
- Use the paradoxical breathing technique (inhale as you descend and exhale as you stand). As you become comfortable with the movement and feel your spinal stability improve, you can switch to anatomical breathing (exhale as you descend and inhale as you stand up).
- Maintaining a neutral spine (slightly arched lower back) along with creased hips is the key to both performance and injury prevention.

| Common error | Error correction |
|---|---|
| Standing too far in front of or too close to the box | Test your distance before you get into your set. You should be able to reach your buttocks to the box easily, but the backs of your knees should not touch the box. |
| Allowing the knees to collapse inward in the bottom squat position, called *valgus collapse* | This occurs frequently and must be avoided because it can lead to ACL tears. It typically is not a knee issue but rather is caused by a lack of hip activation. To help avoid this, press the knees out to the sides as you lower into the squat or take a 20 in. (51 cm) piece of tubing or a light band that is light and easy to stretch and place it around the outside of the knees. This will train you to avoid the knee collapse. |

## KETTLEBELL DEADLIFT

**Figure 6.9** Kettlebell deadlift.

The kettlebell deadlift primarily targets the posterior chain (lower back, glutes, and hamstrings). It is an excellent companion to the kettlebell box squat and additionally helps teach proper hip-creasing mechanics, creating an important foundation for the classical kettlebell exercises (e.g., swing, clean, snatch). With the kettlebell on the ground, stand with your feet shoulder-width apart with the kettlebell just in front of you (see figure 6.9a). Keep your chest lifted as you sit back with your hips until your hands can reach the handle (see figure 6.9b). Grab the handle with both hands and stand up by pressing your feet into the ground until your body is fully upright (see figure 6.9c). Repeat by sitting back to lightly touch the kettlebell to the ground. Do 10 controlled reps with a light weight and then repeat with a more challenging weight (e.g., women start with 8 kg [18 lb] for 10 reps and then use 12 kg [26 lb] for 10 reps; men start with 16 kg [35 lb] for 10 reps and then use 24 kg [53 lb] for 10 reps). This basic exercise teaches you to keep your center of gravity aligned vertically over your base of support. It is important to have control over your center of mass because kettlebell training involves such dynamic movements. A strong and stable base will keep you safe when swinging the kettlebell.

### Key Principles

- Crease at the hips instead of bending at the waist.
- Maintain a neutral spine and slightly arched lower back.
- Legs can be bent or straight depending on the desired training effect. Straight legs will recruit the hamstrings more and bent legs will recruit the quadriceps more.

| Common error | Error correction |
| --- | --- |
| Leading from and rounding the low back | Place a short box behind you with the kettlebell on the floor in front of it. Lightly touch your glutes to the box to ensure leading with the hips. |
| Rounding the shoulders and upper back | Look forward, pinch your shoulders blades together, and keep your chest up. |

## Classical Kettlebell Lifts

Once you have become familiar with a proper warm-up and the introductory kettlebell movements, it's time to learn the classical kettlebell lifts. The classical lifts are those foundational exercises that introduce the mechanical standards and principles used throughout all other kettlebell exercises. Special attention should be paid to smoothly and accurately practicing these exercises, because correct execution of the classical kettlebell lifts will set the foundation for developing fitness safely and effectively.

A sensible approach to learning these movements before putting them into a program is to practice them each several times with a light kettlebell. Think of it as practice, not training or performance. Just get the feel of it and try to get comfortable. Once you have a good idea of how to perform the exercises, you can begin to challenge yourself more, and when you have a strong grasp of a particular exercise, you can put it in a training program.

## SINGLE SWING

**Figure 6.10** Single swing.

The single swing is the foundational movement of all the classical lifts. Within this exercise, you will find many of the universal principles and unique aspects of kettlebell training, such as inertia, pendulum grip endurance, and anatomical breathing. The swing needs to be mastered before moving on to the other classical lift exercises (e.g., clean, snatch). It cannot be understated: All other kettlebell lifts build upon the foundation of the swing.

To perform this exercise, stand with the feet hip-width apart and with one kettlebell on the floor in front of you (see figure 6.10*a*). Sit back with the hips (think box squat) and with one hand, grab the handle with the fingers (see figure 6.10*b*). Thumb positioning for the swing can vary depending on the individual and the training goals. There are three options:

1. Thumb forward, which allows for faster pacing due to minimized motion (creates a shallower downswing) and seems to be more comfortable for those with shoulder tightness because there is no rotation at the shoulder during this position.

2. Thumb back, which provides better grip endurance by distributing some of the stress from the forearm to the triceps and creates more of a momentum-based movement because of the spiral nature of this variation (thus, there is a greater range of motion to reduce and produce force).

3. Neutral thumb, which distributes stress more equally along the grip, arms, and shoulders.

Next, keep the shoulders back and chest lifted as if you are going to do a deadlift, and as you begin to stand, swing the kettlebell between your legs (see figure 6.10*c*). When the swing reaches its end point behind you, stand up completely, extending the ankles, knees, hips, and torso (see figure 6.10*d*). Sustain this pendulum swing through the duration of the set.

When performing this exercise, use one or two cycles of anatomical breathing (a cycle is defined as one exhalation and one inhalation). There are two variations you can use: Exhale at the back of the downswing and inhale during the upswing (one breath cycle), or exhale at the back of the downswing, inhale, exhale as the kettlebell transitions from the horizontal to the vertical plane at the top of the forward swing, and inhale as the kettlebell drops again preceding the next backswing (two breath cycles for every one swing).

## Key Principles

- The pendulum is a perfect analogy for a good kettlebell swing because it relies upon mechanical energy conservation in order to sustain the movement indefinitely. Swinging the kettlebell this way creates a more momentum-based movement, which allows for greater work capacity in addition to less stress on the lower back and grip via efficient deceleration of the bell during the downswing.

- Maximize the connection between the arm and torso on the upswing, ensuring optimal power transfer from the lower body to the kettlebell.

- Relax the arm completely and visualize it as a rope that starts at the base of the neck and ends at the fingertips.

- Deflect back via the hips at the top of the upswing to counterbalance the weight in front of the body and as a catalyst to complete hip extension. Maintain deflection as you drop the kettlebell into the downswing until you feel the triceps come into contact with the rib cage. At that point, softly absorb the downward force with a slight bend of the knees and ankles and then crease the hips into the pendulum spring mechanics.

*(continued)*

| Common error | Error correction |
|---|---|
| No connection between the arm and the hip and torso on the upswing | Use two fingers on the upper arm. If you have a coach or are coaching someone, the verbal cue "Stay connected" is helpful. Also use a mini resistance band around the swinging arm and the body, which will hold the arm against the body. |
| Lack of deflection on the upswing and while dropping the kettlebell into the downswing | If you have a coach or are coaching someone, the verbal cue "Deflect back!" is helpful. It is also helpful to swing in front of an object (e.g., wall, mat) at arm's length; if you don't deflect back, you will hit the object. |
| The kettlebell drops too far below the pelvis on the downswing | Do swings with a yoga block or similar object between the legs or place a second kettlebell on the floor between the legs. If you hit the object or second kettlebell, you have dropped too low. |
| The shoulder unpacks and kettlebell trajectory is too far from the body | Swing in front of an object (e.g., wall, mat) at arm's length; if you don't deflect back, you will hit the object. |

## SINGLE CLEAN

The single clean is a natural progression from the swing and is the intermediary point between the swing and many of the overhead lifts. The clean introduces hand insertion, alignment points connected to the rack position, and positioning of the kettlebell in the hand in order to avoid injury and grip fatigue. It also teaches you how to use your legs to transmit vertical power from the lower to upper body. With practice, your clean becomes a smooth, rhythmic movement that you can sustain for extended lengths of time, although it may take hundreds of practice reps before it flows and becomes polished.

Resting the kettlebell on the forearm is a distinguishing characteristic of kettlebells that makes them behave differently than dumbbells and makes them effective for developing the fitness that comes with high-repetition resistance training. By placing most of the load on the forearm, the muscles of the hand and grip are able to relax. It takes practice before the kettlebell will move smoothly in your hand and into position. Sometimes you will have bad reps and the kettlebell will crash into your forearm. To make this learning process a little kinder, you can wear wrist wraps or wristbands. In time your technique will become more polished and the kettlebell will just float into position on your arm in cleans and snatches, and at that point you may prefer to not use any wraps at all. However, it is an option for those with more tender arms—no sense giving yourself bruises if you don't need to.

With the kettlebell on the floor, sit back with your hips and grip with the handle with the fingers of one hand (see figure 6.11a and b). Swing the kettlebell back through your legs as you did in the one-handed swing (see figure 6.11c) and as it swings forward, keep your forearm braced against your body (see figure 6.11d). During the swing, your arm comes away from the body as inertia pulls the kettlebell forward and up. During the clean, on the other hand, the arm does not disconnect from body, and at the point where the arm would disconnect during the swing, it instead moves vertically along the front of your body. Imagine you are standing inside a chimney. The walls of the chimney block you so that you cannot move out or to the side; you can only move the kettlebell up and down the chimney wall. When the hips reach forward extension, pull with the hip on the working side and give a gentle tug with your trapezius on the same side, pulling the kettlebell up the chimney (see figure 6.11e). Before the kettlebell settles to the chest, loosen your grip and open your hand to insert your fingers as deeply into the handle as you can at a curved angle until the medial portion of your forearm, the ulna, blocks you from inserting the hand any further (see figure 6.11f). Complete the vertical pull by letting the kettlebell rest on your chest and arm (see figure 6.11g) into what is called the *rack*

**Figure 6.11** Single clean.

*(continued)*

**SINGLE CLEAN**  *(continued)*

*position.* This is the top position of the clean. Here are the key alignment points in the top rack portion of the clean technique:

- The kettlebell is medial to the lateral shoulder (toward the midline). If the kettlebell shifts away from the midline, it will bring the load outside your base of support and require more effort to hold.
- Find the ideal placement of the kettlebell between your chest and shoulder and your upper arm. One useful tip is to put the kettlebell in the triangle that is formed with the elbow, forearm, and chest. Keep the kettlebell between the forearm and the chest by moving the upper body back and rotating the palm away from you to about a 45-degree angle.

This rack position works well with the single kettlebell but is much more difficult with double kettlebells because of the flexibility demands and limited range of motion of the doubles. The goal of the rack position is to be comfortable and stable in the position and able to control the top portion of the clean. Now complete the lift by turning your palm faceup and deflecting the force by moving the shoulders back (see figure 6.11*h*). Remember you are standing inside a chimney, so the kettlebell can only move down, not forward. Your elbow stays braced to your body. As the kettlebell is falling, just before the elbow reaches full extension, pull the hand back to catch with the fingers, then tighten the grip to complete the backswing (see figure 6.11*i*). As in the swing, you can use any of the three positions in the bottom portion of the clean—thumb forward, thumb backward, or neutral thumb. Continue this smooth pendulum motion throughout the set.

When performing this exercise, use anatomical breathing with three or more breathing cycles. Starting from the rack position, inhale as you deflect back and drop the kettlebell into the downswing, exhale at the back of the downswing, inhale during the transition into the forward swing, exhale at completion of the forward swing, inhale with hand insertion, and exhale as the kettlebell lands in the rack position. This equals three breath cycles. During a long set, or anytime you are very tired during a set, you can take additional recovery breaths while the kettlebell is resting in rack position.

### Key Principles

- Begin hand insertion at approximately hip level and ensure that the angle of the hand as it begins insertion is 45 degrees. Note that hand insertion is also used in the snatch and many other lifts. The starting and ending of each rep use the same hand position as the swing, and the hand moves in and out of the kettlebell during the up and down phases of the movement.
- Experiment with a variety of thumb positions to find the configuration that feels most comfortable for you.

| Common error | Error correction |
| --- | --- |
| Banging your wrist or forearm on the kettlebell | You are most likely inserting your hand too early, too late, or at an incorrect angle. Use a hand-insertion drill where you visualize a ladder with four rungs in front of you on the vertical plane. Gradually climb the ladder, inserting your hand with a claw grip. Rung 1 is chest level, rung 2 is face level, rung 3 is just over your head, and rung 4 is near the top just before your arm reaches full extension. Clean up and release the fingers to insert the hand at each level, and then drop down into the backswing between each insertion. |
| Crush gripping, or squeezing the handle too hard, in rack position | Keep the hand in a light claw position to reduce heat (friction) and grip fatigue. |
| Cleaning too far out in front or too far laterally | Clean in front of or next to a wall where a bad rep will hit the wall. Imagine you're standing inside a chimney where the kettlebell can only move up and down, not forward or laterally. |

The rack position, where the kettlebell rests against your forearm and chest, is one of the most important skills of kettlebell training—and one of the most difficult to master. Lack of flexibility is usually the main limitation to learning the proper position. Here is an overview of some useful flexibility drills for improving the rack.

### Rack Hold

Stand with a kettlebell on the chest, with hand inserted fully into the handle, forearm resting on the body, legs fully extended, and with the kettlebell vertically aligned over the foot on the same side (see figure 6.12). Hold this static position for 1 minute and work up to 3 minutes before moving up to a heavier kettlebell to target key areas of the shoulders, spine, and hips.

**Figure 6.12**   Rack hold.

### Wall Push

Stand in front of a wall with your palms flat against the wall and elbows bent and touching your ribs (see figure 6.13a). Without moving your feet, push against the wall with your palms. Because the wall will not move, your body has to move back without moving the feet or the hands. Keep pushing until your elbows are fully extended (see figure 6.13b). Your shoulders will end up behind your hips, and you will feel a nice stretch in your lower back. To increase the challenge, move your feet closer to the wall and repeat the drill.

**Figure 6.13**   Wall push.

### Bridging

For the bridging progressions, start with the most basic and work slowly into the progressions, never forcing range of motion and always paying attention to breathing, never holding your breath. The more you can relax your mind and breathing, the easier your muscles will relax and enable you to assume the positions.

For basic bridging, lie flat on your back with your feet flat and knees bent (see figure 6.14a). Press your heels through the floor and lift your pelvis as high off the ground as you can (see figure 6.14b). Keep your shoulders and head flat on the floor. Hold the position for 30 to 60 seconds.

*(continued)*

**Figure 6.14**   Basic bridging.

For intermediate bridging, place your palms flat on the floor with your elbows pointing up toward the ceiling (see figure 6.15a). You will need sufficient flexibility in the shoulders to comfortably place the hands. Press up with your hands and feet and place the top of your head on the floor (see figure 6.15b). Use your head, hands, and feet as wedges and press firmly, lifting your pelvis as high as possible (see figure 6.15c). Progress to 30- to 60-second holds.

**Figure 6.15**   Intermediate bridging.

For advanced bridging, from the intermediate bridge position, lift your head off the floor and extend your arms fully. Use your legs to press your body back as you lift your chest and straighten your elbows (see figure 6.16). You need excellent flexibility of the spine, hip flexors, shoulders, and chest to get into a correct bridge, and this will help you greatly in finding a comfortable rack position.

**Figure 6.16**   Advanced bridging.

## Hanging From Bar

With hands shoulder-width apart or closer, grab a pull-up bar and hang, allowing the body to completely relax (see figure 6.17). Hold for 15 seconds or longer and feel the chest, shoulders, and upper back lengthening.

## Yoga Eagle Stretch

From standing or seated position, reach both arms out to the sides (see figure 6.18a) and then cross one arm over the other in front of you (see figure 6.18b). Fold both elbows in toward your body. If crossing the left arm on top, the right hand will reach up and grab the left wrist or palm (see figure 6.18c). Point your left thumb directly toward your forehead. Hold this position for 30 seconds and then repeat on the other side. To further progress this stretch, assume the eagle stretch position as just described. Keep your palms firmly pressed together and either push both elbows down toward your hips or lift both arms up.

For the yoga eagle stretch, if you currently lack the shoulder flexibility to bring your palms together or to grab your opposite wrist or thumb, hold one end of a small towel, rope, or stretch band in the hand that crosses over, and once you cross the opposite hand under the top arm, reach and grab the other end of the towel, rope, or band and pull on that to perform the stretch.

**Figure 6.17**  Hanging from bar.

**Figure 6.18**  Yoga eagle stretch.

## SINGLE PRESS

**Figure 6.19**  Single press.

The single press is a total upper-body movement that is the beginning progression for more advanced overhead exercises. It teaches proper alignment in the overhead position while simultaneously conditioning the arms, shoulders, and back, and it is the foundational lift for vertical pushing or pressing movements.

To perform this exercise, clean a single kettlebell to your chest into the rack position (see figure 6.19*a*). This is the start position for the press. Before pressing up, compress your rib cage on the side of the pressing arm. As you recoil to the downward compression, press the kettlebell directly up until your elbow is completely extended in the lockout position (see figure 6.19*b*). In this overhead position, the optimal position of the hand and shoulder is such that your thumb is pointing directly back. A slight rotation of the palm is acceptable, but avoid overrotating so that you have the most efficient path, which is a straight line. Any additional rotation or deviation from the straight line is wasted effort and nonoptimal alignment.

To lower the kettlebell, move your body back slightly so that the kettlebell can fall directly down the centerline and all the way to the hip (see figure 6.19*c*) and back to the rack position to complete the lift (see figure 6.19*d*). The drop from the overhead lockout position back to rack position should be a smooth, relaxed movement. Imagine you are being supported from a string and a puppeteer is lifting your arm and kettlebell. When the string is cut, the kettlebell just free-falls back to the rack position. With practice you will be able to absorb the force from the drop so that the kettlebell smoothly slides into place.

When performing this exercise, use anatomical breathing with four breathing cycles. Starting from the rack position, inhale deeply before the initial compression, and then exhale as you drop or flex your thoracic spine. Inhale as you bump with the rib cage, and exhale as you lock out. Take one full breath cycle while in lockout and add more recovery breaths if needed. Inhale as you begin to drop the kettlebell, and exhale as it lands back in the rack position.

## Key Principles

- The rack is important in creating a virtual bench—the rack position is a position of both rest and power generation, ensuring connectivity between the arm and the torso so there is a solid power transfer.

- Use the whole body to press versus just the shoulders. Due to the influence of bodybuilding, many people think that the correct way to press is via isolating the deltoid muscles. The focus of kettlebell training is movement efficiency instead of isolation, so you want to distribute the work among multiple movers. Thus, it's important to create an initial compression and then a bumping action of the spine to add power and work capacity to the movement. Imagine your rib cage as an accordion that opens and closes as you press up and drop down.

| Common error | Error correction |
| --- | --- |
| Only using the arms and shoulders versus the whole body while pressing the kettlebell overhead | Without a kettlebell, practice flaring the lats to raise the hand without pressing from the shoulder. The hand should start to move up just from the flaring of the lats. |
| Pressing the kettlebell using a triangle-like trajectory | Press laterally next to a wall to ensure you are pressing up the centerline. Again, visualize that you are lifting inside a chimney. |
| Incorrect overhead positioning or crush gripping (squeezing the handle too hard) in the rack and overhead positions | Use lockout holds or walks by extending the arm fully overhead and hold the position for time. Also keep the hand in a light claw position to reduce heat (friction) and fatigue in grip. |

## PUSH PRESS

**Figure 6.20** Push press.

The push press is identical to the press but includes a leg drive. The lift initiates from the legs and is completed through the arm and hand. This allows more diversified conditioning in addition to significantly increasing the ability to work at higher volume and intensity. Once you find the max load you can use in the press, the use of your legs will allow you to do more than you can in a strict press. The use of the legs also allows greater endurance because you are distributing effort over more of your body.

To perform this exercise, clean the kettlebell to your chest (see figure 6.20a). Load the stance by sinking your knees downward as you compress your rib cage (see figure 6.20b). Immediately follow the slight downward knee bend with fast and explosive lifting, pressing your feet vigorously into the ground (see figure 6.20c). From the extension of the legs, the kettlebell will already be more than halfway to the top. Complete the lift by pressing through the triceps into the overhead lockout position, identical to the top position of the press (see figure 6.20d). To drop the kettlebell back to your chest, rise up slightly on your toes as you move your body back in order to allow the kettlebell to fall straight down the chimney (see figure 6.20e). Your feet are planted again as the kettlebell reaches your chest and your elbow slides on top of your hip (see figure 6.20f).

When performing this exercise, use anatomical breathing with four breathing cycles. Starting from the rack position, inhale deeply before the initial compression, and then exhale as you drop into a half squat. Inhale as you extend the legs and bump with the rib cage, and exhale as you lock out. Take one full breath cycle while in lockout and add more recovery breaths if needed. Inhale as you deflect the trunk backward to drop the kettlebell, and exhale as the kettlebell lands back in the rack position.

### Key Principles

- During the half squat, stay connected with the heels flat on the ground and the elbows and forearms pressed against the torso. The connectivity keeps the body linked and improves the transfer of energy from the ground up.

- Use the whole body in the push press—following a rapid half squat, create an initial compression and then a rapid extension into the bumping action of the spine, with the arm finishing the lift.

| Common error | Error correction |
| --- | --- |
| Losing the connection between the elbow and hip and the heel and floor when descending into the half squat | Practice the half squat without pressing, paying attention to keeping your forearms against your torso throughout the up and down portions of the half squats. |
| Not fully extending the legs and pressing too early with the arms | Practice thoracic bumps, allowing you to focus on the legs without arm involvement. |

## SNATCH

**Figure 6.21** Snatch.

The kettlebell snatch is a total-body exercise with special emphasis on the entire posterior chain. It simultaneously develops strength, explosiveness, structural integrity, cardiorespiratory capacity, and virtually every attribute on the athletic continuum. There are six stages to the snatch:

1. Inertia swing
2. Acceleration pull with hip and trapezius
3. Hand insertion deep into the handle
4. Overhead lockout
5. Direction change into the drop
6. Grip change into the backswing

To perform this exercise, with the kettlebell on the floor in front of you, load your hips and grip the kettlebell with your fingers as you would for the swing (see figure 6.21*a*). Swing the kettlebell back between your legs as you begin to stand, further loading the hips (see figure 6.21*b*). As with the swing and clean, various thumb positions can be used in the downswing and upswing portion of the snatch. The most common is to rotate the thumb back at the end of the downswing and transition to a 45-degree angle (thumb up) at the beginning of the acceleration pull. Keep your arm connected to your body and extend your knees and hips, allowing the inertia of the kettlebell to pull your arm forward (figure 6.21*c*). Just as the arm begins to separate from the body, accelerate the kettlebell vertically as fast as you can by rapidly pulling with the hip, followed by a shrug of the trapezius.

If you are snatching with your right hand, push forcefully with your left leg, pull back your right hip, and shrug with your right trap (see figure 6.21*d*). As the kettlebell is accelerating upward, release your fingers and insert your palm deeply into the handle (see figure 6.21*e*). Allow the momentum to carry the kettlebell all the way to the top and lock out your arm in the fully extended elbow position (see figure 6.21*f*). This overhead lockout position is identical to the overhead position in the push or push press (thumb facing back, no or minimal rotation). To drop the kettlebell back down, first shift your weight to the opposite foot (if snatching with the right hand, shift to the left foot) and lean your upper body back (see figure 6.21*g*). Keep your hips and torso extended maximally and let your triceps connect to your torso. Finish the downswing by changing grips and pulling your hand back to catch the handle with your fingers (see figure 6.21*h*), and tighten the fingers as you follow the kettlebell between your legs into the backswing (see figure 6.21*i*). Use the rhythmic motion to continue the snatch for the desired repetitions.

Note that the half snatch can be used as a variation when getting familiar with the snatch or as a segue into using heavier loads. The upward part of the snatch is as previously described; however, in the half snatch, you will drop the kettlebell from the overhead lockout position straight down to the chest into the rack position, then drop the kettlebell from the chest, identical to the lower portion of the clean. This reduces the range of motion and therefore the speed of the kettlebell on the downward portion, giving you more time to learn proper control of the movement. Later you will move to the full snatch, dropping from the overhead position in one continuous movement into the backswing.

When performing this exercise, use anatomical breathing with three or more breathing cycles. You can start from the overhead position, inhale as you deflect back and drop the kettlebell into the downswing, exhale at the back of the downswing, inhale as you upswing, and exhale on lockout. Or, you can start from the overhead position, inhale as you deflect back and drop the kettlebell, exhale into the downswing, inhale, exhale as you begin the acceleration pull, inhale, and exhale on lockout. For both variations, you can take recovery breaths in the overhead position.

*(continued)*

**SNATCH** *(continued)*

### Key Principles

- Ensure a connection between the torso and arm on the upswing for maximal leverage and power transfer. Having your full body mass behind the acceleration of the kettlebell will enable you to move the kettlebell faster and therefore with more power and ease.

- Hand insertion should occur when the kettlebell is higher than head level, and before your elbow fully extends. Inserting too early or too late interferes with smooth timing and transfer of force.

- Overhead alignment and the position of the kettlebell on the hand is an important factor in work capacity, grip endurance, and injury avoidance. Finding the position that allows you to relax makes managing the breath easier. An incorrect position creates excessive tension, which brings fatigue sooner.

- As with the swing and clean, maintain deflection when dropping the kettlebell from the overhead position into the backswing. This is necessary for proper balancing, safety, and load distribution. Do not crease the hips until the triceps comes into contact with the rib cage.

- Time the torso and hip creasing with the moment your triceps touches the rib cage, allowing you to absorb a greater percentage of the decelerating load through the strong muscles of the legs and torso.

| Common error | Error correction |
|---|---|
| No connection between the arm and the hip and torso on the upswing | Use a resistance band around both arms and the body, which will hold the snatching arm against the body, teaching you the feeling of keeping the arm in contact with the body. |
| Lack of deflection on the upswing and dropping the kettlebell into the downswing | Swing in front of a wall at arm's length. If you don't deflect back, you will hit the wall. |
| Banging your wrist or forearm on the kettlebell | You are most likely inserting your hand too early, too late, or at an incorrect angle. Use a hand-insertion drill where you visualize a ladder with four rungs in front of you on the vertical plane. Gradually climb the ladder, inserting your hand with a claw grip. Rung 1 is chest level, rung 2 is face level, rung 3 is just over your head, and rung 4 is near the top just before your arm reaches full extension. Clean up and release the fingers to insert the hand at each level, and then drop down into backswing between each insertion. This will give you the feel of the perfect timing, which will be at the rung 3 to rung 4 level. |
| Using a vertical versus horizontal trajectory on the backswing | Precede the snatch with a low swing to instill proper hip pendulum mechanics. The snatch is an extension of the swing, and by starting with one or two low swings, you will create the inertia to lead into the full snatch. |
| Lack of fixation in the overhead position | Use lockout holds or walks where you hold the kettlebell in overhead lockout for time. Stand in one place, walk in clockwise and counterclockwise circles, or move around the room in any pattern. |
| Exaggerated trajectory on the upswing and downswing | Snatch in front of a wall as you visualize that you're lifting inside a chimney. If the kettlebell hits the wall, you are doing it incorrectly (too much horizontal movement). |

## SQUAT

**Figure 6.22**   Squat.

The squat is a primal movement pattern and one of the most important strength and conditioning exercises for all-around good function and health. Watch a young child and you will see that she can squat with perfect mechanics without any instruction at all. To train the squat, it is important to have correct movement before adding kettlebells or any other external load. The goals for a quality squat movement are as follows:

- Feet flat on the ground
- Knees aligned vertically over the feet with no inward collapsing of the knees (valgus collapse)
- Hips sit back to carry some of the load so that the load is not placed excessively on the knees
- Trunk upright as much as possible, if not completely vertical
- Balanced and stable body in both the upward and downward portions of the movement

   To perform this exercise, stand with your feet about shoulder-width apart with the toes pointing forward (see figure 6.22a). In some cases, tightness in the hip joints will require that the toes are turned out to the sides. If this applies to you, it is OK to do so up to about 30 degrees. Sit back by leading with the hips as if you were sitting on a chair or box (review the box squat in the Introductory Kettlebell Moves section earlier in this chapter). Actively descend into the bottom position by pulling yourself down with your hip flexors as you drop your center of mass until the tops of your thighs are parallel with the floor or slightly below parallel (see figure 6.22b). Open the hips to achieve maximal depth. Try to avoid flexing your trunk forward too much. Pushing your arms out in front of you serves as a counterbalance to help you sit back with the trunk. Throughout the movement, your feet stay flat on the floor. From the bottom position, push your feet firmly into the floor and extend straight up, straightening the legs fully (see figure 6.22c). Once you have the feel of this movement, and if you have no pain or discomfort, you can begin loading. Paradoxical or anatomical breathing can be used depending on weight and volume.

   Progressing in the squat is best done in stages. Stage 1 is called the *goblet squat*, which uses a single kettlebell held with two hands. Hold a kettlebell in front of you with both hands facing

*(continued)*

**SQUAT** *(continued)*

palms up and with your forearms against your body (see figure 6.23*a*). The shape of the hands looks like a goblet or giant drinking glass. Squat down (see figure 6.23*b*) and stand up while holding the kettlebell in front of you (6.23*c*). Many people find that holding a light kettlebell in the goblet position makes the squat easier because the front-loaded position acts as a counterbalance, enabling you to sit further back. To progress from the goblet squat to stage 2, the front squat, clean one kettlebell to the rack position (see figure 6.24*a*). Keep the arm against the body as you squat down (see figure 6.24*b*) and stand up. This is the front squat. Your nonloaded hand will be out to the side acting as a counterbalance. In the next chapter you will learn the front squat with double kettlebells.

**Figure 6.23**  Goblet squat.

**Figure 6.24**  Front squat.

## Key Principles

- Initiate the movement in the hips, not in the knees.
- The trunk remains as upright as possible throughout.
- Aim for maximal range of motion at the top and bottom positions of the squat.

| Common error | Error correction |
|---|---|
| Knees press out to the sides without hip movement | The knees should stay vertically aligned over the feet and the hips open out to the sides. Wrap an exercise band firmly around both legs just above the knees to create lateral pressure. Press your knees out as you sit into the squat to prevent the band from slipping. |
| Exaggerated rounding of the spine | Stand with the tips of your toes touching the wall. Looking straight ahead, pull your arms behind you by pinching your shoulder blades together. Sit back and down into the squat, and then stand up. The wall will prevent you from moving forward, so you have to sit back and keep an arch in the spine. Initially you may need to move your toes away from the wall a bit. As you improve, you can move the toes closer. |
| Can't descend into a full squat due to lazy hip flexors | Lie on your back with palms on the floor and legs extended and pull your toes toward you into dorsiflexion. While a partner holds one foot in each hand by grabbing the tops of the insteps, pull your knees toward your chest. Now extend your legs straight without any resistance from your partner. This drill activates your hip flexors so you can learn to use them to pull yourself into the bottom position of the squat. |
| Heels lift up toward the bottom of the squat, shifting excessive load to the knees | Insert a small weight plate or block 2 to 4 in. (5-10 cm) tall under the heels to enable you to sit down further. Progress using a shorter lift and eventually you will be able to squat with none. Perform an ankle mobility exercise as a warm-up and between sets. In an extended lunge position, kneel on one knee on a mat with the other foot in front; palms are flat on the floor about shoulder-width apart in front of the front foot. Shift weight to the hands and lift the rear knee. Point the toes of the rear foot into maximal plantar flexion while firmly pressing the ankle into the floor. Press your shoelaces into the floor to feel the stretch along the front of your ankle, foot, and shin. Immediately change to maximal dorsiflexion by pushing firmly back with the hands and front foot, driving the rear heel into the floor. Alternate between laces down and heel back. |

The six classical kettlebell lifts of the swing, clean, press, push press, snatch, and squat form the foundation of your kettlebell training and are the most important lifts to practice and master. By learning them well, you will develop a strong base to build upon, and because the key concepts of kettlebell lifting are contained within these classical lifts, learning new lifts will be much easier.

# INTERMEDIATE EXERCISES

The exercises in this chapter are categorized as intermediate because they increase in neurological complexity and load, thus requiring more balance, power, coordination, and body awareness. You will notice repetition in some of the key points because many of the guiding principles of kettlebell lifting apply regardless of whether the exercise is beginning, intermediate, or advanced. Do not be distracted by the categorization of an exercise as basic, intermediate, or advanced. Those labels are simply for the sake of organization as your knowledge of exercise variation grows. The principles taught in the basic lifts in chapter 6 are found throughout all other kettlebell exercises, whether single or double, basic, intermediate, or advanced. That is why they are basic—they are foundational to the entire system of movements.

A review of the basic exercises taught in chapter 6 emphasizes the key principles that are contained throughout all kettlebell exercises. These principles include the following:

- In the swing, you are introduced to the pendulum, which is the action of inertia and involves hinging and extending the hips. You also begin to train the grip dynamically.

- In the clean, you learn acceleration, insertion of the hand, and deflection of the body in addition to the inertia and dynamic grip contained within the swing.

- In press and push press, you learn how to lock out the joints of the legs and arms (fixation) and how to deflect force in the lowering phase.

- In the snatch, you are exercising the grip and use inertia, acceleration, insertion, fixation, and deflection all together in a single exercise.

- In the squat, you learn to lower and raise your center of mass over your base of support, and you extend the range of the hips, knees, and trunk moving through flexion and extension.

As mentioned, these core principles of the classic lifts are contained in all the other lifts in one form or another. Therefore, the importance of mastering the basic exercises found in chapter 6 cannot be overstated. Also, keep in mind the need for a thorough warm-up before integrating the following exercises into your training program.

## SINGLE-LEG KETTLEBELL DEADLIFT

The one-legged kettlebell deadlift demands balance and core stability. Unilateral, or single-leg, exercise is important in a training program because the increased balance requirements recruit the muscles of the hips and glutes. In bilateral or two-legged training, there is a tendency to use the quads and knees as the dominant movers, making it is easy to build an imbalance between the quads and glutes if only bilateral squatting motions are trained. The hips have to be used properly in order to maintain safe mechanics and healthy posture. When the hips are not fully or properly engaged, movements such as the squat or swing (or any exercise that loads the posterior chain) become knee dominant and your body will compensate for the poor movement in the joints above and below the working joint. That means the lumbar vertebrae (lower back) above and the knees below the hips will work harder because the hips are not working adequately. Single-leg exercises are hip-dominant exercises that engage the glutes and hamstrings to maintain balance. Another important benefit of single-leg training is the high activation of the deep core musculature that is required to stabilize on one leg. Increased core stabilization gives you a more solid platform to build your strength from.

Following are four variations of the single-leg kettlebell deadlift.

**Two-Arm Single-Leg Kettlebell Deadlift**   Shift all your weight to one leg and lift the other leg off the ground with the knee bent (see figure 7.1*a*). Fold at the hips by sitting back and flexing the trunk toward the ground, and grab the handle with both hands (see figure 7.1*b*). Complete the lift by pulling with your hamstrings until your support leg and trunk are fully extended (see figure 7.1*c*). Be sure to complete the hip extension. If you lose balance, touch your nonweighted leg to the floor to recover.

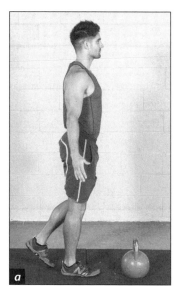

**Figure 7.1**   Two-arm single-leg kettlebell deadlift.

**One-Arm Contralateral Single-Leg Kettlebell Deadlift**   Set up the same as in the previous variation (see figure 7.2*a*), but this time as you sit back with the hips and flex the trunk, grab the handle with your opposite hand only (see figure 7.2*b*) and stand up to the top position (see figure 7.2*c*). Once you master the balance in this movement, increase the challenge by loading and unloading on alternating reps. This method of varying the resistance mimics a more real-world function. On the first rep, flex forward to pick up the kettlebell, stand up with it, put it back down, and stand up without it. Repeat this loaded–unloaded pattern for each rep and you will find that you have to constantly adjust to the change in load, which makes this variation more proprioceptively challenging than doing all reps under a constant load.

**Figure 7.2**   One-arm contralateral single-leg kettlebell deadlift.

## One-Arm Ipsilateral Single-Leg Kettlebell Deadlift

Set up the same as in the previous variation (see figure 7.3*a*), but this time as you sit back with the hips and flex the trunk, grab the handle with your same-side hand only (see figure 7.3*b*) and stand up to the top position (see figure 7.3*c*).

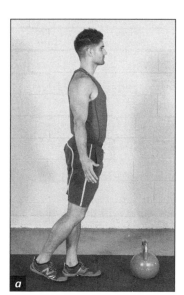

**Figure 7.3**   One-arm ipsilateral single-leg kettlebell deadlift.

*(continued)*

**SINGLE-LEG KETTLEBELL DEADLIFT** *(continued)*

**Two-Arm Single-Leg Double Kettlebell Deadlift** Once you start to get into heavier kettlebells with the one-leg and one-arm variations, you will find that grip and hand strength will be the limiting factor in your progress. Your hips and legs are stronger than your grip. At this point if you want to increase load, you must switch to using two kettlebells. For example, if you have a hard time holding 48 kilograms (106 lb) in one hand, you can achieve the same level of glute and hamstring activation by doing using two kettlebells of 24 kilograms (53 lb) each so you have less weight in each hand but the same total weight. It is also easier to balance since the load is distributed bilaterally through the two arms.

Shift all your weight to one leg and lift the other leg off the ground with the knee bent (see figure 7.4*a*). Fold at the hips by sitting back and flexing the trunk toward the ground, and grab one handle in each hand (see figure 7.4*b*). Complete the lift by pulling with your hamstrings until your support leg and trunk are fully extended (see figure 7.4*c*). Be sure to complete the hip extension. If you lose balance, touch your nonweighted leg to the floor to recover.

**Figure 7.4** Two-arm single-leg double kettlebell deadlift.

### Key Principles

- Crease at the hips rather than bending at the waist.
- Maintain a neutral spine and slightly arched lower back.
- Because you are standing on one leg and your balance is being challenged, tense your whole body during this movement to maintain structural integrity and linkage.
- Breathing can be anatomical or paradoxical depending on whether the load is submaximal or maximal. If it's submaximal, use anatomical breathing where you exhale as you descend, inhale as you come up, and exhale at the top or final position. If it's maximal, use paradoxical breathing where you inhale as you go down, hold your breath for a few seconds as you tighten everything, and exhale as you come up.
- Legs can be bent or straight depending on the desired training effect. You will find a particular angle that suits your structure most comfortably. Start with a 20-degree bend and adjust slightly from there.

| Common error | Error correction |
|---|---|
| Keeping the support leg too soft | Shift all of your weight onto the support leg and push the kneecap back, tightening the quads. |
| Overextending the center of mass beyond the foot during the forward bending | Place the kettlebells directly in front of the support foot and not too far forward. |
| Not finishing the hip extension | Tighten the glutes at the top of the movement, activating the opposing muscles and thereby fully extending the hips. |

## DOUBLE SWING

**Figure 7.5**  Double swing.

Just as the single kettlebell swing is the foundation of all the other single kettlebell exercises, the double kettlebell swing is the foundation of all the other double kettlebell exercises, and the mechanics and alignment developed in this exercise ensure that you will be able to transition effectively into more advanced movement patterns.

To perform this exercise, place two kettlebells of equal weight on the floor in front of you. Load the hips by sitting back and grab the handles of each kettlebell with the fingers (see figure 7.5a). Keep the handles of the kettlebells in vertical alignment. Keep your shoulders pulled back with the chest lifted. Note that thumb positioning is significant and depends on the lifter's anatomical structure, skill set, and goals. If the thumb is forward, it allows for faster pacing, minimizes shoulder activity (good for those with pain or discomfort during rotation of the shoulders), and is more reliant upon leg drive versus momentum. Leaner athletes with strong legs tend to prefer this variation. If the thumb is back, there is more momentum via a greater range of motion. This is ideal for enhancing grip endurance and displacing load over the whole body. Lighter athletes tend to prefer this variation. If the thumb is neutral (palm facing back),

*(continued)*

### DOUBLE SWING  *(continued)*

it distributes stress more equally along the grip, arms, and shoulders. Experiment with all three hand positions to determine which is most comfortable. As with other techniques, find a flow that works well with your body structure and keep with it. Try changing grip positions when your grip fatigues in order to prolong a set.

As you begin to stand, swing the kettlebells between your legs with your forearms connecting to your torso (see figure 7.5b). When the swing reaches its end point behind you, stand up completely, extending the ankles, knees, hips, and torso (see figure 7.5c). Sustain this pendulum swing through the duration of the set. In your stance the legs will have to be farther apart. The degree to which this happens depends on your body levers and the length of your upper and lower legs. The key is to make just enough room for the kettlebells to comfortably pass between the legs. A stance that is too wide will negatively affect leverage and power, making it more difficult for you to move easily. Learn how to open your hips by pushing your knees out to the sides rather than directly forward.

When performing this exercise, use one or two cycles of anatomical breathing (a cycle is one exhalation and one inhalation). One variation is to exhale at the back of the downswing and inhale during the upswing. Another variation is to exhale at the back of downswing, inhale, exhale as the kettlebell transitions from the horizontal to the vertical plane, and inhale as the upswing continues. For maximal loads (5 reps or fewer), use paradoxical breathing due to the increased spinal stability it provides. Inhale as you go into the backswing, and exhale as you transition into the upswing.

### Key Principles

- As mentioned in chapter 6, the squat mechanic of swinging is applicable for low volume and general fitness work. It's ideal for creating a quick spike in heart rate due to the simplistic mechanics and large muscle groups used. However, for sets beyond 30 seconds in length, the pendulum spring technique creates a more momentum-based mechanic, which allows for greater work capacity in addition to less stress on the lower back and grip.

- During the backswing and upswing, keep the kettlebells close to your center of mass (hips). This creates better alignment, control, and power.

- Maximize the connection between the arm and torso on the upswing.

- Deflect back via the hips at the top of the upswing to act as a counterbalance to the weight in front of the body and as a catalyst to complete hip extension. This is more critical compared with the single kettlebell swing due to the increased load. Insufficient extension of the hips during the upswing results in loss of balance, poor alignment, and poor power transfer.

- Maintain deflection as you drop the kettlebell into the downswing and time the creasing of the hips. (Maintain deflection until you feel the triceps come into contact with the rib cage. At that point, softly absorb the downward force with a slight bend of the knees and ankles and then crease the hips into the pendulum spring mechanics.) Refer to chapter 6 for determining the angle of the hip crease.

- The kettlebells will most likely bang together on the downswing and upswing. This is not a problem as long as it's minimal. Look for a smooth groove in which the kettlebells lightly brush each other rather than clang together.

| Common error | Error correction |
|---|---|
| No connection between the arm and the hip and torso on the up-swing | Fasten a resistance band around both arms to keep the arms connected to the torso. |
| Lack of deflection on the upswing and while dropping the kettlebell into the downswing | If you have a coach or are coaching someone, a verbal cue of "Deflect back" is helpful. It is also helpful to swing in front of an object (e.g., wall, mat) at arm's length; if you don't deflect back, you will hit the object. |
| The kettlebell drops too far below the pelvis on the downswing | Do swings with a yoga block or similar object between the legs or place a second kettlebell on the floor between the legs. If you hit the object or second kettlebell, you have dropped too low. |
| The shoulder unpacks and the kettlebell trajectory is too far from the body | Swing in front of an object (e.g., wall, mat) at arm's length; if you don't deflect back, you will hit the object. |

## DOUBLE CLEAN

The double clean is a valuable standalone exercise in addition to being an essential transition point to pressing, jerking, and other overhead movements. Before moving on to the double clean, you should be able to demonstrate a solid rack position and good hand-insertion technique. If are not yet comfortable with the one-arm clean, you will struggle with the double clean. The increased challenge comes not only from the increased load but also the increased coordination required to synchronize bilateral loading. More than anything, the reduction in mobility presents the greatest challenge. With the one-arm clean, even if you are stiff in the upper body and have not perfected the rack position, you can sustain it because only one side of your diaphragm and chest is compressed, so the open side can breathe easily. When you introduce doubles, you greatly reduce the space for your diaphragm and lungs to expand. Your technique must be precise in order to produce optimal results.

The rack position with two kettlebells is significantly more difficult than with one, so you need to be sure to establish a good rack position. Set up by standing behind the kettlebells so that when you flex the trunk to pick them up your hips are already loaded. The handles should be placed vertically. When cleaning to the chest, optimal timing occurs when the elbows reach the hips at the same moment that the kettlebells reach your chest. The postural keys for a good rack position are as follows:

- Knees are fully extended.

- Elbows are connected to the torso and dropped toward the hips. Optimal position is with both elbows sitting on top of the pelvis and the upper-body muscles able to relax under load.

- Hands are inserted deep into the handles and wrists are in relaxed, neutral position. The sides of the handles each contact two points on the hand, one side sitting in webbing between the thumb and index finger, dropping down at an angle, and the other side braced against the ulna.

- Kettlebells are medial to the lateral shoulder and toward the midline as much as possible to achieve a vertical alignment of the combined center of mass over the base of support. Women with large breasts will have difficulty achieving a midline rack position and will have to move the kettlebells more laterally in order to stabilize them against the body. Don't allow the kettlebells to move too far laterally.

As mentioned, finding the ideal placement of the kettlebells is more challenging with double kettlebells than it is with a single kettlebell. It takes time and practice to find the best alignment for your body levers. The standard alignment is to stack one handle directly above the other so that the two become one, so to speak. Instead of holding the two kettlebells side by side, as shown in figure 7.6a, you stack one handle directly over the other, as shown in figure 7.6b. Secure the handles by hooking the

**Figure 7.6** Holding the kettlebells in (a) a nonoptimal side-by-side position and in (b) an optimal stacked position.

fingers of the bottom hand between the palm and kettlebell handle of the top hand. Once this self-tightening grip is in place, you can relax the hands and arms and the position will secure the two kettlebells on the midline. This particular midline alignment requires the least amount of energy to hold and is therefore considered optimal positioning. Continue to work on mastering the rack position by adding static holds to your training. At first you may find even 30 seconds of the rack hold to be challenging because of muscular tension and poor alignment. With more practice you will be able to relax in this position because your postural muscles will be supporting the kettlebell load, allowing the larger prime-mover muscles to relax and recover between reps.

To perform this exercise, begin as in a double kettlebell swing, swinging the kettlebells back through your legs (see figure 7.7a). As they swing forward, keep your forearms braced against your body (see figure 7.7b). Your arms stay connected to your body, and at the point where the arm would disconnect during the double swing, the arms move vertically during the clean. Imagine you are standing inside a chimney and the walls of the chimney block you, so you can only move the kettlebell up and down. As your hips reach forward extension, pop up onto the toes and give a tug with your trapezius muscles, pulling the kettlebell up the chimney (see figure 7.7c). Before the kettlebell settles to the chest, loosen the grip and open the hands to insert them deeply into the handles (see figure 7.7d). Complete the vertical pull by letting the kettlebell rest on your chest and arm into the rack position (see figure 7.7e). Complete the lift by turning your palms faceup and deflecting the force by moving your shoulders back as you quickly rise again onto the toes (see figure 7.7f). Your elbows stay braced to your body. As the kettlebells are falling, just before your elbow reaches full extension, pull your hands back to catch with the fingers and tighten the grip to complete the backswing (see figure 7.7g). Continue the smooth pendulum motion throughout the set (see figure 7.7h).

Popping onto the toes after the backswing and the first part of the forward swing, at the completion of the inertia phase and during the start of the vertical acceleration, gives you additional extension in the lift and uses the high-endurance musculature of the calves. By using the calves to facilitate the vertical transfer of force, you will be able to last longer and use less energy on each rep. The feet must return to flat just preceding the arrival of the kettlebells to the chest. The pop onto the toes must be quick, and up and down is done as one movement. Do not go up on the toes and stay up; instead, lift up on the toes and immediately let the heels drop again. It is a timing issue that will come with practice. For every double clean repetition, you will pop up onto toes then drop to flat feet two times—once at the beginning of the upward movement and once at beginning of the drop.

When performing this exercise, use anatomical breathing with three or more breathing cycles. One variation is to start from the rack position, inhale as you deflect back and drop the kettlebells into the downswing, exhale at the back of the downswing, inhale during the upswing and hand insertion, and exhale as the kettlebells land in the rack position (two breath cycles). Another variation is to start from the rack position, inhale as you deflect back and drop the kettlebells into the downswing, exhale at the back of the downswing, inhale, exhale as you begin hand insertion, inhale, and exhale as the kettlebells land in rack position (three breath cycles). You can take recovery breaths in the rest position to allow for proper recovery and pacing.

*(continued)*

**Figure 7.7** Double clean.

## Key Principles

- The hand insertion begins at approximately hip level, and the angle of the hands as they begin insertion is 45 degrees. Hand insertion happens via two movements—a subtle but quick pulling motion followed by inserting the hands forward and upward into the bells. When done correctly, the bells will be weightless, easy to manipulate, and with no traumatic impact to the wrist and forearm.

- As the kettlebells are cleaned to the rack position, it's crucial to open the hands into a light claw to avoid trapping the fingers between the two kettlebells. Failure to do so can result in broken fingers or fingernails.

- To help absorb the force of the downward fall, you can add further deflection by rising onto your toes at the start of the drop and then dropping your heels preceding the backswing. By rising onto your toes during the start of the drop, you increase the extension of your trunk and simultaneously raise your center of mass closer to the kettlebells, thereby reducing the distance the kettlebells and arms have to travel. In other words, the legs and trunk work more so that the arms have to work less.

| Common error | Error correction |
| --- | --- |
| Banging your wrist or forearm on the kettlebell | You are most likely inserting your hand too early, too late, or at an incorrect angle. Use a hand-insertion drill where you visualize a ladder with four rungs in front of you on the vertical plane. Gradually climb the ladder, inserting your hand with a claw grip. Rung 1 is chest level, rung 2 is face level, rung 3 is just over your head, and rung 4 is near the top just before your arm reaches full extension. Clean up and release the fingers to insert the hand at each level, and then drop down into backswing between each insertion. |
| Incorrect rack position or difficulty achieving the rack position | Hold two kettlebells in rack position for time (duration). Also perform mobility and flexibility drills targeting key areas, such as the shoulders, spine, and hips, as described in chapter 6. |
| Gripping the handles too hard in the rack position (crush gripping) | Keep your hand in a light claw position to reduce heat (friction) and grip fatigue. |
| Cleaning too far out in front or too far laterally | Clean in front of or next to a wall where a bad rep will hit the wall. As mentioned previously, visualize that you are standing inside a chimney where the kettlebell can only move up and down, not forward or laterally. |

## DOUBLE FRONT SQUAT

**Figure 7.8** Double front squat.

The double front squat is more advanced than the regular squat in that the load has increased and maintaining alignment of the kettlebells is more challenging. A front squat with two kettlebells is significantly more challenging than a front squat with a single kettlebell because of the restricted breathing that occurs with the load of two kettlebells on your chest and abdomen. It's important to be proficient in the mechanics of the goblet squat and single kettlebell front squat before performing the double front squat.

To perform this exercise, stand in your normal squat stance with the toes forward (see figure 7.8a), or you can slightly evert your toes if necessary to open tighter hips and achieve maximal depth. It is a good idea to simulate the same stances you will use in the snatch, clean, and clean and jerk for precise practice of motor patterns. Sit back with your hips and lower your center of mass until the tops of your thighs are parallel with the floor or slightly below parallel (see figure 7.8b). The front load will naturally try to pull you forward into a flexed position, especially with increasing loads. You counteract this forward pull by sitting way back onto your heels and strongly arching your back, pinching the shoulder blades together and lifting the chest, while keeping your forearms firmly against your body. Avoid flexing your trunk forward too much. With the correct body alignment, the load of the kettlebells in front of you acts as a counterbalance to allow you to sit back onto your heels. Throughout the movement your feet are flat on the floor. From the bottom position, push your feet firmly into the floor and drive up from the heels to stand up, straightening the legs fully (see figure 7.8c). When performing this exercise, use paradoxical or anatomical breathing depending on weight and volume.

Those who are less flexible will tend to disengage the arms from the body toward the bottom position and end up holding the kettlebells with just the arms, instead of placing the arms against the body to gain support from the body mass. Until you develop the shoulder flexibility to keep your arms against your body and the back flexibility to really arch your back and lift your chest, it will be difficult to control heavier kettlebells in the front squat. Revert to the rack holds and bridging exercises to improve your shoulder and trunk flexibility for good arm–body connection.

There is a variation of the front squat that you can use for heavy kettlebells if you have a hard time holding them in rack. Instead of cleaning the kettlebells to the chest as in the traditional rack position, you can clean the kettlebells directly on top of the shoulders (see figure 7.9). Instead of being in front of you, the load is pressing directly down and the alignment is more similar to that of a back squat with a barbell. The position allows you to get more leverage on the kettlebells and makes it much easier to breathe since the load is not compressing the lungs and diaphragm. This means you can go heavier and get more repetitions, which makes this an excellent variation for strength development.

### Key Principles

- Actively descend into the bottom position via hip flexor recruitment.
- For muscular strength development, use heavier loads for a few reps (e.g. 5 sets of 5 reps).
- Avoid allowing your knees to collapse inward by pressing the knees out to the side and placing your hips inside the spacing between your hips in the bottom position.

**Figure 7.9** Heavy kettlebell squat position.

| Common error | Error correction |
| --- | --- |
| Weight on the toes and not the heels | Practice the box squat—sitting back onto a box to teach sitting back with the hips. |
| Exaggerated rounding of the spine | Stand with the tips of your toes touching the base of the wall, look straight ahead, and pull your arms back behind you by pinching your shoulder blades together. Without adjusting your head position, sit back and down into the squat, and then stand up. The wall will prevent your body from moving forward, so you have to learn to sit back and keep a nice arch in the spine. Initially you may need to move your toes away from the wall a bit. As you improve, you can move the toes closer. |
| Can't descend into a full squat due to lazy hip flexors | Lie flat on your back with your palms on the floor and legs extended, and pull your toes toward you into dorsiflexion. A partner holds one foot in each hand by grabbing the tops of the insteps. Against your partner's resistance, pull your knees toward your chest. Now extend the legs straight again without any resistance from your partner. This drill helps to recruit your hip flexors so you can learn to use them to pull yourself into the bottom position of the squat. |
| Kettlebells fall out of the rack position | Maintain vertical alignment as much as possible between the hips and torso while descending into the squat. |

*(continued)*

## DOUBLE FRONT SQUAT *(continued)*

| Common error | Error correction |
| --- | --- |
| Heels lift toward the bottom of the squat, shifting excessive load to the knees | To help correct this, insert a 2 to 4 in. (5-10 cm) weight plate or block under the heels. Eventually you will be able to squat without it. Use this ankle mobility exercise as a warm-up and between sets. In an extended lunge position, kneel on one knee on a mat with the other foot in front and both facing forward. Hands are on the floor shoulder-width apart in front of the front foot. Shift your weight to the hands and lift the rear knee. Point the toes of the rear foot while firmly pressing the front of the ankle into the floor. Press your shoelaces into the floor to stretch the front of your ankle, foot, and shin. Then push firmly back with the hands and front foot to drive the rear heel into the floor. Alternate between laces down and heel back. |

# ONE-ARM JERK

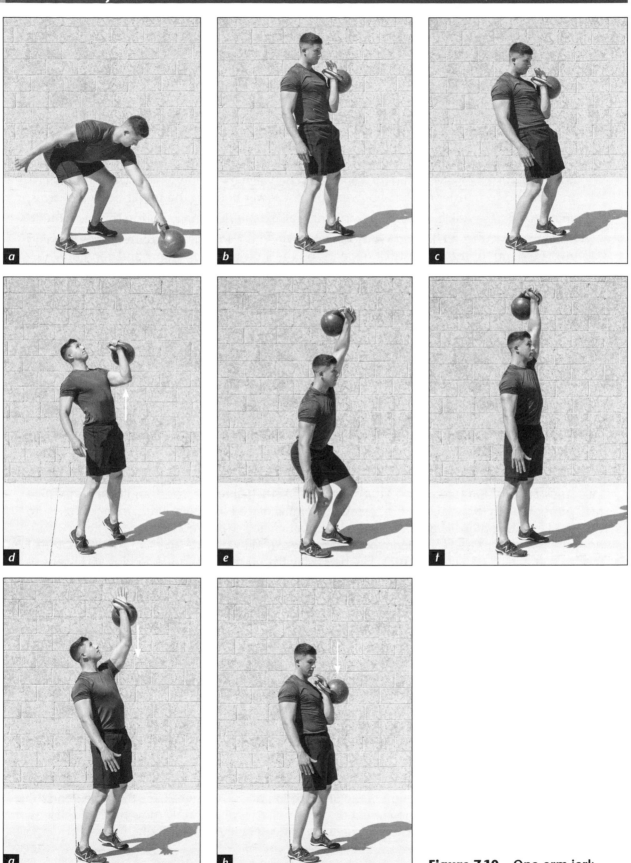

**Figure 7.10** One-arm jerk.

*(continued)*

**ONE-ARM JERK** *(continued)*

The jerk is a full-body exercise that requires a high degree of coordination, timing, and ability to generate maximum power in a short range of motion. Multiple athletic qualities are called upon in the correct performance of the jerk, and therefore it is considered the most technical of all the kettlebell lifts. The one-arm jerk (and eventually the double jerk, which you will learn in the next chapter) is a high-value exercise not only for its conditioning benefits but also because it involves the practice of many key principles of kettlebell lifting. With each rep you practice the rack and lockout positions and strengthen those positions that are crucial to performance in the other classical lifts of the clean and the snatch. In addition to that reinforcement, a complex coordination between upper body and lower body is needed to develop a crisp, fast, powerful jerk. The jerk has five primary movement components:

1. *Half squat (first dip)*—Maintain the connection between the elbows and torso and the heels and ground to transfer maximal power from the lower body to the upper body and arms.

2. *Bump (sendoff)*—Ankle, knees, hips, and torso all extend maximally during this movement.

3. *Undersquat*—Arms are locked via dropping down into a squatting posture versus pressing up. The depth of the undersquat depends on the individual's anatomy and conditioning.

4. *Fixation (stand to lockout)*—There are two parts to the fixation. First, stand up to the overhead posture. Second, perform a knee roll, which involves keeping the hips at the level of the undersquat and only rolling the knees backward to lockout. The fixation in the final lockout position involves fully extending the elbow, keeping the arm close to the centerline of the body, externally rotating the shoulder (triceps facing forward and thumb back at an angle) and keeping the rib cage open.

5. *Drop to the rack position*—The triceps are turned off and the bells are lowered to the rack position via a smooth, controlled drop. The force of the bells coming down is absorbed by rising onto the toes and bringing the chest toward the bells. As the elbows begin to land in the rack position, the heels are lowered and the thoracic spine rounded to safely diffuse the load.

To perform this exercise, with the kettlebell on the floor, grab the handle and load the hips into the start position (see figure 7.10*a*). Clean the kettlebell to the chest and establish a solid rack position, with legs straight, hips extended, elbow placed on pelvis, hand inserted fully into the handle, and kettlebell vertically aligned over your feet (see figure 7.10*b*). From the rack position, the jerk is preceded by a deep inhalation. Then, rapidly dip the knees in a half squat (first dip) as you exhale (see figure 7.10*c*). The heels stay flat on the floor and the hips and knees sit forward. Do not sit the hips back on the first dip; this will cause a disconnect between the arm and kettlebell and the body. Because the kettlebell load is in front of you, you must slide your hips and knees forward to keep them aligned under the kettlebell.

From the rapid half squat, immediately straighten the legs and drive up maximally onto the toes while lifting the chest and extending the torso maximally. Deflect your head back and keep your eyes on the kettlebells (see figure 7.10*d*). This phase of the movement is called the *bump* or *send-off* and is the major component of the jerk. Just at the completion of the bump, when the ankles, knees, hips, and torso are all maximally extended, the momentum from the half squat into the bump will launch the kettlebells directly vertical. At this moment, the elbows disconnect from the torso and you rapidly drive the heels down and back in coordination with the sitting back of the hips (see figure 7.10*e*). This phase of the movement is called the *under-squat* or *second dip*. At the same moment that the heels drive into the ground, the arm is fully straightened and the elbow is locked (cannot have one without the other). The arm is now fully locked and stable. From completion of the undersquat, press the knees back to fully extend the legs. There is no independent movement of the arms in this phase, only movement of the legs. Your entire body is now fully locked out—elbow and knees are both straight.

The completion of the upward portion is called *fixation*, which means there is no movement and you have total control over both your body and the load. Optimal alignment is to have the biceps directly next to the ear, not by moving the head to the arm, but by placing the arm next to the head, which remains in neutral position (see figure 7.10*f*). Depending upon your body structure and degree of upper-back and shoulder flexibility, the arm may be slightly in front or slightly behind the head. Someone who is very flexible may have the arm behind the head, whereas someone who is less flexible may have the arm slightly in front. Ultimately you have to find the sagittal placement that feels most comfortable and allows you to relax in the lockout position.

The final phase is the drop, which returns the kettlebell to the chest. From fixation, the arm relaxes, the kettlebell falls in a smooth motion to the chest, and the elbow returns to the pelvis. It is helpful to rise onto the toes at the beginning of the drop to reduce the distance that the arm and kettlebell have to travel to get the elbow to the hip (see figure 7.10*g*). As soon as the arm connects to the body, the feet plant to complete the motion. You are now in the rack position in preparation for the next rep (see figure 7.10*h*). It is not a requirement to rise onto the toes at initiation of the drop. Heavier lifters or those using light kettlebells may prefer to stay flat-footed throughout the drop; however, for lighter lifters or those using heavier kettlebells, the elevation of the toes will help to reduce the impact of the drop.

When performing this exercise, use anatomical breathing with four or more cycles. Inhale before the first dip and exhale during the half squat, inhale on the bump, exhale upon landing to the undersquat and then to lockout, do an additional breathing cycle in the top position, inhale at the beginning of the drop, and exhale as the elbows make contact into the rack. If a deep undersquat is used, take an additional breath cycle between completion of the undersquat and fixation (i.e., five total cycles with a deep undersquat and four total cycles with a shallow, quick undersquat).

### Key Principles

- The three phases of half squat, bump, and undersquat must all be performed with maximum speed.
- The key to an effective jerk is leg power; to improve the strength and endurance of the jerk, improve strength and endurance of the legs.
- Maintain arm contact with body throughout the completion of the bump phase.
- Timing is key; establish full extension of the elbow as the heels hit the floor during the undersquat.

| Common error | Error correction |
| --- | --- |
| Losing connection between the elbow and hip and the heel and floor when descending into the half squat | Practice the half squat without jerking to focus on keeping your arms glued against your body. |
| Descending too slowly when dropping into the half squat | Focus on dropping into the half squat to activate a stretch reflex to facilitate a stronger bump. |
| Slow transition from the undersquat to lockout | Using the lockout squat, isolate and practice the motion of ascending quickly from the undersquat to lockout. See double overhead squats in chapter 8 for a detailed description of this exercise. |

## ONE-ARM CLEAN AND JERK

**Figure 7.11** One-arm clean and jerk.

The one-arm clean and jerk is truly a full-body strength and conditioning maneuver. You can develop a high degree of fitness doing just this exercise because it combines a pull, a push, and a squat into one movement and therefore works many muscles simultaneously. Here we combine the pulling motion of the clean with the pushing motion of the jerk into one exercise rather than separating them into two exercises. In the sport of kettlebell lifting, this is called *cycling* because of the cyclical nature of doing this exercise in high repetitions. Like the jerk, it is best to first become familiar with the one-arm version before tackling the double long cycle, which is presented in chapter 8. The term *long cycle* refers to the clean and jerk, and the terms can be used interchangeably when referencing the kettlebell exercise.

To perform this exercise, from the kettlebell resting on the floor (see figure 7.11*a*), clean to the rack position (see figure 7.11*b*), and then jerk overhead with the same arm (see figure 7.11*c*). Drop the kettlebell back to rack position (see figure 7.11*d*), and then drop again into the back-swing (see figure 7.11*e*). For the grip in the clean portion, you can use thumb forward, thumb backward, or neutral thumb depending on your preference.

When performing this exercise, use anatomical breathing with eight or more breathing cycles. Starting from the rack position, inhale as you deflect back and drop the kettlebell into the downswing, exhale at the back of the downswing, inhale during the transition into the forward swing, exhale at completion of the forward swing, inhale with hand insertion, and exhale as the kettlebell lands in the rack position. This equals three breath cycles for the clean component. From the rack position, inhale before the first dip, exhale during the half squat, inhale on the bump, exhale upon landing to the undersquat and then to lockout, take an additional breath cycle between completion of the undersquat and fixation and an additional breathing cycle in the top position, inhale at the beginning of the drop, and exhale as the elbows make contact into the rack. This equals five breath cycles for the jerk component, totaling eight breath cycles for each single repetition of the clean and jerk.

There are no technical differences between doing the clean and jerk as one exercise or as two, but there is a consideration of timing. When dropping from the fixation in the jerk, do not pause in the rack position before the downswing. Instead, drop to the rack position and immediately use the same inertia to drop into the backswing, and then clean to the chest. It has only to do with conservation of energy, relating once again to Newton's first law of motion, that is, a body set in motion stays in motion. Kettlebell sport athletes who compete in the long cycle will find that it burns slightly less energy to do the drop in one motion instead of two. You can rest as long as needed once you reclean the kettlebell to chest.

## Key Principles

- Clean and jerk is a rhythmic exercise so move smoothly and evenly from one movement to the next.
- Take continuous breaths to maintain a stable breath and heart rate; never hold your breath.
- Reduce the arc of the drop from chest to backswing by deflecting body backward at the beginning of the drop.

*(continued)*

**ONE-ARM CLEAN AND JERK** *(continued)*

| Common error | Error correction |
|---|---|
| Banging your wrist or forearm on the kettlebell | You are most likely inserting your hand too early, too late, or at an incorrect angle. Use a hand-insertion drill where you visualize a ladder with four rungs in front of you on the vertical plane. Gradually climb the ladder, inserting your hand with a claw grip. Rung 1 is chest level, rung 2 is face level, rung 3 is just over your head, and rung 4 is near the top just before your arm reaches full extension. Clean up and release the fingers to insert the hand at each level, and then drop down into backswing between each insertion. |
| Insufficient flexibility to extend the hips in the rack position | Practice the flexibility and mobility exercises from chapter 6 or rack holds later in this chapter. |
| Losing connection between the elbow and hip and the heels and floor when descending into the half squat | Practice the half squat without jerking to focus on keeping your arms glued against your body. |
| Descending too slowly when dropping into the half squat | Focus on dropping into the half squat to activate a stretch reflex to facilitate a stronger bump. |
| Slow transition from the under-squat to lockout | Using the lockout squat, isolate and practice the motion of ascending quickly from the undersquat to lockout. See double overhead squats in chapter 8 for a detailed description of this exercise. |

## KETTLEBELL JUMP SQUAT

**Figure 7.12**    Kettlebell jump squat.

*(continued)*

**KETTLEBELL JUMP SQUAT** *(continued)*

As the name implies, this is a kettlebell squat that involves jumping via a powerful ankle, knee, and hip extension. The jump squat is one of the most taxing anaerobic exercises you can do. It is used by athletes of many sports to develop explosive, fast-twitch legs and by kettlebell athletes to develop strength, power, and endurance. It is used extensively to train, reinforce, and condition the kettlebell jerk pattern because of the identical patterns between the two exercises. Almost all athletes talk about the legs being the first thing to go, and in kettlebells it is no different. You can only go as far as your legs will take you, and nowhere is this more true than in kettlebell jerks. So, the kettlebell jump squat is one of the most important finishers that a kettlebell athlete can do.

To perform this exercise, grab a single kettlebell by the horns (see figure 7.12*a*) and bring it behind you by doing the first half of the halo exercise as you learned in chapter 6 (see figure 7.12*b*). Holding the kettlebell behind your upper back, pinch your shoulder blades together so that your trapezius muscles form a shelf and the kettlebell rests on the upper-back muscles (see figure 7.12*c*). Drop all the way down into a maximal-depth squat (see figure 7.12*d*) and then rapidly jump as high as you can with your feet leaving the ground (see figure 7.12*e*). Absorb the landing softly through the balls of the feet and immediately descend into the squat again. Do each rep to maximal range up and down and also at maximal speed. In others words, go fast but do not shorten the range of the reps!

When performing this exercise, you can use paradoxical or anatomical breathing depending on weight and volume. Due to the speed of the exercise, one breathing cycle will be used.

## Key Principles

- Use the proper firing sequence—hip extension, knee extension, and then ankle extension.
- Due to the dynamic and ballistic nature of the movement, it is important to maintain proper alignment of the joints throughout the exercise. With the forces involved, a bad landing can cause a strain or sprain of the lower-body joints and muscles.
- When landing and descending into the squat, do so with proper mechanics and a slightly slower tempo to main control and safety.

| Common error | Error correction |
| --- | --- |
| Landing off balance when descending from the jump | This compromises the leverage and safety of the repetitions that follow. To help avoid this, maintain proper vertical alignment of the torso, hips, knees, and feet as you land to achieve optimal posture and positioning for the next jump. Do not lean forward or back. |
| Kettlebell bouncing and banging your neck | Hold the kettlebell firmly by the sides of the handles (horns) and pinch the muscles of the upper back to form a shelf for the kettlebell to rest upon, thereby avoiding direct contact with spine. |

## FARMER'S CARRY

**Figure 7.13** Farmer's carry.

Nothing signifies the hard work of manual labor like the full-body conditioning exercise of the farmer's carry, and there may be no greater test of mental fortitude and the ability to endure discomfort. Although it is possibly the least technical exercise from a motor pattern perspective, it has enduring value for developing grip endurance and core stability while also enhancing flexibility in the cervical and thoracic spine. The concept is simple—pick up something heavy and hold it for as long as you can or walk with it as far as you can, that is, until you can no longer hold it and it drops out of your hands. This can be done with one hand or two, and if you have a kettlebell with a thicker handle, that makes it all the more challenging. You can almost never go wrong by adding one set of heavy reps at the end of the main training.

To perform this exercise, squat to pick up the kettlebells, which should be shoulder-width apart (see figure 7.13a). Using the finger grip with thumb lock as used in the swing, clean, and snatch, lift the kettlebells with a deadlift and hold onto the kettlebells to the sides of your body for a period of time or for a maximum effort (see figure 7.13b). Breathe normally and continuously, with equal inhalation and exhalation. If you are in a place where a drop would damage the floor, place the kettlebells down just before your grip fails. Otherwise, keep holding them until they drop.

(continued)

**FARMER'S CARRY**   *(continued)*

Exerting maximum effort in the farmer's carry will surely fry your grip, which is why it is recommended as a finishing exercise. Because of the intense forearm contractions in a max or near-max effort, it is a good idea to stretch the forearm and fingers for a few minutes after this exercise to help your grip recover faster. Here is a favorite way to stretch the deep forearm flexors after a challenging set of the farmer's carry: Kneel on the floor with a mat under your knees. Spread your fingers out as wide as possible and touch the insides of the pinkies together (see figure 7.14a). Press both palms flat onto the floor, with the hands turned so that the pinkies are pointing backward directly toward you (see figure 7.14b). You may feel this stretching right away if you have tight forearms. Breathe and relax for 30 to 60 seconds. Keeping the palms flat as the priority, move deeper into the stretch by walking your lower body away from the hands and lowering your center of mass (see figure 7.14c). See how deep you can move into the stretch. Shake out your hands afterward to let the muscles relax.

**Figure 7.14**   Forearm and finger stretch.

## Key Principles

- Maintain proper alignment throughout the duration of the exercise. You will be handling heavier loads, which can strain your muscles of your upper back, neck, and traps if you let the load pull you out of upright posture.
- Grip is both firm and relaxed; excessive squeezing of the handles will make the forearms fatigue more quickly.
- Remain mentally relaxed throughout; steady breathing will help you to stay calm for the duration.

| Common error | Error correction |
| --- | --- |
| Failure to maintain proper alignment, especially in the cervical spine (rounding) and lumbar spine and pelvis (tilting) | Look forward and slightly up during the entire exercise. Head and eye position are strongly connected to proper posture. Also keep your hips level, even, and square to the direction you are facing and keep your abdominal and gluteal muscles stable. Never let the weight pull or twist you. |
| Squeezing the grip too hard with the center of your palm | Use the finger-lock position by wrapping the thumb over the first two fingers on each hand. |
| Bending to put the kettlebells down | Bend your legs to place the kettlebells on the floor upon completion of each set. |

## RACK HOLDS AND OVERHEAD HOLDS

Rack holds and overhead holds are static or isometric holds used to develop structural integrity, flexibility, and conditioning in both of these important positions. In addition to the conditioning effects, the static holds help teach you to relax in the postures through proper positioning so that the structure of your postural muscles holds the load rather than the prime movers, which will fatigue quickly.

**Rack Hold**   To perform this exercise, with the kettlebells resting on the floor, clean them to rack position and hold (see figure 7.15). With the kettlebells held in rack position, keep the legs straight with knees fully extended. Hold your arms against your torso and keep your elbows down toward or resting on top of the pelvis. Your hands are fully inserted into the handles. The proper rack position aligns the kettlebells vertically over your hips and your hips vertically over your stance.

**Figure 7.15**   Rack hold.

**Figure 7.16**   Overhead hold.

**Overhead Hold**   To perform this exercise, with the kettlebells resting on the floor, clean them to rack position and then jerk them into an overhead lockout position and hold (see figure 7.16). Your hands are fully inserted into the handles. The arms are held overhead with elbows fully extended and the biceps next to the ears. The proper position for the overhead hold aligns the kettlebells vertically over your shoulders, your shoulders vertically over your hips, and your hips vertically over your stance.

## Key Principles

- In addition to holding these positions statically, it's also beneficial to do both while walking in order to learn how to relax optimally, alternating from rack to lockout positions and holding each position for a few seconds before changing.
- With the rack holds, the flexibility and conditioning benefits will be greater when using heavier kettlebells because the load will allow you to more easily drop your elbows to your hips.
- During the overhead hold, it is important to ensure the triceps are facing forward instead of to the sides (and thumbs facing back), because this is a more structurally stable position for the shoulders. If the triceps are not facing forward and you fail to maintain elbow lock, the bells could fall on top of your head, causing severe injury.

| Common error | Error correction |
| --- | --- |
| Letting the elbows drift away from the centerline in a rack hold | Hang from a bar for increased time to improve shoulder and back flexibility so that the elbows can relax into the ideal alignment. |
| Racking to one side in a rack hold | This overly fatigues one arm and negatively affects pacing due to the increased time and motion needed for readjustments. To avoid this, improve flexibility and practice rack holds with load equally distributed on both sides. |
| Arms falling out of vertical alignment to the front in an overhead hold | This overly fatigues the shoulders. To help avoid this, improve shoulder and spinal flexibility so that proper alignment and range of motion can be attained. See chapter 6 for flexibility exercises. |

## RENEGADE ROWS

**Figure 7.17**  Renegade rows.

The renegade row is a unique strength exercise that combines stability and mobility of the anterior core muscles in a horizontal pulling movement. The majority of kettlebell exercises involve vertical lifts and emphasize the posterior chain (glutes, hamstrings, back), which are important for power development. However, to develop well-rounded conditioning, it is important to also train the front side of the body to balance out the rear-side dominance. The ability to maintain stability while moving and to create mobility while remaining stable is called *dynamic stability*, and the renegade row is one of the best exercises for developing that control. This exercise trains the anterior core strength needed to prevent extension of the lumbar spine and to keep the low back stable. Renegade rows combine elements of a front plank, a frontal-plane stability exercise, with horizontal rowing, a sagittal-plane mobility exercise.

To perform this exercise, place two heavy kettlebells on the floor shoulder-width apart (see figure 7.17*a*). It is important to use heavy kettlebells that will not flip or roll while supporting your body weight, so use kettlebells that are at least 16 kilograms (35 lb), and preferably heavier. Grab a handle with each hand and squeeze tightly (see figure 7.17*b*). Place your body in a plank position as in the top position of a push-up, balancing on the balls of your feet and with the spine level; do not arch or collapse the hips (see figure 7.17*c*). With your body weight balanced evenly between your hands and feet, shift your weight to one hand, making sure to press that hand firmly down through the kettlebell so that it is stable. With the other hand, pull the other kettlebell up until it touches to your rib cage (see figure 7.17*d*). Slowly lower that kettlebell, and then shift to that side and repeat the row (pull) on the other side. Go back and forth, one side up and down at a time. Inhale as you pull the kettlebells to the hips and waist, and exhale as you lower them back down.

## Key Principles

- Pay equal attention to the stabilizing arm and the pulling arm.
- Keep the shoulders of both arms connected into the socket via contraction of the latissimus dorsi muscles.
- Pull the kettlebell to the rib cage or abdomen and focus on pulling the elbows up and toward the center of the spine.

| Common error | Error correction |
|---|---|
| Rotating the torso during the pull | Prevent rotation of the hips during the rowing movement by keeping the abdominal muscles firm and hips stable. |
| Pulling primarily with the biceps instead of the back muscles | Keep the rib cage expanded and focus on pulling the elbow toward the ribs. |
| Letting the hips sag | Activate the core muscles to ensure proper alignment via a straight line from the head to the heels. |
| Bending the stabilizing arm | This results in poor control and loss of leverage and power. To avoid this, focus on keeping the stabilizing arm locked. |

## WINDMILL

The windmill is an exercise that simultaneously targets the core and lateral hip while improving stability and strength in the overhead position. It is also an excellent way to enhance overall flexibility. The windmill has some similarities to the yoga triangle posture, except it adds dynamic stabilization to the shoulder in the overhead position. The movement can seem complex if not understood in sequence, so it is advisable to practice this lift in stages, as you will see as the exercise is described.

First, there are two common setups with regard to stance. The stance can have either the toes pointing to one side at an angle or pointing forward.

**Toes-Angled Stance**   Start with the feet pointing forward, shoulder-width apart (see figure 7.18a). Pivot on the heels to the left approximately 45 degrees (see figure 7.18b). The left foot is now the front foot and the right foot is the rear foot.

**Figure 7.18**   Toes-angled stance for the windmill.

**Toes-Forward Stance**   Start with your feet pointing forward, shoulder-width apart (see figure 7.19). Because you have a bilateral stance, you will have to balance the load directly over the center of the base. When performing the windmill motion, your body will naturally rotate more to compensate for the reduced angle of the hips in the toes-forward position.

**Figure 7.19**   Toes-forward stance for the windmill.

**Stage 1: Windmill Preparation**   Holding a rope, exercise band, or stick by both ends, assume a toes-forward stance, with one hand high, one hand low, and the rope, band, or stick behind the back (see figure 7.20*a* for an example with a rope). Keep the chest open and facing upward as you push the rear hip out to the side and pull down with the bottom hand (see figure 7.20*b*). Rise to top position by pulling the rear hip back to start position and simultaneously pulling with the top hand (see figure 7.20*c*). You should feel the use of rope, stick, or band opening your chest and stabilizing your scapulae by pinching them together behind you. Keep this elongated and stable feeling throughout the full range of motion. This is the control you are looking for, and this same level of control has to be present when you add a greater load. This is the windmill movement; adding a weight should not change the positioning. You have to learn the alignment first with this drill and then maintain the alignment as you add progressively heavier loads.

**Figure 7.20**   Windmill preparation.

*(continued)*

**WINDMILL**  *(continued)*

**Stage 2: Low Windmill**  You can perform the low windmill with either toes-angled or toes-forward stance (here we will use the toes-angled stance). Raise your right arm overhead with the biceps touching your ear and turn your left palm forward so that the back of your left hand is against the inside of your left thigh (see figure 7.21*a*). Your weight shifts maximally to the rear (right) leg and you push your lateral hip to the side (see figure 7.21*b*). Your weight will stay maximally on the rear leg throughout the windmill movement. Do not shift to the forward leg at any portion of the movement. Now look up to the high hand and as you look up, rotate your upper torso toward the hand such that you feel your chest lifting and facing up toward the ceiling (see figure 7.21*c*). You are now set in the upper body with a kettlebell on the floor between your feet. Looking up at the top hand, as you descend, the bottom hand, which is braced against your inner thigh with palm facing forward, will slide down the inside of the leg until it reaches the handle of the kettlebell (see figure 7.21*d*). Grab the kettlebell and pull up by extending the body vertically (see figure 7.21*e*). Lower yourself under control and repeat for the desired reps. Even though this is a low windmill, keep your chest lifted and facing upward and your eyes on the upward hand.

**Figure 7.21**  Low windmill.

**Stage 3: High Windmill**  With the high windmill, you have an added shoulder stabilization component. The chest has to remain open and lifted in order to pack the shoulder, which means to maintain a position in which the arm is firmly protracted into the shoulder socket, the latissimus dorsi is fully engaged, the arm is connected to the body, and the scapulae are adducted, providing a stable upper-body platform. Once the shoulder girdle is stabilized in this way, the fulcrum of motion is performed only with the hip joint. You have learned the importance of lockout and shoulder stabilization through the overhead lifts. The same things apply in the high windmill.

Again, you can perform the high windmill with either the toes-angled or toes-forward stance (here we will use the toe-angled stance). Clean a kettlebell to the chest with your right arm and feet pointing forward, shoulder-width apart (see figure 7.22a), and then pivot on your heels to the left approximately 45 degrees (see figure 7.22b). The left foot is now the front foot and the right foot is the rear foot. Raise your right arm overhead with the biceps touching your ear and turn your left palm forward so that the back of your left hand is against the inside of your left thigh (see figure 7.22c). Shift your weight maximally to the rear (right) leg and push your lateral hip to the side. Your weight will stay maximally on the rear leg throughout the windmill movement. Do not shift to the forward leg at any portion of the movement. Now look up to the high hand, and as you look up, rotate your upper torso toward the hand such that you feel your chest lifting and facing toward the ceiling (see figure 7.22 d and e). Lower yourself by pressing your rear (right) hip out to the side and lift up by pulling with the rear hip to return to the start position.

**Figure 7.22**  High windmill.

(continued)

**WINDMILL** *(continued)*

**Stage 4: Double Windmill**   The double windmill is a way to increase the load on your core musculature when it starts becoming too heavy to easily control in the overhead position. The shoulder is the limitation, not the core, so there will be a point where the risk far outweighs the reward in the high windmill. If you like the feel of heavy windmills, and some people do, then it is far safer to distribute heavier loads over both hands. The trade-off is that in exchange for a heavier load, you will have a reduced range of motion, because the low kettlebell will limit the range of motion of the bottom hand.

Double windmills can be performed with either the toes-angled or toes-forward stance (here we will use the toe-angled stance). With your right arm, clean one kettlebell to your chest into the rack position. The second kettlebell is on the floor. Start with your feet pointing forward, shoulder-width apart (see figure 7.23*a*), and pivot on your heels to the left approximately 45 degrees (see figure 7.23*b*). The left foot is now the front foot and the right foot is the rear foot. Press your right arm overhead with the biceps touching your ear and turn your left palm forward so that the back of your left hand is against the inside of your left thigh (see figure 7.23*c*). Shift your weight maximally to the rear (right) leg and push your lateral hip to the side. Your weight will stay maximally on the rear leg throughout the windmill movement. Do not shift to the forward leg at any portion of the movement. Now look up to the high hand, and as you look up, rotate

**Figure 7.23**   Double windmill.

your upper torso toward the hand such that you feel your chest lifting and facing toward the ceiling (see figure 7.23*d*). Lower yourself by pressing the rear (right) hip out to the side as your left hand slides down along the inside of your left leg until the fingers touch the handle of the kettlebell on the floor. Grab the handle with your left hand and lift up by pulling with the rear hip to return to the up position (see figure 7.23*e*). Repeat the double windmill by repeating the lateral bending and standing for the desired number of repetitions, and then repeat on the other side.

**Stage 5: Extended Windmill**   You may already have extreme flexibility through naturally good range of motion or through years of training and will not be challenged at all by the windmill from a flexibility standpoint. Or, you may be challenged by a high windmill, but with the double windmill your range is too limited to get an effective stretch. In either case, if you have the ability to do so safely and effectively, you can extend the range you have to move in by standing on two boxes of equal height. The more flexible you are, the higher the boxes you will use. Make sure you only use loads you can safely control, and use sturdy boxes with wide bases so you minimize the chances of losing your balance.

**Key Principles**

- Focus on creasing at the hips.
- Keep the arms locked into the shoulder socket via contraction of the latissimus dorsi and adduction of the scapulae.
- Keep the rib cage open and expanded.
- Keep your eyes focused on the kettlebell.
- When first learning the windmill, it's advisable to have a partner spotting you during the lift.
- For all stages, inhale into your belly as you descend and exhale as you come up. To achieve a greater range of motion, add an extra exhalation in the bottom position.

| Common error | Error correction |
|---|---|
| Excessive bending of the legs in the bottom position | Although a slight bending of the legs is acceptable, the ideal is to have both legs straight. Make sure to extend your knees fully. |
| Shifting weight to the front leg during the downward portion of the lift | Shift weight to the rear leg by pushing your rear hip up and back. |
| Reaching your bottom hand outside the base of support during the bottom portion of the lift | Slide the back of the bottom hand along the inside of the front leg while lowering the body into the bottom portion of the lift. |
| Creasing at the waist during the descent | Focus on creasing at the hips instead by pushing the outside of the hip out and to the side. |

## GET-UP

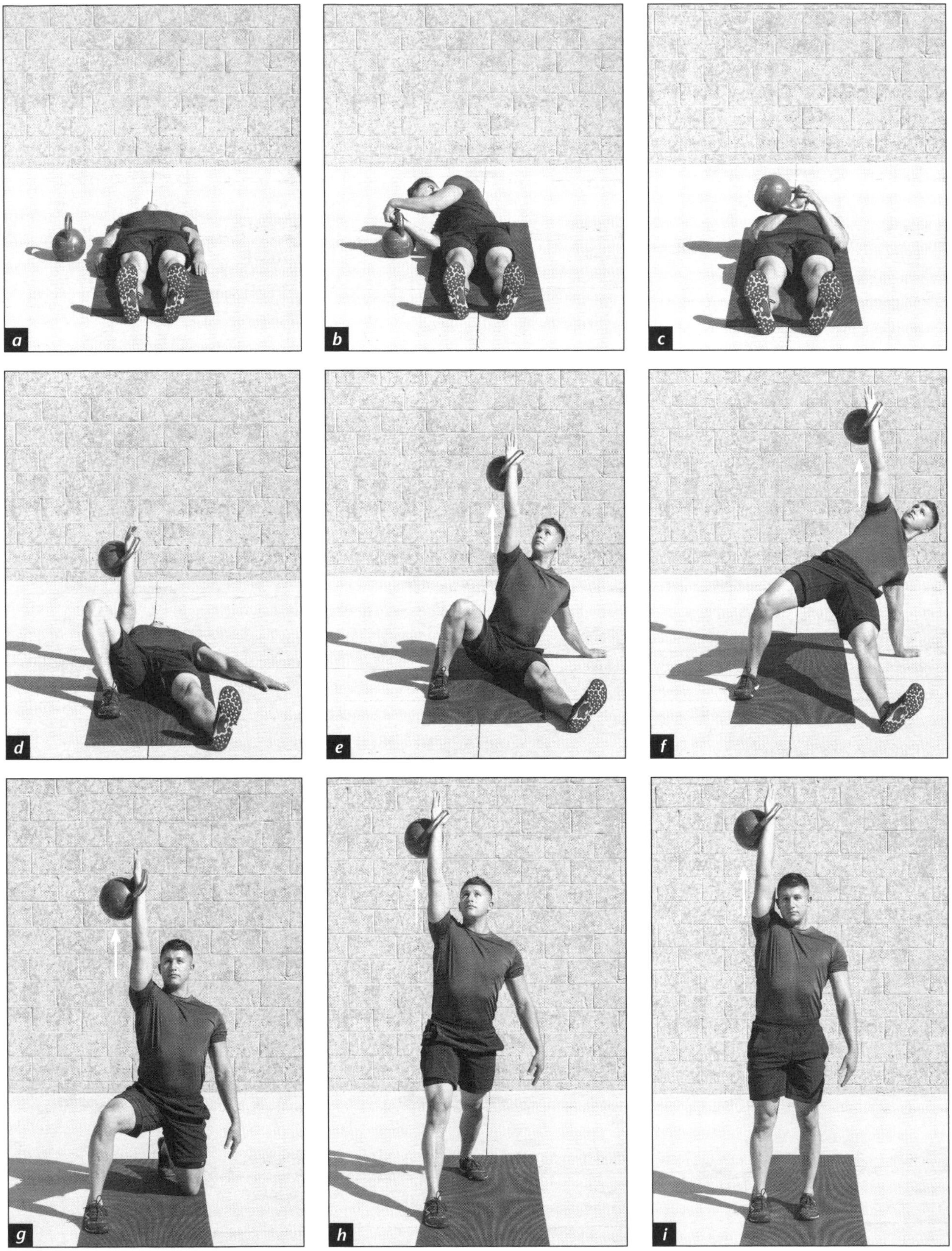

**Figure 7.24** Get-up.

This exercise has its lineage in Turkish grapplers using it as a full-body conditioning movement that also develops the ability to make effective and strong transitions from the ground to standing and vice versa, and thus the original name for this exercise is *Turkish get-up*. In current applications, the get-up is appreciated for its similarities to primal rolling patterns, which are early movement patterns that infants master in the process of rolling from front to back, from back to front, and from lying to sitting, kneeling, and standing patterns. As such it has value in movement education, and it is becoming a popular drill for assessing movement quality because of the complex series of movements that the body performs in the exercise. It addresses all planes of motion and combines mobility with stability requirements, as well as combining basic movement patterns such as lying, rolling, kneeling, lunging, squatting, and standing into one movement. The individual movements within the get-up are not particularly complex. Its basic coordination is more simplistic than a double jerk, for instance. Yet stringing them together into a seamless movement symphony brings the get-up a lot of attention in the kettlebell fitness community.

Although the get-up can certainly be practiced with heavy loads, there may be much greater value in its mobility and stabilization challenges. A starting practice is to put a light object on top of your fisted hand and go through the entire movement. The object is on your fist and not clutched in your hand in order to develop the control of motion in the vertical plane. Any sway forward, back, or to the sides will cause the object to tip, so you quickly adapt to keep balance. A shoe or a water bottle is usually handy and makes a convenient object for this practice. A progression in the development of control is to fill a small plastic or paper cup with water and do your best not to spill it on yourself. Once you have developed some skill in the weightless version of the get-up and have a solid understanding of the vertical transfer of power and stability needed, you can begin performing get-ups with a kettlebell.

To perform this exercise, start by lying flat on your back with the kettlebell on the floor to the right of your body (see figure 7.24*a*). To get the kettlebell into position, roll your body to the right, insert your right hand fully into the handle (see figure 7.24*b*), and use two hands to pull the kettlebell to your chest. Roll back to your left so you are flat on your back (see figure 7.24*c*). Raise your right arm straight up over your chest and bend your right knee so that the right foot is flat on the floor; the left arm is flat on the floor at about a 45-degree angle (see figure 7.24*d*). Initiate the movement by flexing your abs slightly and then shifting the weight to the left arm, first to the shoulder, then the elbow, then the forearm, and finally the palm. As your body weight transfers to the left palm, the left hand presses firmly into the floor and the left elbow extends, fully locked out (see figure 7.24*e*). This is the first stopping point, and you are completely stable.

Transition by lifting your hips off the floor and maximally extending them (see figure 7.24*f*). It is important that the force moves vertically as your hips extend. Any forward drift of the right arm will cause you to lose control of the kettlebell. Your weight is supported by two points at this stage, the left palm and the right foot. Keep these two points of contact stable and lift the extended left leg off the floor. Keeping the hips lifted, move the left leg back and under your hips by bending the knee and pulling the leg behind you into a lunge position (see figure 7.24*g*). The left knee should be turned out slightly to the side to create a wider base and therefore better balance. Complete this phase by lifting the left hand off the floor and extending the trunk upright. From this lunge position, shift your body weight to the right (front) leg and step up by pushing your right leg into the ground and extending your right knee fully (see figure 7.24*h*). Complete the upward phase of the get-up by stepping your left (rear) foot up to meet the right foot so that your stance is equal and balanced (see figure 7.24*i*).

Now reverse the movement: Step back with the left foot and drop your center of mass by bending both knees and returning to the lunge position with the right foot forward. Place your left palm on the floor, raise your hips high, and extend your left leg out in front. Now lower your mass so that you are seated on the floor. Complete the movement by dropping from left palm to forearm, then to shoulder, and finally to the lying position that you started from. It may feel more natural to slide the bottom arm along the floor as you are lowering yourself.

*(continued)*

**GET-UP**   *(continued)*

### Key Principles

- Keep your eyes on the kettlebell at all times to maintain focus and avoid losing the location of the kettlebell in case of a bad rep.
- Ensure the kettlebell stays vertical throughout the movement so that your body mass is under the load, ensuring better control of the kettlebell.
- Breathe normally throughout.
- Keep your arm packed into your shoulder to create shoulder stability and better control of the kettlebell.
- When first learning the get-up, use a spotter to be prepared to save a bad rep.

| Common error | Error correction |
|---|---|
| Bringing the kettlebell over the face when transitioning the hands | Using both hands, bring the kettlebell around the top of the head to the other side. |
| Trying to sit up during the first segment of the movement | Roll up at a 45-degree angle using the elbow and foot as levers. |

## RUSSIAN TWIST

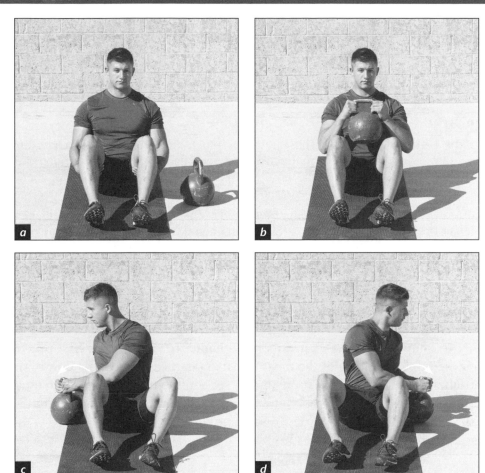

**Figure 7.25** Russian twist.

This exercise is a phenomenal core conditioning movement that focuses on creating rotation in the thoracic region while resisting or limiting rotation in the lumbar region. The function of resisting rotation in the lumbar spine is to stabilize the lower back. As a general rule, excessive rotation in the lumbar spine, especially while under additional load, can strain the low back. The joints above (thoracic spine) and below (hips) the lumbar spine are responsible for rotation. This is another key component of what is referred to as *dynamic core stability*, that is, preventing or limiting rotation in the lumbar spine (stability) while creating movement in the surrounding body segments.

Sit on the floor with your trunk upright (see figure 7.25a). You will have to keep your abdominal muscles tight in order to avoid falling or leaning back too far. Pick up the kettlebell with two hands, holding it by the sides of the handle (see figure 7.25b). Keep your feet anchored to the floor and twist to one side until the kettlebell lightly touches the floor on one side (see figure 7.25c). Maintain tension in the abs while twisting and lightly touching the kettlebell to the floor on the other side (see figure 7.25d). Keep your hips stationary and create the rotation from the upper spine and thoracic muscles.

You can also perform this exercise by raising the feet off the floor to balance on your sit bones. You are less stable in this variation, and without the feet anchored you will have more movement in the hips. As your upper body twists one way, the hips counterbalance by twisting to the opposite direction. Exhale as the kettlebell touches the ground on either side and inhale on the transitions between these two points.

*(continued)*

**RUSSIAN TWIST**  *(continued)*

### Key Principles

- Keep the trunk angled back 45 degrees to keep the core muscles engaged.
- Keep the abdominal muscles tight throughout the exercise.
- Avoid shifting your weight from one hip to the other—keep the hips in a fixed position.

| Common error | Error correction |
|---|---|
| Bouncing the kettlebell off the ground | This creates too much momentum, which compromises the contraction and conditioning of the core muscles. To avoid this, ensure the kettlebell completely decelerates after touching the ground. |
| Using the biceps instead of the core to move the kettlebell | At the beginning of the motion (while the kettlebell is still on the ground), focus on deactivating the arms and initiating the motion with the muscles of the trunk. |

Along with the chapter 6 basic exercises, you now have a strong foundation of the most important kettlebell lifts that can be used in various combinations to form the backbone of your fitness or strength and conditioning programs. Just as with the basic exercises from chapter 6, take time to first practice these new lifts. Start easy, learn the flow of the movement, get confident that you understand it, and then start to challenge yourself and include it in your program.

CHAPTER

8

# ADVANCED EXERCISES

The exercises in this chapter are advanced because they all require an enhanced emphasis on breath control, coordination, flexibility, stability, raw strength, and absolute power. Each of the lifts reflects an extreme progression. Some movements emphasize an increase in multiple athletic attributes simultaneously. Due to the increased demands of these advanced exercises, a strong foundation in the basic and intermediate exercises is a prerequisite for incorporating them into your training programs. As always, special attention must be paid to safety by attending to mechanics, alignment, and breathing.

## BOTTOMS-UP CLEAN

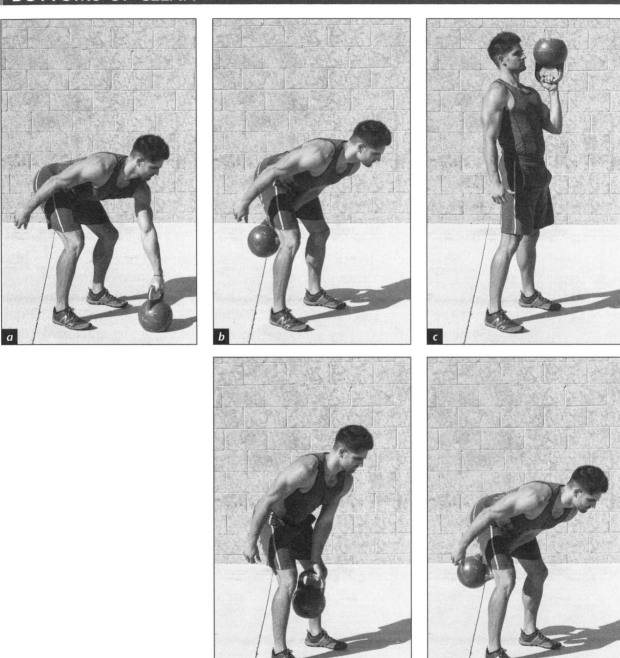

**Figure 8.1**    Bottoms-up clean.

The bottoms-up clean is the same as the conventional clean in terms of the hip and knee mechanics. However, the final position is different—instead of the kettlebell resting against the forearm, it is held statically with the bottom facing up. This necessitates a higher level of mental focus and dramatically works the grip and core muscles.

With a single kettlebell on the floor, sit back to load the hips and grab the handle with the finger-hook grip (see figure 8.1a). As with the one-arm clean, you swing the single kettlebell back through your legs to load your hips (see figure 8.1b) and then extend and pull the kettlebell up toward the chest (see figure 8.1c). Although a thumbs-back or thumbs-forward position can be used on the backswing, keeping the thumbs forward will create the smoothest transition to the bottoms-up position. Instead of inserting your hand into the handle, take a tight, crushing grip, squeezing the handle as tightly as you can to keep the bottom of the kettlebell facing up and prevent it from flipping. In addition to the intense grip, the kettlebell must remain vertically aligned over your feet with the forearm kept in a vertical plane in order to maintain the balanced position. While squeezing the grip tightly, also squeeze the abdominal and gluteal muscles, creating a full-body tension. To lower the kettlebell, let it fall and catch with the fingers as in a standard one-arm clean (see figure 8.1d), and follow the kettlebell down and back into a backswing (see figure 8.1e).

When performing this exercise, use the paradoxical breathing method to create extra tension in your core. Inhale as you swing the kettlebell through your legs, and exhale as the kettlebell reaches the top position as you squeeze your muscles to control it in the bottoms-up position; inhale again as the kettlebell swings back down.

## Key Principles

- In the final position, focus on tensing four primary areas to help stabilize the kettlebell by turning the body into one solid supporting structure. These areas are the grip, core, buttocks, and latissimus dorsi muscles. When tension is generated in these areas, it will spread and create full-body connectivity.

- While executing the other parts of the movement (upswing and downswing), focus on being maximally relaxed while maintaining proper alignment.

- Use your free hand as a spotting tool to increase safety and avoid the bell falling into your face.

- The bottoms-up clean can be performed with single or double kettlebells, although the double bottoms-up clean requires greater coordination than the single version.

- If the kettlebell falls to one side or the other, quickly reposition your feet to the other side to prevent the falling kettlebell from colliding with your knee.

| Common error | Error correction |
| --- | --- |
| Inability to maintain the bottoms-up positioning of the kettlebell | Keep the elbow connected to the torso and tense the grip, core, buttocks, and lats to stabilize the entire body. Chalk the kettlebell and ensure your hand is placed in the center of the handle with the thumb forward on the backswing and upswing. |
| Maintaining a strong crush grip throughout the drop | Loosen the grip as the kettlebell drops into the backswing to allow the grip to recover before the next bottoms-up clean. |
| Allowing the arm and kettlebell to drift too far forward in the top position, causing loss of control | Keep the kettlebell, elbow, hip, and feet in vertical alignment. |

## BOTTOMS-UP PRESS

Upon mastering the bottoms-up clean, you are ready to progress to the bottoms-up press. As with the bottoms-up clean, this positioning challenges the grip and overall body linkage while still activating the pressing muscles of the upper body.

**Single Bottoms-Up Press**   With a single kettlebell on the floor in front of you, grab the handle with a finger-lock grip and sit back to load the hips (see figure 8.2a). Clean the kettlebell to the bottoms-up position (see figure 8.2b). Maintain total-body tension and press the kettlebell directly up so that the load remains vertically aligned over your base of support (see figure 8.2c). The mechanics are identical to kettlebell press. Lower the kettlebell to chest level under control (see figure 8.2d). You can press repeatedly from the bottoms-up position or allow the kettlebell to swing down and reclean between each rep.

**Figure 8.2**   Single bottoms-up press.

**Double Bottoms-Up Press**   The double bottoms-up press is more challenging than the single variety, using twice the load and requiring more coordination to control and balance the kettlebells with both hands. With both kettlebells on the ground in front of you, grab the handles with finger-lock grips and sit back to load the hips (see figure 8.3*a*). Clean both kettlebells to the bottoms-up position (see figure 8.3*b*). Maintain total-body tension and press the kettlebells directly up so that the load remains vertically aligned over your base of support (see figure 8.3*c*). Lower the kettlebells to the clean position to complete each rep.

**Figure 8.3**   Double bottoms-up press.

*(continued)*

**BOTTOMS-UP PRESS** *(continued)*

**Alternating Bottoms-Up Press** The alternating bottoms-up press adds an additional coordination component to the double bottoms-up press. With both kettlebells on the ground in front of you, grab the handles with finger-lock grips and sit back to load the hips (see figure 8.4*a*). Clean both kettlebells to the bottoms-up position (see figure 8.4*b*). Maintain total-body tension and press one kettlebell directly up while maintaining the other kettlebell in the bottoms-up clean position (see figure 8.4*c*). Lower the kettlebell to the bottoms-up clean position while simultaneously pressing the other kettlebell to the top position (see figure 8.4*d*). On last rep, lower the top kettlebell before attempting to place the kettlebells on the floor.

**Figure 8.4** Alternating bottoms-up press.

**Key Principles**

- While pressing, maintain tension in all the aforementioned areas to keep the body connected and maximize power.
- As with the bottoms-up clean, when using a single kettlebell, it's important to spot the kettlebell with the free hand.
- When performing any of the double kettlebell variations, if the bells fall out of vertical position, step to the opposite side from the falling kettlebells to avoid collision.

| Common error | Error correction |
| --- | --- |
| Inability to maintain the bottoms-up positioning of the kettlebell | Keep the elbow connected to the torso and tense the grip, core, buttocks, and lats to stabilize the entire body. Also be sure to chalk the kettlebell and ensure your hand is placed in the center of the handle with the thumb forward on the backswing and upswing. |
| Pressing the kettlebells up with the body excessively deflected back and remaining in that position during lockout | After deflecting back to initiate the press, bring the body and head into vertical alignment. |
| Failing to manage the kettlebell falling from the bottoms-up position | Reposition your feet to one side or the other to prevent a falling kettlebell from smashing your knee or body. |

## DOUBLE ALTERNATING CLEAN

The double alternating clean is an advanced exercise that requires a high degree of body aware-ness, power, and coordination. There are two tempo-based variations for this exercise: two count and one count.

**Two-Count Variation**   For the two-count variation, start with both kettlebells on the floor in front of you, sit back to load the hips, and grip both handles with finger locks (see figure 8.5a). Clean one to the chest and let the other hang (see figure 8.5b). Next, let the top kettlebell drop (see figure 8.5c) and then clean the other kettlebell to the chest (see figure 8.5d). The timing of the two-count variation is the same as the one-arm clean except you alternate hands every rep. The greater challenge is that you will not be able to have much of a backswing and will have to pull the kettlebell up from a more static position, called the *hang position*, as shown in figure 7.13. This means you will not have the benefit of momentum the way you do in the one-arm or double clean and instead will have to use a more quad-dominant thrusting force to lift the bells. Because this is more of a dead start and requires greater effort to move the kettlebells, the double alternating clean is most commonly used as a power exercise, doing fewer reps and using challenging loads.

**Figure 8.5**   Double alternating clean: two-count variation.

When performing the two-count double alternating clean, use anatomical breathing with three or more breathing cycles. One variation is to start from the rack position, inhale as you deflect back and drop the kettlebell into the downswing, exhale at the back of the downswing, inhale during the upswing and hand insertion, and exhale as the kettlebell lands in the rack position. Another variation is to start from the rack position, inhale as you deflect back and drop the kettlebell into the downswing, exhale at the back of the downswing, inhale, exhale as you begin hand insertion, inhale, and exhale as the kettlebell lands in the rack position. Recovery breaths can be taken in the rest position to allow for proper recovery and pacing.

**One-Count Variation**   The one-count variation is much more challenging and requires more precise timing and coordination. In the two-count variation, there is a natural pause as the kettlebell comes to rest in the rack position, so in effect you are still moving only one side of your body at a time. For the one-count variation, however, there is no stopping point and one side must pull as the other is pushing. The up and down is continuous throughout the set and you must sustain a rhythm to sustain the set. The key is to focus only on the pulling hand since you cannot have your attention on two things at one time. Once you start the pull with the right hand, the momentum carries it to the rack. In a standard clean, the legs straighten as the kettlebell comes to the rack. However, in this one-count variation, just as the right-hand kettlebell comes to the rack, you bend your legs and drop your center of mass, and as you let the right kettlebell fall into the drop, the left arm pulls and the legs bend as the left kettlebell comes to the rack. Continue this pattern throughout the set.

When performing the one-count double alternating clean, use paradoxical breathing with one breathing cycle due to the accelerated movement and tempo. Exhale as you lower one kettlebell and simultaneously bring the other up to the rack position. Inhale quickly in the rack position and repeat the sequence.

### Key Principles

- For the two-count variation, use the pendulum spring mechanics in regard to hip and knee activity. For the one-count variation, it becomes necessary to use a squat-based mechanic due to the trajectory and fast-paced tempo.

- For the two-count variation, the trajectory of upswing and downswing is best described as the letter *J*. Thus, there is a circular component to the movement. For the one-count variation, the upswing and downswing follow a vertical groove (straight up and down). For the two-count variation, focus on both the cleaning arm and the arm that is not cleaning. For the latter, the primary goal is connectivity—keep the arm in contact with the torso.

- An important mechanic during the one-count variation is a drop to the squat position that initiates the motion for *both* kettlebells—the kettlebell that is descending and the kettlebell that is accelerating up.

| Common error | Error correction |
|---|---|
| Not deflecting back before dropping the kettlebell into the backswing for the two-count variation | Swing in front of an object (e.g., wall, mat) at arm's length; if you don't deflect back, you will hit the object. |
| Letting the noncleaning arm drift away from the torso in the two-count variation | Practice the movement without kettlebells, keeping your elbows glued to your body throughout the entire set. |
| Struggling with the timing of simultaneously pulling one kettlebell up as the other drops in the one-count variation | Bend your legs and drop your center of mass rapidly as you let the kettlebell fall into the drop. |

## DOUBLE SNATCH

The double snatch is one of the best exercises for increasing explosiveness, hip drive, and overhead stability. This exercise has two variations: the double half snatch (racking on the drop from overhead) and the double full snatch (no racking on the drop from overhead). *Half snatch* means to snatch the kettlebell or kettlebells overhead and then lower them to rack position before executing the downswing. *Full snatch*, or just *snatch*, means to snatch the kettlebells overhead and drop into the backswing from the top. The full snatch requires extensively more core stability, which is your stance. The bells fall a lot faster and more forcefully from the top. Therefore a natural progression for any double snatch is to first practice the double half snatch, and only progress to the double full snatch after you have full control over the movement.

**Double Half Snatch**   Start with both kettlebells on the floor in front of you. Sit back to load the hips and grip both handles with finger locks (see figure 8.6*a*). Swing the kettlebells back between your legs (see figure 8.6*b*) and then rapidly extend the knees and hips as you drive your body forward, with your forearms still connected to your body (see figure 8.6*c*). As the kettlebells swing forward and up, the kettlebells (and arms) pull away from your body. At this moment, shrug your trapezius muscles and pull with the arms, moving the kettlebells vertically up an imaginary chimney (see figure 8.6*d*). As the kettlebells are moving up, insert your hands into the kettlebells when they are between your neck and the top of your head. Proper overhead positioning is important for efficiency and thus work capacity. Your triceps are facing forward, thumbs are pointing back at a 45-degree angle, biceps are close to the ears, arms are vertical, and rib cage is open. From the overhead fixation position (see figure 8.6*e*), deflect the trunk backward and rise up onto the toes slightly as you let the kettlebells fall to the chest in the rack position (see figure 8.6*f*). From the rack, deflect the trunk again as you drop the kettlebells down and into the backswing to complete the rep. As with the double swing and double clean, various thumb positions can be used in the downswing and upswing portion of the double half snatch. The ideal is to turn the thumb back at the end of the downswing and transition to a 45-degree angle (thumb up) at the beginning of the acceleration pull.

When performing this exercise, use anatomical breathing with three or four breathing cycles. One variation with three cycles is to start from the overhead position, inhale as you deflect back and drop the kettlebells, exhale as they land into the rack position, inhale as you drop from the rack, exhale at the back of the downswing, inhale as you upswing, and exhale on lockout. Another variation with four cycles is to start from the overhead position, inhale as you deflect back and drop the kettlebells, exhale as they land into the rack position, inhale as you drop from the rack, exhale at the back of the downswing, inhale, exhale as you begin the acceleration pull, inhale, and exhale on lockout.

**Figure 8.6** Double half snatch.

*(continued)*

**DOUBLE SNATCH**  *(continued)*

**Double Snatch**  The double kettlebell snatch is more similar to a barbell snatch than it is to a one-arm kettlebell snatch. Use the double snatch for strength and power training, and keep the reps lower. The double snatch is a great exercise, but it should be used sparingly and only by strong lifters who have good flexibility, strength, and fitness. This is because the shoulder girdle and torso can rotate and absorb force well in the one-arm snatch. With the double snatch, the range of motion is much more restricted for the shoulders, scapulae, and spine. It puts much more stress on the body to swing both arms overhead together with such force. This is not to scare you; it is simply to show you the forces involved and make sure you respect them. You can do the double snatch, but do not do bad reps. Keep them crisp and powerful and make sure that you have the fitness to be able to demand perfect form. Avoid discomfort in this or any lift.

Start with both kettlebells on the floor in front of you. Sit back to load the hips and grip both handles with finger locks (see figure 8.7*a*). Swing the kettlebells back between your legs (see figure 8.7*b*), and then rapidly extend the knees and hips as you drive your body forward with your forearms still connected to your body (see figure 8.7*c*). As the kettlebells swing forward and up, the kettlebells (and arms) will pull away from your body. At this moment, shrug your traps and pull with your arms, moving the kettlebells vertically up an imaginary chimney (see figure 8.7 *d* and *e*). As the kettlebells are moving up vertically, insert your hands when the two kettlebells are between your neck and the top of your head. Alignment in overhead position is with triceps facing forward, thumbs pointing back at a 45-degree angle, biceps close to the ears, arms vertical, and rib cage open. Due to the extreme inertia of the double full snatch, it's critical to maintain deflection when dropping the kettlebell from the overhead position into the backswing. As you deflect the trunk backward, rise onto the toes slightly as you let the kettlebells fall (see figure 8.7*f*). When the triceps come into contact with the rib cage, sit back with the hips and keep your eyes on the kettlebells as they swing back behind you to complete the rep (see figure 8.7*g*). Failing to deflect or incorrectly time the hip crease could result in a loss of balance, injury, and so on. Pay extra attention to sitting back with the hips into the backswing. As with the double half snatch, various thumb positions can be used in the downswing and upswing.

**Figure 8.7**  Double Snatch.

**Figure 8.7**    *(continued)*

When performing this exercise, use anatomical breathing with two or three breathing cycles. One variation with two cycles is to start from the overhead position, inhale as you deflect back and drop the kettlebells, exhale at the back of the downswing, inhale as you upswing, and exhale on lockout. Another variation with three cycles is to start from the overhead position, inhale as you deflect back and drop the kettlebells, exhale at the back of the downswing, inhale, exhale as you begin the acceleration pull, inhale, and exhale on lockout.

*(continued)*

**DOUBLE SNATCH** *(continued)*

### Key Principles

- Maintain the connection between the torso and arm on the upswing for maximal leverage and power transfer.
- Some lifters will extend up on both toes at the beginning of the acceleration pull and dip just before the kettlebells reach fixation. These additional actions are appropriate for heavier kettlebells because they shorten the distance the load has to travel and accelerate the power output.

| Common error | Error correction |
|---|---|
| No connection between the arm and the hips and torso on the up-swing | If you have a coach or are coaching someone, a verbal cue of "Stay connected" is helpful. Fasten a resistance band around both arms to keep the arms connected to the torso. |
| Lack of deflection on the upswing and while dropping the kettlebell into the downswing | If you have a coach or are coaching someone, a verbal cue of "Deflect back" is helpful. It is also helpful to swing in front of an object (e.g., wall, mat) at arm's length; if you don't deflect back, you will hit the object. |
| Banging your wrist or forearm on the kettlebell | You are most likely inserting your hand too early, too late, or at an incorrect angle. Use a hand-insertion drill where you visualize a ladder with four rungs in front of you on the vertical plane. Gradually climb the ladder, inserting your hand with a claw grip. Rung 1 is chest level, rung 2 is face level, rung 3 is just over your head, and rung 4 is near the top just before your arm reaches full extension. Clean up and release the fingers to insert the hand at each level, then drop down into the backswing between each insertion. |
| Vertical rather than horizontal trajectory on the backswing | Use pendulum hip and knee mechanics. It is also helpful to precede the double snatch with a double low swing. |
| Lack of fixation in the overhead position | Hold the kettlebells in lockout position for time. Stand in one place, walk in clockwise and counterclockwise circles, or move around the room in any pattern. |
| Exaggerated trajectory on the up-swing and downswing | Snatch in front of a wall as you visualize yourself lifting inside a chimney. If you hit the wall, you're doing it incorrectly. |

# DOUBLE ALTERNATING SNATCH

The double alternating snatch is one of the most advanced movements you can do in kettlebell training and is highly beneficial in multiple regards (e.g., speed, power, coordination). High levels of body awareness, power, and coordination are necessary to safely perform the double alternating snatch, so special attention must be paid to alignment, breathing, and movement mechanics. There are two variations of this exercise: two count and one count.

**Two-Count Variation** For the two-count variation, deadlift two kettlebells from the floor (see figure 8.9a), sit back with the hips to swing both kettlebells between your legs (see figure 8.9b), and accelerate and snatch one kettlebell over your head (see figure 8.9c). Deflect the torso back to drop the kettlebell down (see figure 8.9d), again swing both kettlebells between your legs (see figure 8.9e), and snatch the other kettlebell over your head (see figure 8.9f).

**Figure 8.9** Double alternating snatch: two-count variation.

*(continued)*

## DOUBLE ALTERNATING SNATCH *(continued)*

When performing this exercise, use anatomical breathing with three or more breathing cycles. One variation is to start from the overhead position, inhale as you deflect back and drop the kettlebell into the downswing, exhale at the back of the downswing, inhale during the upswing and hand insertion, and exhale as the kettlebell lands in the overhead position. Another variation is to start from the overhead position, inhale as you deflect back and drop the kettlebell into the downswing, exhale at the back of the downswing, inhale, exhale as you begin hand insertion, inhale, and exhale as the kettlebell lands in the overhead position. Also note that during the two-count variation, recovery breaths can be taken in the overhead position to allow for proper recovery and pacing.

**One-Count Variation**   The one-count variation is more intense, and its more precise timing and coordination leave little margin for error. In the two-count variation, there is a natural pause as the kettlebell comes to fixation in the overhead lockout position. During the one-count variation, however, there is no stopping point, and one side must pull as the other is dropping. The one-count variation requires a continuous rhythm to sustain the set.

For the one-count variation, deadlift two kettlebells from the floor (see figure 8.10*a*), sit back with the hips to swing one kettlebell between your legs (see figure 8.10*b*), and accelerate and snatch the kettlebell over your head (see figure 8.10*c*). As the kettlebell completes the overhead fixation, bend your legs and drop your center of mass (see figure 8.10*d*); as you let the top kettlebell fall into the drop, the other arm pulls and the legs bend as the kettlebell is pulled to fixation between the legs (see figure 8.10 *e* and *f*). Focus only on the pulling hand while letting the overhead arm relax into the drop. Once you start the pull with the one hand, the momentum carries it to the overhead lockout (see figure 8.10*g*).

**Figure 8.10**   Double alternating snatch: one-count variation.

**Figure 8.10** *(continued)*

When performing this exercise, use paradoxical breathing with one breathing cycle due to the accelerated movement and tempo. Exhale as you lower one kettlebell and simultaneously bring the other up to the overhead position. Inhale quickly and repeat the sequence. There is no place for recovery breaths during the one-count variation because it is a continuous movement.

### Key Principles

- For the two-count variation, as in the alternating clean, you will not have much of a backswing and will have to pull the kettlebell up from the more static hang position using a quad-dominant thrusting force to accelerate the bells.

- The two-count variation is also similar to the alternating clean in that it is more appropriate as a power exercise, doing fewer reps and using challenging loads.

- As with the alternating clean, use pendulum spring mechanics in the two-count variation and squat mechanics in the one-count variation.

- For the one-count variation, the motion initiates with the drop into the squat. This creates the momentum for both the bell that is traveling up and the bell that is descending.

| Common error | Error correction |
|---|---|
| Not deflecting back before dropping the kettlebell into the backswing for the two-count variation | Swing in front of an object (e.g., wall, mat) at arm's length; if you don't deflect back, you will hit the object. |
| Not keeping the nonsnatching arm connected to the hips and torso in the two-count variation | Fasten a resistance band around the nonsnatching arm and torso to reinforce the arm staying connected to the torso. Practice with one side and then switch the band to the other arm and practice with the other side. |
| Struggling with the timing of simultaneously pulling one kettlebell up as the other drops in the one-count variation | Bend your legs and drop your center of mass rapidly as you let the kettlebell fall into the drop. |

## DOUBLE JERK

The double jerk is a premier power-generation exercise that develops multiple attributes on the athletic conditioning continuum, including explosiveness, flexibility, structural integrity, strength, timing and coordination, breath capacity, and bilateral symmetry. It is a classic exercise, but it is listed here as an advanced exercise because it requires a high degree of timing and control, which can only develop after establishing a solid foundation in the basic movements, such as the press, push press, and squat. The key limitation in performance of the double jerk is the bilateral deficit, or the disparity in range of motion, strength, and coordination between one hand and the other. In other words, you can only go as far as your weakest hand takes you.

Remember, as we learned in the previous chapter, the jerk has five primary movement components:

1. Half squat (first dip)
2. Bump (send-off)
3. Undersquat (second dip)
4. Fixation (stand to lockout)
5. Drop to rack position

To perform this exercise, with the kettlebells on the floor, grab the handles with the finger-lock grip and load the hips into the start position (see figure 8.11a). Clean the kettlebells to the chest into the rack position (see figure 8.11b). From the rack position, move rapidly into the half squat or first dip as you exhale (see figure 8.11c). It's important to maintain the connection between the elbows and torso and the heels and ground when executing the half squat in order to maximize power transfer from the lower body to the upper body. From the half squat, immediately extend the ankles, knees, hips, and torso into the forceful bump (send-off), making sure to keep the elbows connected to the torso (see figure 8.11d). The bump involves what is called *quadruple extension*, where the ankles, knees, hips, and torso all extend

**Figure 8.11** Double jerk.

**Figure 8.11** *(continued).*

maximally. The final position involves the hips being up and forward while the shoulders are held down and back.

From completion of the bump, drop immediately into the undersquat or second dip (see figure 8.11*e*). Again, be aware that the half squat, bump, and undersquat must all be performed with maximum speed and that the elbows should maximally lock out in the undersquat at same time that the heels strike the ground. To maximize efficiency, the arms are locked via dropping down into a squatting posture versus pressing up when executing the undersquat. The depth of the undersquat depends on your anatomy and conditioning. People with strong legs and triceps will drop deeper, whereas lighter competitors whose primary advantage is speed will likely use a shallower undersquat.

Press the knees back to fully extend the legs into fixation, with elbows and knees straightened (see figure 8.11*f*). There are two primary movement mechanics to accomplish fixation, or stand to lockout. First, simply stand up to the overhead posture. Second, perform a knee roll, which involves keeping the hips at the level of the undersquat and only rolling the knees backward to lockout. The fixation in the final lockout position involves fully extending the elbow, keeping the arm in close proximity to the centerline of the body, externally rotating the shoulder (triceps facing forward and thumb back at an angle), and keeping the rib cage open. Depending on mobility, the body can be aligned in a straight line or positioned with the chest forward and pelvis tilted to the rear. Optimal fixation is with the biceps directly next to the ears. Each lifter must find the best sagittal alignment for her structure.

Drop the kettlebells back to the rack position (see figure 8.11*g*). The triceps relax and the bells are lowered to the rack position via a smooth, controlled drop. The force of the bells coming down is absorbed when you rise onto your toes and bring your chest toward the bells. As the elbows begin to land in the rack position, the heels are lowered and the thoracic spine rounded to safely diffuse the load. The knees may be bent slightly as well. It is optional to rise onto your toes at beginning of the drop or to stay flat-footed throughout the drop.

When performing this exercise, use anatomical breathing with four or five cycles. Inhale before the first dip, exhale during the half squat, inhale on the bump, exhale upon landing

*(continued)*

**DOUBLE JERK**   *(continued)*

to the undersquat and then to lockout, take an additional breathing cycle in the top position, inhale at the beginning of the drop, and exhale as the elbows make contact into the rack. If a deep undersquat is used, take an additional breath cycle between completion of the undersquat and fixation (i.e., five total cycles with a deep undersquat and four total cycles with a shallow, quick undersquat).

### Key Principles

- Move the legs as fast as possible to maximize power transfer from the ground up.
- Maintain the connection between the torso and arms as long as possible through the bump phase of the jerk.
- Decelerate the kettlebells as much as possible during the drop to reduce body impact.

| Common error | Error correction |
|---|---|
| Losing the connection between the elbow and hip and the heels and floor when descending into the half squat | Practice the half squat without jerking to ingrain the movement as a reflex. |
| Descending too slowly when dropping into the half squat | Focus on dropping into the half squat to activate a stretch reflex to facilitate a stronger bump. |
| Pressing to lockout instead of dropping to the undersquat to lock the arms | Lockout overhead an empty bar or 5 ft (1.5 m) PVC pipe. From a standing position, practice rapidly dropping into the undersquat without bending or pressing with the arms. |
| Slow transition from the undersquat to lockout | Using the lockout squat, isolate and practice the motion of ascending quickly from the undersquat to lockout. See kettlebell jump squat in chapter 7 for a detailed description of this exercise. |

## DOUBLE CLEAN AND JERK

**Figure 8.12** Double clean and jerk.

*(continued)*

**DOUBLE CLEAN AND JERK**  *(continued)*

The double clean and jerk is the most comprehensive kettlebell lift. The entire kinetic chain is involved in the execution of this all-body lift, and a joint-by-joint analysis of the movement will show a perfect mixture of stability and mobility. Furthermore, all phases of the stretch–shortening cycle are present in a given repetition, making this lift truly plyometric and perfect for increasing explosive power, or the ability to accelerate rapidly. Because of this, the double clean and jerk is used for power development in cross-training for many sports.

To perform this exercise, start with two kettlebells on the floor in front of you. Grip each with the finger-lock grip and sit back to load the hips (see figure 8.12*a*). Pick up and swing both kettlebells between the legs (see figure 8.12*b*), then swing forward and up to clean the kettlebells to the chest and establish your solid rack position (see figure 8.12*c*). Half squat and immediately extend the legs and torso as you rise maximally onto the toes to bump the kettlebells off the chest (see figure 8.12*d*), then immediately sit the hips into an undersquat while the arms extend fully into lockout (see figure 8.12*e*). Finish the fixation of the jerk so that the legs and arms are fully extended. Deflect the torso back and drop the kettlebells to the rack position (see figure 8.12*f*). Rising onto the toes at the beginning of the drop is optional. Drop from the rack position into a backswing (see figure 8.12*g*). Most lifters will use a thumbs-forward position for the double clean and jerk; however, the thumbs-backward and neutral-thumb positions are also acceptable. Reclean the kettlebells to rack position (see figure 8.12*h*).

When performing this exercise, use anatomical breathing with eight or more breathing cycles. From the rack position, inhale before dropping into the half squat, exhale during the half squat, inhale as you extend your legs and body during the bump, exhale as you sit your hips back and drop into the undersquat, inhale as your legs extend into fixation, exhale at completion of the fixation, take one breath cycle while holding fixation, inhale as the body deflects back, exhale as the kettlebells fall into the rack position, take one breath cycle while in the rack position, inhale as you deflect back to drop the kettlebells, exhale with the backswing, inhale and exhale as the kettlebells swing forward, and inhale and exhale as the kettlebells are cleaned to the chest. Takes as many recovery breaths as needed before the next repetition.

**Key Principles**

- Use pendulum hip mechanics.
- Maximize the connection between the arms and torso.
- Move the legs as fast as possible to maximize power transfer from the ground up.
- Maintain the connection between the torso and arms as long as possible through the bump phase of the jerk.
- Decelerate the kettlebells as much as possible during the drop to reduce body impact.
- Take multiple, continuous breaths (eight or more breath cycles per rep) to keep your breathing and heart rate under control.

| Common error | Error correction |
|---|---|
| Performing the clean to the chest in two movements instead of one | Bring your elbows to the ilia at same moment the kettlebells touch the chest. |
| Insufficient flexibility to extend the hips in the rack position | Practice the flexibility and mobility exercises from chapter 6 or rack holds later in this chapter. |
| Descending too slowly when dropping into the half squat | Focus on dropping into the half squat to activate a stretch reflex to facilitate a stronger bump. |
| Pressing to lockout instead of dropping to the undersquat to lock the arms | Lockout overhead an empty bar or 5 ft (1.5 m) PVC pipe. From a standing position, practice rapidly dropping into the undersquat without bending or pressing with the arms. |
| Slow transition from the undersquat to lockout | Using the lockout squat, isolate and practice the motion of ascending quickly from the undersquat to lockout. See kettlebell jump squat in chapter 7 for a detailed description of this exercise. |
| Loss of grip during the clean component | Practice the farmer's carry for time in order to improve grip endurance. |

## BOTTOMS-UP PUSH-UP

**Figure 8.13** Bottoms-up push-up.

The bottoms-up push-up is an upper-body conditioner that simultaneously develops horizontal pressing strength and anterior core stability due to the positioning and instability of the kettlebell and the added balance needed to perform it. It is considered an advanced exercise because skill is involved in performing it correctly and it is risky for anyone who lacks sufficient core stability to control the kettlebell and prevent it from tilting and falling.

To perform this exercise, place the kettlebell so that it is balanced on the handle (see figure 8.13a). You can position the handle either in vertical or horizontal alignment to exert more of a sagittal- or frontal-plane challenge, respectively. Use a floor surface that is not too slick so that the kettlebell does not slide around. Place both palms firmly on the bottom of the kettlebell. People with larger hands will have to turn the fingers outward so that only the base of the palm is placed on the bottom and the fingers wrap around the sides of the bell. Those with smaller hands can place both palms directly on the flat bottom of the kettlebell. Pressing firmly down through the center of the kettlebell, set your body in a plank position, supported on your hands and the balls of your feet (see figure 8.13b). Hold this balance and lower your body until your chest lightly touches your hands (see figure 8.13c), then press straight up until your arms are fully extended, with the elbows completely locked in the top position (see figure 8.13d). Proper alignment is with the palms in line with the center of the chest, elbows connected to the torso, and scapulae retracted, with a straight line running from the base of the neck to the heels. Keep the shoulders packed into their sockets by corkscrewing the arms into external rotation and contracting the lats. Note that the riskiest part of the exercise is dismounting from the kettlebell after your last set. Because the kettlebell is supporting your body weight, you should place your knees on the floor first to shift the body weight away from the kettlebell, and then let the kettlebell fall to the floor.

When performing this exercise, use anatomical or paradoxical breathing depending on your conditioning level. For the less conditioned, this exercise could approximate maximal effort with a few reps, so paradoxical breathing will keep the spine safe by creating high pressure in the thoracic cavity; inhale on the way down and exhale on the way up (one cycle). For those who are more conditioned, anatomical breathing is the better match and will facilitate better endurance; exhale on the way down and inhale on the way up.

A more advanced variation of this exercise is the double bottoms-up push-up. In this variation, do your push-up with one bottoms-up kettlebell supporting each palm. Setting up is a bit tricky, but you will figure out a method that works for you with a bit of trial and error. I like to rest one bottoms-up kettlebell against my thigh while I use two hands to set the other kettlebell bottoms up. Then slide the second kettlebell into position once the first is stable. It's a fun way to mix in some horizontal pressing to help balance out the high volume of vertical pressing contained in most kettlebell lifts.

### Key Principles

- "Claw" the kettlebell. As mentioned earlier, both relaxation and tension tend to lead to more of the same. Thus, in this exercise, generate high degrees of tension via the grip, core, glutes, and lats to maximize structural integrity, body connectivity, and power.
- Due to the possibility of the kettlebells tipping, make sure your training area is configured safely—there should be no sharp, pointy, or fragile objects in the vicinity, and there should be a soft area to land (such as a rubber mat) in case you slip.

| Common error | Error correction |
|---|---|
| Not tensing sufficiently to maximize body connectivity, strength, and alignment | Irradiate tension throughout the body by tensing the hands, lats, glutes, and core. |
| Hands out of alignment with the chest and too far forward | This compromises shoulder stability and performance. Keep the hands in line with the center of the chest. |
| Not packing the shoulder | Pack the shoulder by pressing both palms firmly and screwing them into the kettlebell. |
| Failing to keep the scapulae retracted | This deactivates the chest and puts too much stress on the shoulders. Focus on scapular retraction via rib cage expansion. Think to yourself, "Big chest." |

## SQUAT METHOD GET-UP

As mentioned in chapter 7, the get-up has its lineage in Turkish grapplers using it as a full-body conditioning exercise that enhances the ability to make efficient and strong transitions from the ground to standing and vice versa. Though you may not be a grappler, the fairly complex movement patterns of the get-up may carry over nicely into your overall movement ability or agility. Chapter 7 presented a lunging pattern in the transitional posture between lying and standing. Here, the transition is a squat pattern, and this variation will be more challenging for most people because it demands greater mobility in the hips, upper spine, and shoulders.

Just as you did for the get-up in chapter 7, to perform this exercise, start by lying flat on your back. Raise your right arm straight up over your chest and bend your right knee so that the foot is flat on the floor; your left arm is flat on the floor at about a

**Figure 8.14**  Squat method get-up.

45-degree angle (see figure 8.14*a*). Initiate the movement by flexing your abs slightly and then shifting your weight to your left arm, first to the shoulder, then the elbow, then the forearm, and finally the palm (see figure 8.14*b*). As your body weight transfers to your left palm, your left hand presses firmly into the floor and your left elbow extends, fully locked out (see figure 8.14*c*). This is the first stopping point and you are completely stable. Transition by lifting your hips off the floor and maximally extending them (see figure 8.14*d*). It is important that the force moves vertically as your hips extend; any forward drift of the right arm will cause you to lose control of the kettlebell.

Now, for the squat method, this is where the movement changes. Your weight is supported at two points at this stage—the left palm and the right foot. Keep these two points of contact stable and lift the extended left leg off the floor. Keeping your hips lifted, move your left leg directly under your left hip and plant it firmly on the floor (see figure 8.14*e*). Because this is a much narrower base compared with the lunge variation, your weight will be centered behind on your left palm. To complete this phase, you will need to push your body weight forward with your left palm until your weight is balanced solely on both feet. Complete this phase by lifting the left hand off the floor and extending the trunk upright (see figure 8.14*f*). From this squat position, complete the upward phase of the get-up by standing straight up (see figure 8.14*g*).

Now reverse the movement: Squat directly down to drop your center of mass by sitting back with your hips and bending both knees. Place your left palm flat on the floor behind you and sit back to shift your weight to the palm. Drop your hips further to sit on the floor. Complete the movement by dropping from left palm to forearm and then to shoulder while simultaneously extending both legs out in front of you to return to the lying position that you started from. It may feel more natural to slide the bottom arm along the floor as you are lowering yourself.

When performing this exercise, use natural breathing. Don't hold your breath at any point, but don't try to time the breath in any particular pattern.

## Key Principles

- Review the overhead squat to familiarize yourself with the key alignment points of that phase of the get-up.
- Keep your eyes on the kettlebell at all times.
- When first learning the get-up, practice it without a kettlebell and use an object such as a yoga block, water bottle, or shoe to simulate holding a bell and ensure vertical alignment is used at all times.
- Ensure the kettlebell stays vertical throughout the movement.
- Keep your arm packed into your shoulder when the arm is fully extended overhead.
- When first learning the get-up, use a spotter.
- When transitioning from the ground to the beginning of the squat, it's important to brace with the free hand behind the torso to avoid falling backward.

*(continued)*

**SQUAT METHOD GET-UP**  *(continued)*

| Common error | Error correction |
|---|---|
| Bringing the kettlebell over your face when transitioning the hands | Using both hands, bring the kettlebell around the top of your head to the other side. |
| Trying to sit up during the first segment of the movement | Roll up at a 45-degree angle using your elbow and foot as levers. |
| Rolling or pronating one or both ankles | Press both feet flat to the floor. |
| Allowing the knees to collapse inward in the bottom squat position (valgus collapse) | This occurs frequently and must be avoided because it will lead to injury to the medial (inside) ligaments of the knees. This is typically caused by a lack of hip activation, not a problem with the knees. To help avoid this, press your knees out to the sides as you lower yourself or place a 20 in. (51 cm) piece of tubing or a light band that is easy to stretch around the outside of the knees. You will have to press your knees out to the sides to prevent the band from falling, thereby avoiding the knee collapse. |

# CHAIR PRESS

**Figure 8.15**  Chair press.

*(continued)*

**CHAIR PRESS** *(continued)*

A tremendous test of upper-body strength and endurance, the chair press demands additional core stability because it removes the assistance from the leg that is given in the standing press. The chair press is a nice way to include some periodic variation in your program and can be selected as a vertical pressing component in any well-rounded fitness program. We will show this exercise using two kettlebells, but you may also perform a single-arm chair press with one kettlebell.

Start with two kettlebells on the floor in front of you and grip with the finger lock (see figure 8.15a). Sit back with your hips to swing the kettlebells back between your legs (see figure 8.15b) and then to your chest (see figure 8.15c), and finally sit on a sturdy box or chair with no back support (see figure 8.15d). Keeping your feet flat on the floor, press directly up into lockout (see figure 8.15e). Lower the kettlebells to your chest to complete the rep (see figure 8.15f).

When performing this exercise, use anatomical breathing with four breathing cycles. Starting from the rack position, inhale deeply before the initial compression, and then exhale as you drop and flex your thoracic spine. Inhale as you bump with the rib cage, and exhale as you lock out. Take one full breath cycle while in lockout and add more recovery breaths if needed. Inhale as you begin to drop the kettlebell, and exhale as it lands back in the rack position. Take recovery breaths while in the rack position before the next rep.

### Key Principles

- Maintain total-body tension during the pressing action by squeezing the grip, abs, and glutes. Use irradiation for heavy lifting and grinding movements like the chair press, amplifying the effect of the working muscles by tensing the muscles surrounding them.
- Keep the arm packed into the shoulder when pressing.

| Common error | Error correction |
| --- | --- |
| Leaning back during the press | Keep the abdominal muscles firm and braced, as if preparing to take a punch. |
| Hips shifting from one side to the other | Keep your feet flat on floor, hips squared to the front of the room, and abdominal muscles firm. |
| Bilateral deficiency, the limitation of the strength and endurance from the weaker, nondominant arm | Train the standing press and chair press with one arm at a time to develop more equality between the dominant and nondominant arms. |

## OVERHEAD SQUAT

The overhead squat is a great exercise for well-rounded development, simultaneously training balance, flexibility, coordination, stability, mobility, and strength. As a prerequisite, you should feel comfortable with the front squat, because the lower-body mechanics involved are identical. The overhead squat has the added challenge of stabilizing the upper body by supporting the load overhead while squatting.

In the unloaded version, using just a stick, the overhead squat is a standard test that is effective in developing the range of motion needed for the kettlebell version. The overhead squat and its variations are also often used for movement screening and assessment of movement quality. Thanks to the combination of movement and stabilization involved in this movement, a well-trained eye can spot assorted movement deficiencies just by having the athlete, patient, or client do a few repetitions with only a stick overhead. This movement pattern can be tested regularly to note improvement as verification of a well-designed program. Now put a kettlebell overhead, and especially two kettlebells, and the demands change this movement from a basic assessment, to an advanced (single kettlebell) exercise, to a super advanced (double) exercise.

Before trying the kettlebell overhead squat, you should test the movement pattern with a stick, rope, or PVC pipe. You want to have great control in the unloaded version before spending any time with the kettlebell versions. Truthfully, the single kettlebell will be easier than just the stick alone once you get the hang of it. This is because the unilateral overhead squat allows for a significant amount of rotation in the hips, shoulders, and torso, and the additional rotation creates slack throughout the body, which allows for postural compensations in order to get vertically underneath the load.

Before performing the overhead squat with a kettlebell, you must first be able to perform it correctly with no load. The phases of progression for the overhead squat are described next.

**Phase 1**   Holding a broomstick or PVC pipe, place your hands approximately one-and-a-half shoulder-widths apart. Your feet should be slightly wider than shoulder-width apart. Extend your arms directly overhead and straighten them completely (see figure 8.16a). Keeping your chest lifted and shoulders pulled back, sit back with your hips and do a full squat (see figure 8.16b). Make sure to keep your feet flat on the floor. If your heels start to drift up, you will need to practice the overhead squat with your heels elevated slightly, such as with a 5- or 10-pound (2.25 or 4.5 kg) weight plate under each heel (see figure 8.16c). Work on increasing ankle mobility until you can perform an overhead squat with feet flat. This is phase 1 of the overhead squat, called *hands apart, feet apart*. Once you have mastered phase 1, increase the challenge with phase 2.

**Figure 8.16**   Phase 1 of the overhead squat: hands apart, feet apart.

*(continued)*

**OVERHEAD SQUAT** (continued)

**Phase 2** Hold the stick with your hands together and feet slightly wider than shoulder-width. Extend your arms directly overhead and straighten them completely (see figure 8.17a). With your chest lifted and shoulders pulled back, sit back with your hips and do a full squat (see figure 8.17b). Make sure to keep your feet flat on the floor. This is phase 2 of the overhead squat, called *hands together, feet apart*. Once you have mastered phase 2, increase the challenge with phase 3.

**Figure 8.17** Phase 2 of the overhead squat: hands together, feet apart.

**Phase 3** Hold the stick with your hands approximately one-and-a-half shoulder-widths apart and feet together. Extend your arms directly overhead and straighten them completely (see figure 8.18a). With your chest lifted and shoulders pulled back, sit back with your hips and do a full squat (see figure 8.18b). Make sure to keep your feet flat on the floor. This is phase 3 of the overhead squat, called *hands apart, feet together*. Once you have mastered phase 3, give phase 4 a shot.

**Figure 8.18** Phase 3 of the overhead squat: hands apart, feet together.

**Phase 4** Phase 4 is extremely challenging, and mastering it shows a high degree of flexibility and core stability in the overhead squat. Hold the stick with hands together and feet together. Extend your arms directly overhead and straighten them completely (see figure 8.19*a*). Keep your chest lifted and shoulders pulled back, sit back with your hips, and do a full squat (see figure 8.19*b*). Make sure to keep your feet flat on the floor. This is phase 4 of the overhead squat, called *hands together, feet together.*

**Figure 8.19** Phase 4 of the overhead squat: hands together, feet together.

**Phases 5 Through 8** To fine-tune and perfect the overhead squat, you can combine phases 1 through 4 with the face-the-wall squat that you first learned as a supplement to the front squat. For phases 5 through 8, then, face the wall and go through the overhead squat progressions using a stick or PVC pipe. The wall will completely prevent any deviation on the sagittal plane, because it will block the stick from moving forward, thereby forcing your trunk to maintain maximal extension in order to complete the squat. Anyone who can perform phase 8—face the wall, hands together, feet together—has a very high level of flexibility and total-body control in the overhead squat pattern and can safely perform any variation of the squat.

With the overhead squat progression phases as a prep, you can now integrate the kettlebell overhead variations. Phases 1 through 8 described previously will develop the flexibility and body control needed to master the overhead squat and should be practiced regularly. Once you have mastered the eight phases, you can move on to the single overhead squat with a kettlebell, as described next.

*(continued)*

**OVERHEAD SQUAT** *(continued)*

**Single Overhead Squat**   Set your stance as you would for the front squat, with feet approximately shoulder-width apart. Evert the toes as much as necessary to be able to sit in a full squat position. Once your stance is set, bring a kettlebell in the overhead lockout position and keep your eyes on it (see figure 8.20a). You can press, jerk, push press, or snatch the kettlebell to lockout, whichever method you choose. Keep your arm locked out and your eyes on the kettlebell. Squat until the bottoms of your thighs are parallel with the floor (see figure 8.20b). The nonworking arm is out to the side, counterbalancing the load. Drive up from the bottom position by pressing your feet into the ground and return to standing position (see figure 8.20c). Repeat on the other side.

**Figure 8.20**   Single overhead squat.

In the single kettlebell overhead squat, it is perfectly acceptable to rotate the trunk toward the working arm (see figure 8.21a). This will allow the torso to take up some of the range that you may be lacking in the shoulder girdle and upper back. It is also acceptable to have some lateral flexion toward the nonworking arm (see figure 8.21b), again for the purpose of creating range or space so that you can keep the kettlebell vertically centered over your base of support.

**Figure 8.21**   Body position variations for the single overhead squat: *(a)* rotating trunk toward working arm and *(b)* flexing laterally toward the nonworking arm.

**Double Overhead Squat** If the single kettlebell overhead squat is advanced, the double kettlebell overhead squat is even more advanced because it requires a great deal more flexibility to get into position. Set your stance as you would for the single kettlebell overhead squat (see figure 8.22a). Bring both kettlebells to lockout via the clean and jerk, clean and press, clean and push press, or double snatch. Keep your chest lifted and scapulae pinched together (see figure 8.22b). Squat by sitting your hips back and down (see figure 8.22c). Drive up by pressing your feet into the ground and return to standing position (see figure 8.22d). Many people will not have developed the range of motion necessary to perform the double kettlebell overhead squat safely or effectively, meaning with good form. In that case, spend time on the overhead squat variations with a stick only.

**Figure 8.22** Double overhead squat.

(continued)

**OVERHEAD SQUAT** *(continued)*

When performing both the single and double overhead squat, use paradoxical breathing. From the start position, inhale into your belly as you squat down and exhale as you stand up. Another variation is two breath cycles per rep, where you inhale at the top, exhale as you squat down, inhale in the bottom position, and exhale as you stand up.

**Key Principles**

- Actively descend into the bottom position by pulling yourself down with your hip flexors.
- Be aware of alignment and posture at all times.
- Keep the elbows locked out completely and kettlebells fixated in overhead position.
- Keep your chest lifted and shoulders pulled back and down.
- Keep your knees vertically aligned over the feet throughout the motion.
- Open the hips to achieve maximal depth.
- Drive up from the heels to stand up.
- Fully extend the knees and hips in the top position.

| Common error | Error correction |
|---|---|
| Allowing a knee valgus position during the descent | Press your knees to the sides during the descent. Use a light exercise band around the outsides of the knees. Mobilize your ankles and hips before squatting. |
| Lifting the heels in the bottom range of the squat | Press your heels back and down into the floor Insert a 5 or 10 lb (2.25 or 4.5 kg) weight plate under the heels and perform the squat. |
| Arms drifting forward on the sagittal plane during the descent | Practice the face-the-wall squat. Practice the overhead squat mobility drills from this chapter. |

Practice the advanced kettlebell exercises for increased strength, power, endurance, and coordination. The exercises in chapters 6, 7, and 8 provide all the variety you need to explore the full range of benefits that kettlebell lifting has to offer. In the next chapters, you will learn how to combine kettlebells with other popular functional training tools to bring more variety to your programs and how to put kettlebells and various tools together to develop effective strength and conditioning programs.

# CREATING A CUSTOMIZED FITNESS PROGRAM

The correct training techniques and the quality of your practice are important, but equally important is the way you put the various exercises together into a fitness program. However, we need to make a distinction here. A program in itself calls for a schedule, a plan. Is it necessary to have a plan in order to achieve fitness? It really depends on—you guessed it—your goals.

One training concept is called *instinctive training*, which means doing whatever you feel like doing. Study the materials and learn the techniques, but when it comes time to go into your personal training dungeon and pick up those bells, do you want to just leave it to how you're feeling, or do you need a schedule to keep you on a precise path? This is an interesting question because there are all kinds of people who find success just doing something every day, without a great deal of structure. A concept along the lines of instinctive training is found in the credo that if something is important, you should do it every day. Are squats important? If so, squat every day. Are pressing movements important? Do them every day! This is a great concept in theory. In practice, however, it may become burdensome. Cardio is important, strength is important, balance is important, and flexibility is important. Squatting, pressing, pulling, and lunging are all important.

Obviously you cannot do everything that is important every day.

On the other end of the spectrum from instinctive training are highly respected strength and conditioning professionals who have definite programs that their athletes follow. Sets, reps, rest periods, frequency, volume, and intensity are precisely delineated in a periodized program.

Which approach is most appropriate for you, the instinctive method or the structured method? In my opinion, it is not a rigid program that determines success in fitness. For athletes in a team setting, it is necessary to have specific schedules because you are dealing with a group of people. As individuals, they have their own needs, strengths, and weaknesses, but a coach is limited in how much one-on-one teaching can be done in a group environment. The program addresses some general principles that the whole team follows throughout the season.

For lifelong fitness and injury-free training, a philosophy of how you want to move and how you want to feel will keep you on the path. As a teacher or coach, the most valuable advice I can give you is to put an emphasis on quality first, then quantity, and to learn how to analyze and adapt various factors in order to adjust your training results to fit your changing goals. There is no perfect program, but there are programs that can work perfectly if they are infused with the knowledge of what works for specific objectives or goals. Many of these programs will work for you if you follow them to the letter, at least for a little while. Some of them may need to be tweaked a little or maybe even a lot.

Practice, experimentation, recording (logging a training journal is crucial), revision—these are all necessary steps along the path to lifelong strength and fitness. With that aim in mind, the sample programs listed here are as much food for thought as they are rules. They will work, but they eventually will stop working without the knowledge of how to adapt them.

# TYPES OF TRAINING PROGRAMS

For general health and fitness, the most common focal points for training programs are fat loss, muscular strength and endurance, and strength and power. While there are many possible programs which will effectively accomplish these goals, there are some guidelines for addressing each of these popular health and fitness objectives. The most effective fat-loss programs are based upon a high-intensity circuit-type workout; muscular strength programs rely upon lower volume and heavier loads; strength and endurance programs depend upon moderate loads and longer duration/higher volume workouts. Here are some guidelines for developing training programs for fat loss, muscular strength and strength and endurance, respectively.

## Fat-Loss Programs

Traditional fat-loss programming involved long, slow cardiorespiratory training, such as running, cycling, and other forms of steady-state aerobics. Dr. Kenneth Cooper, founder of the famous Cooper Institute, was instrumental in promoting aerobic conditioning for a healthy heart and lungs, circulation, and weight control. Dr. Cooper developed both the term *aerobics* and the aerobic method of training. James Fixx

wrote the best-selling book *The Complete Book of Running* in the mid-1970s, which helped to further establish the fitness craze via running. To this day, running is one of, if not the most, common form of exercise for health- and weight-conscious advocates. It requires only a pair of running shoes and off you go.

Although running and other aerobics are certainly effective for weight loss, beyond a certain point at least some of the weight lost will be muscle. This is because long-duration aerobic exercise elevates your levels of cortisol, which is a stress hormone. The longer the workout lasts, the more cortisol is released. Cortisol has a catabolic effect on muscle tissue, which means it can cause breakdown, or wasting, of the muscles. In addition, prolonged aerobic training can increase inflammation and does little to increase fat loss. Because of the catabolic nature of long-duration aerobic activity, the introduction of high-intensity, short-duration interval training has proven to be very effective for fat-loss programs. These short, intense bursts of power, repeated several times with little or no rest between sets, have a more anabolic or muscle-building quality with little or none of the catabolic effects found in long-duration aerobic training.

Generally speaking, optimal hormonal response to exercise occurs up to about 45 minutes of exercise. The most important hormones for strength and muscle gains and fat loss are testosterone and growth hormone. After 45 minutes or so of prolonged exercise, these hormonal levels begin to drop and cortisol starts to surge. Cortisol does the opposite of the anabolic growth hormones and testosterone, causing the catabolic breakdown of muscle tissues. As such, the prolonged, slow, distance type of endurance training can be counterproductive for fat loss and can even make you fatter as the body starts losing hard-earned muscle tone.

An interesting and influential study was performed by Dr. Izumi Tabata in 1966. In his study, Dr. Tabata selected seven subjects and had them perform a training exercise 5 days per week for 6 weeks. Each session included 8 sets of one specific exercise and was performed at a high intensity. Each training set was 20 seconds long followed by 10 seconds of rest, and in total, each Tabata workout was 4 minutes in duration. The other group performed 60 minutes of cardiorespiratory (aerobic) training 5 days per week for 6 weeks. Upon completion of the 6-week study, Tabata found that the cardio group that trained for a longer duration at a moderate intensity showed only a minor improvement in aerobic capacity and no improvement in anaerobic capacity. On the other hand, the HIIT (high-intensity interval training) group showed improvements in both aerobic and anaerobic capacities.

These Tabata protocols have become a popular form of high-intensity training for serious exercise enthusiasts and athletes alike. The original Tabata protocol consisted of a 5-minute warm-up, 8 minutes of 20-second maximal intensity exercise followed by 10 seconds of rest, and a 2-minute cool-down. However, Dr. Tabata's study was done on highly trained endurance athletes. For the general population, it is too intense and most people are not likely to stick with it. Therefore, most adaptations of the Tabata protocols use 8 intervals (4-minute sets after warming up). The shorter, more intense interval-based training such as Tabata or circuit training burns a lot of calories but avoids the cortisol spikes associated with muscle loss, thereby allowing more recovery while you rest after the workout, which is when the strength- and growth-producing anabolic phase of recovery takes place.

There are advantages and disadvantages of both aerobic- and anaerobic-based fat-loss programs. Most effective fat-loss programs thus incorporate a mixture of anaerobic and aerobic exercises.

## Muscular Strength and Endurance Programs

In my experience, nothing works more effectively than kettlebell training for muscular strength and endurance goals, a point that has been emphasized throughout the book. It is precisely the blend of load, speed, and duration that gives such versatile utility to kettlebell training. If your goal is a blend of strength and endurance, a consistent, progressive kettlebell program is probably all you need. Dumbbells, barbells, and body-weight protocols can also be performed for increased muscular strength and endurance.

## Strength and Power Training Programs

For maximal strength, barbells reign supreme because they can achieve heavier loads in all the basic lifts, including the squat, deadlift, bench press, clean, snatch, and overhead press. Kettlebells have a place, as do sandbags and strongman-type training methods, but barbells are definitely the foundation if your goal is to achieve maximal strength and power through your training program.

To improve power, you have to move a load as quickly as possible through a full range of motion. Medicine balls are a great tool for this because they can be accelerated with maximal velocity and then released at the point of full extension, thereby fully expressing your power in the movement. Remember that *power* is defined as the amount of work performed per unit of time and therefore there is a distinction between strength and power. Strength, or the amount of force that is produced, is a component of power, and it is the speed of movement that differentiates power from strength. Therefore, programs for power development must include full-speed movements.

# FITNESS PROGRAM DESIGN

Starting a fitness program is an important step for your health and well-being. Before you begin training with kettlebells, it is a good idea to create a program that you can follow. Designing a program requires some consideration of your goals and your current capabilities. Here are some guidelines to keep in mind when designing your kettlebell training program.

- Have an idea of your current fitness level so you have a starting point from which to measure your progress. There are some simple tests you can do to determine your starting points, as we learned in chapter 4.

- Before you write your own program or follow a prescribed program template, you need to clarify your focal point or most important goal for that period of time. Do you want to lose weight? Or do you have some performance goal, such as completing a triathlon? Having a specific goal will keep you focused on your progress. If, for example, you need to drop 20 pounds (9 kg), you may want to prioritize a program that emphasizes fat loss for the next 3 months or so. If you reach your fat-loss goals, your next program can focus on strength and endurance progression. Further, it is helpful to have an overall approach that allows you the flexibility to mix and match training tools and methods while addressing your fundamental fitness goals.

- It's important to start slowly and progress gradually. If you have any injuries or medical conditions, be sure to first consult a doctor to understand appropriate guidelines for your fitness program. Select kettlebells that are appropriate for your current level and will allow you to make progress for the next 3 to 6 months. Listen to your body. If you feel pain, shortness of breath, dizziness, or nausea, take a break. You may be working out too often or too intensely.

- You'll need a well-rounded program that addresses strength, endurance, and range of motion. Keep track of your goals and progress using a journal or logbook. If you find that your progress stalls, you may have to increase the frequency or intensity of your workouts. Set new goals to stay motivated over time.

- Allow time for recovery between sessions so you can adequately rest and recover, and always allow time for an adequate warm-up at the start of the workout and for a cool-down at the end. If you're not feeling well, you may need to take a day or two of rest before your next workout.

When I design general fitness programs, the guiding philosophy I follow is to address all the major movement patterns. If we look at all of the movement types that are demanded of you, we can come up with a classification system. This classification helps you group the various conditioning exercises so that you can be sure to use complementary movements to exercise your body in each of the range of motion: vertical pushing, vertical pulling horizontal pushing, horizontal pulling, hip hinging, knee hinging and midline (core) stability and dynamic mobility.

There are several classes of movements that your body makes and there are at least a few high-quality, functional exercises for each movement, as you can see in table 9.1. These examples are by no means exhaustive; however, you will find that by sticking to the movement groups shown in the table, you will address all your strength and conditioning needs and will not lack variety.

If you understand the concept of the seven movement patterns, you can substitute kettlebells with any other kind of loaded resistance such as barbells or dumbbells.

For health and fitness, it is my experience and professional opinion that a primary goal is to strive for balance in developing the body as well as your skill set. Kettlebell training is a specialization that offers particular advantages to your overall fitness level. A kettlebell program of any type is going to naturally emphasize vertical pulling and pressing more than horizontal pulling and pressing. With the predominance of vertical movements in kettlebell training, you want to add some horizontal movements to give attention to other angles of motion. There is also a predominance of movement in the sagittal and frontal planes, so including some movements in the transverse plane is a good idea for balance.

With this guiding philosophy and a rich assortment of functional exercises to choose from, we can easily construct effective, well-rounded exercise programs to meet any fitness goal.

**Table 9.1  Movement Classifications**

| | |
|---|---|
| **Vertical push** | One-arm press, double press, one-arm push press, double push press, one-arm jerk, double jerk, one-arm seated press, double seated press, standing or seated alternating press, dips, handstand push-ups on floor or parallette bars |
| **Vertical pull** | One-arm snatch, one-arm clean, double clean, pull-up, deadlift |
| **Horizontal push** | Floor or bench press, any push-up variation |
| **Horizontal pull** | One-arm bent row, bent row, renegade row, horizontal row, one-arm horizontal row, inverted pull-up |
| **Lower body—knee emphasis** | Front squat, front squat onto toes, squat swing, kettlebell jump squat |
| **Lower body—hip emphasis** | Two-hand swing, one-hand swing, one-leg deadlift, good morning, pistol (one-leg squat), hand-to-hand swing |
| **Core stability and dynamic mobility** | Overhead squat, one-arm overhead squat, windmill, get-up, lying pullover, bottoms-up plank holds, side planks |

## CREATING A TRAINING LOG

There are several ways to log your progress. The important thing is that you do it and that you use a system that makes it easy to track your workouts. Then when your progress stalls, you can look back over the previous weeks and months to see exactly what you did and what you may need to change to restart your progress. My suggestion is to keep a log with the following information:

- Date
- Name of exercise
- Load selected
- Number of repetitions
- Number of sets

- Duration of sets
- Duration of rest between each set
- Total time of workout
- Total tonnage

With the information recorded in your workout log, you can see exactly how much work you did, what weight you used, and total volume and total duration. Over time you should see some or all of those numbers go up, such as heavier loads, same loads with more reps or more sets, shorter rest periods, and so on. This will allow you to see your progress easily. You also can record your total tonnage for each workout, each week, and each month. As a general trend, the total tonnage should increase at least a bit each month. When it stops increasing, it is a good indication that you need to take a week or two off to let your body recover. Then you can go back to training refreshed and renewed.

# SAMPLE TRAINING PROGRAMS

Following are some sample training programs that address the common concerns of fat loss, muscular strength and endurance, and strength and power development. You can follow each of the programs exactly, modify the weight, reps, sets or duration of any exercise, or make up new programs. These sample workouts are to get you started so you have an idea of what to do in your workouts. With experience, you will have the knowledge and confidence to create some of your own training programs. The possibilities are limitless.

## Sample Fat-Loss Programs

This section describes three programs that focus on fat loss. One is for beginners, one is for intermediate exercisers, and one is for advanced exercisers (see figures 9.1-9.3.)

| **Figure 9.1** | Beginner Fat-Loss Program |
|---|---|
| **Warm-up** | 1. *Around-the-body pass (pg. 77):* 30 s each direction with light kettlebell |
| | 2. *Halo (pg. 78):* 30 s each direction with light kettlebell |
| | 3. *Kettlebell deadlift (pg. 81):* 10 reps |
| | 4. *Goblet squat (pg. 97):* 10 reps |
| | 5. *Joint mobility exercises (pg. 46):* Rotate all major joints (shoulders, hips, neck) 10-20 times. |
| **Main session** | 1. *Single swing (pg. 82):* Tabata protocol as described on page 178 for 20 s with 10 s rest before alternating arms. Repeat for 4 sets with 1 min recovery between sets. |
| | 2. *Single press (pg. 90):* Tabata protocol as described on page 178 for 20 s with 10 s rest before alternating arms. Repeat for 4 sets with 1 min recovery between sets. |
| **Cool-down** | 1. *Easy jog for 10 min* |
| | 2. *Stretch for 5 min*: 30 s each side for each stretch (behind-the-back shoulder stretch, pg. 62; shoulder stretch, pg. 62; triceps pulls, pg. 63; standing knee-to-chest stretch, pg. 64; standing quadriceps stretch, pg. 65) |

| **Figure 9.2** | Intermediate Fat-Loss Program |
|---|---|
| **Warm-up** | 1. *Two-arm single-leg kettlebell deadlift (pg. 102):* 8 reps on each side |
| | 2. *Windmill (pg. 130):* 10 reps on each side |
| | 3. *Joint mobility exercises (pg. 46):* Rotate all major joints (shoulders, hips, neck) 10-20 times. |
| **Main session** | Perform as many rounds as possible in 10 min: |
| | 1. *Double swing (pg. 105):* 15 reps with medium-weight kettlebells |
| | 2. *Double clean (pg. 108):* 15 reps with medium-weight kettlebells |
| | 3. *Double front squat (pg. 112):* 15 reps with medium-weight kettlebells |
| | 4. *Russian twist (pg. 139):* 40 twists with medium-weight kettlebell |
| **Cool-down** | 1. *Easy jog for 10 min* |
| | 2. *Stretch for 7 min*: 1 min per stretch (standing hamstrings stretch, pg. 65; standing knee-to-chest stretch, pg. 64; standing quadriceps stretch, pg. 65; spinal extension, pg. 67; child's pose, pg. 68; knee-to-chest stretch, pg. 67; spinal flexion, pg. 66) |

| **Figure 9.3** | Advanced Fat-Loss Program |
|---|---|
| **Warm-up** | 1. *Easy jog for 5 min*<br>2. *Dynamic mobility exercises (pg. 56):* arm twirls forward and backward for 30 s, dynamic clapping for 30 s, leg swings in each direction for 30 s<br>3. *Single overhead squat (pg. 174):* 30 s each side<br>4. *Spinal flexion (pg. 66):* hold for 1 min<br>5. *Calf stretch (page 66):* 1 min per leg |
| **Main session** | 1. *Double half snatch (pg. 150):* Tabata protocol as described on page 178 for 20 s with 10 s rest. Repeat for 4 sets.<br>2. *Bottoms-up push-up (pg. 164):* Tabata protocol as described on page 178 for 20 s with 10 s rest. Repeat for 4 sets. |
| **Cool-down** | *Static stretches*: 30 s each side or 10 reps each exercise (standing quadriceps stretch, pg. 65; standing hamstrings stretch, pg. 65; standing knee-to-chest stretch, pg. 64; calf stretch, pg. 66; spinal flexion, pg. 66) |

## Sample Strength and Endurance Programs

This section offers three programs that focus on strength and endurance. One is for beginners, one is for intermediate exercisers, and one is for advanced exercisers (see figures 9.4-9.6).

| **Figure 9.4** | Beginner Strength and Endurance Program |
|---|---|
| **Warm-up** | 1. *Easy jog for 5 min*<br>2. *Joint mobility exercises (pg. 46):* Rotate all major joints (shoulders, hips, neck) 10-20 times or for 5 min. |
| **Main session** | Perform 10 reps of each of the following exercises on each side of the body without stopping. Repeat for 3 rounds with 1 min rest between each round. One round consists of the single swing (pg. 82), single clean (pg. 84), single press (pg. 90), snatch (pg. 94), and goblet squat (pg. 97). |
| **Cool-down** | *Stretch for 7 min*: Perform each stretch for 1 min (behind-the-back shoulder stretch, pg. 62; standing knee-to-chest stretch, pg. 64; standing hamstrings stretch, pg. 65; standing quadriceps stretch, pg. 65; spinal extension, pg. 67; child's pose, pg. 68; spinal flexion, pg. 66). |

## Figure 9.5  Intermediate Strength and Endurance Program

| | |
|---|---|
| **Warm-up** | 1. *Easy jog for 5 min* |
| | 2. *Goblet squat (pg. 97):* 1 set of 10 reps with a light- to moderate-weight kettlebell |
| **Main session** | 1. *Double clean (pg. 108):* 10 sets of 10 reps with two moderate-weight kettlebells and 1 min rest between sets |
| | 2. *One-arm jerk (pg. 115):* 5 sets of 10 reps on each arm with a moderate-weight kettlebell and 1 min rest between each set |
| | 3. *Double front squat (pg. 112):* 10 sets of 10 reps with two moderate-weight kettlebells and 1 min rest between sets |
| **Cool-down** | *Stretch for 7 min:* Perform each stretch for 1 min (behind-the-back shoulder stretch, pg. 62; neck flexion stretch, pg. 63; lateral neck stretch, pg. 64; standing knee-to-chest stretch, pg. 64; standing hamstrings stretch, pg. 65; standing quadriceps stretch, pg. 65; spinal extension, pg. 67; child's pose, pg. 68; spinal flexion, pg. 66). |

## Figure 9.6  Advanced Strength and Endurance Program

| | |
|---|---|
| **Warm-up** | 1. *Body-weight squat (pg. 97):* 1 min |
| | 2. *Body-weight push-ups:* 30 s |
| **Main session** | 1. *Single overhead squat (pg. 174):* 5 sets of 5 reps each side with 1 min rest between each set |
| | 2. *Double clean and jerk (pg. 161):* 10 sets of 10 reps with 1 min rest between sets |
| | 3. *Farmer's carry (pg. 123):* 1 set as long as possible with two heavy kettlebells |
| **Cool-down** | 1. *Easy jog for 20 min* |
| | 2. *Stretch for 9 min:* Perform each stretch for 1 min (behind-the-back shoulder stretch, pg. 62; neck flexion stretch, pg. 63; lateral neck stretch, pg. 64; standing knee-to-chest stretch, pg. 64; standing hamstrings stretch, pg. 65; standing quadriceps stretch, pg. 65; spinal extension, pg. 67; child's pose, pg. 68; spinal flexion, pg. 66). |

## Sample Strength and Power Programs

In this section there are three programs that focus on strength and power. One is for beginners, one is for intermediate exercisers, and one is for advanced exercisers (see tables 9.7-9.9).

| **Figure 9.7** | Beginner Strength and Power Program |
| --- | --- |
| **Warm-up** | 1. *Easy jog for 5 min*<br>2. *Figure-eight between-the-legs pass (pg. 79):* 1 min in each direction with a light kettlebell<br>3. *Joint mobility exercises (pg. 46):* 20 reps of each (hip circles, trunk twists, lateral bends, waist bends, shoulder rolls, neck tilts, neck rotations, ankle bounces) |
| **Main session** | Perform 5 sets of 5 reps per hand of each exercise with a moderate-heavy kettlebell, resting no more than 1 min between each set. One set consists of the single swing (pg. 82), single clean (pg. 84), single press (pg. 90), push press (pg. 92), half snatch (pg. 95), and front squat (pg. 98). |
| **Cool-down** | *Stretch for 9 min*: Perform each stretch for 1 min (behind-the-back shoulder stretch, pg. 62; neck flexion stretch, pg. 63; lateral neck stretch, pg. 64; standing knee-to-chest stretch, pg. 64; standing hamstrings stretch, pg. 65; standing quadriceps stretch, pg. 65; spinal extension, pg. 67; child's pose, pg. 68; spinal flexion, pg. 66). |

| **Figure 9.8** | Intermediate Strength and Power Program |
| --- | --- |
| **Warm-up** | 1. *Easy jog for 5 min*<br>2. *Body-weight squat (pg. 97):* 1 set for 30 s<br>3. *Joint mobility exercises (pg. 46):* 20 reps of each (hip circles, trunk twists, lateral bends, waist bends, shoulder rolls, neck tilts, neck rotations, ankle bounces) |
| **Main session** | 1. *Rack hold (pg. 126):* Hold for 2 min with two light kettlebells, rest 1 min, hold 2 min with two moderate-weight kettlebells, rest 2 min, hold 1 min with two heavy kettlebells.<br>2. *Overhead hold (pg. 126):* Hold 1 min with two light kettlebells, rest 1 min, hold 1 min with two moderate-weight kettlebells.<br>3. *Bottoms-up press (pg. 144):* Do 2 sets of 5 reps per hand, resting 1 min between sets.<br>4. *Renegade rows (pg. 128):* Do 3 sets of 10 reps, resting 1 min between sets.<br>5. *Kettlebell jump squat (pg. 121):* Do 3 sets of 15 reps, resting 1 min between each set.<br>6. *Farmer's carry (pg. 123):* Hold two heavy kettlebells for as long as possible for 1 set. |
| **Cool-down** | 1. *Easy jog for 5 min*<br>2. *Stretch for 9 min*: Perform each stretch for 1 min (behind-the-back shoulder stretch, pg. 62; neck flexion stretch, pg. 63; lateral neck stretch, pg. 64; standing knee-to-chest stretch, pg. 64; standing hamstrings stretch, pg. 65; standing quadriceps stretch, pg. 65; spinal extension, pg. 67; child's pose, pg. 68; spinal flexion, pg. 66). |

| **Figure 9.9** | Advanced Strength and Power Program |
| --- | --- |
| **Warm-up** | 1. *Body-weight squat (pg. 97):* 1 set of 30 reps |
| | 2. *Skipping rope (pg. 45):* 1 min |
| | 3. *Dynamic mobility exercises (pg. 56):* 15 reps of each (arm twirls in both directions, pg. 57; chest hollow and expand, pg. 58; vertical chest opener, pg. 58; dynamic clapping, pg. 59; leg swings, pg. 60) |
| **Main session** | 1. *Squat method get-up (pg. 166):* 5 reps each arm |
| | 2. *Double overhead squat (pg. 175):* 5 sets of 5 reps, resting 1 min between sets |
| | 3. *Double alternating clean (pg. 148):* 1 min, rest 1 min |
| | 4. *Double alternating snatch (pg. 155):* 1 min, rest 1 min |
| | 5. *Double clean and jerk (pg. 161):* 5 sets of 10 reps, resting 1 min between sets |
| **Cool-down** | 1. *Easy jog for 10 min* |
| | 2. *Stretch for 9 min*: Perform each stretch for 1 min (behind-the-back shoulder stretch, pg. 62; neck flexion stretch, pg. 63; lateral neck stretch, pg. 64; standing knee-to-chest stretch, pg. 64; standing hamstrings stretch, pg. 65; standing quadriceps stretch, pg. 65; spinal extension, pg. 67; child's pose, pg. 68; spinal flexion, pg. 66). |

Following the philosophy of total-body integration, being mindful of the seven common movement patterns, and using the rich assortment of beginner, intermediate, and advanced kettlebell exercises described in this book, you can easily put together your own constantly varied exercise programs to keep motivated and prevent boredom. When you combine the kettlebell exercises with other great training tools, you have a virtually unlimited range of movements and tools to choose from. Your health and fitness are important, and with *Kettlebell Training* as your guide, you have all the practical information you need to reach your fat-loss, strength and endurance, or strength and power training goals.

# SPORT-SPECIFIC TRAINING PROGRAMS

Kettlebell training is not only beneficial for improving general fitness, it can also be an important addition to the strength and conditioning preparation of athletes from many sports. Though some sports have a narrow focus, emphasizing one quality above all others, most sports require an assortment of skills, ranges of motion, and energy systems. For example, powerlifting focuses on the singular quality of developing maximal, or limit, strength, and marathon running focuses on maximizing cardiorespiratory fitness and stamina. But many other sports require an integrated blend of qualities. For this reason, kettlebell training is a great complement to the conditioning of most athletes—it is by nature a blend of strength, power, endurance, and mobility. At the same time, for a kettlebell (or any other) cross-training program to be effective, the energy systems and movement patterns of the particular sport need to be taken into account while also adhering to physiological principles.

A truism of most training programs is that everything works until it stops working. What this means is that doing something different will have an adaptive effect up to a certain point. If you are not used to training in a particular way, with practice you improve your strength, conditioning, and coordination. These initial adaptations are largely neurological, meaning early improvements can be attributed to the improved synchronization of nerve cells and muscle fibers rather than to muscle hypertrophy (increased muscle size). But after a certain amount of time, maybe a few weeks or maybe a month or more, you reach a plateau and measurable progress slows down or even stops. You are no longer able to use a heavier kettlebell or perform more reps. Once your body adjusts to this new level, your strength or endurance may even decrease a bit. Your body has adapted to the program you are following, and you have to modify something in order to progress.

Through the selected exercises and set and rep ranges, the following sport-specific programs train the primary movement patterns and energy systems of the particular sport and work the body in an integrated manner that complements the sport. Before we get into the specific programs, let's review some basic exercise principles.

## BASIC EXERCISE PRINCIPLES

Before proceeding to program recommendations for specific sports, a quick review of important exercise principles is in order so that you can understand how the body adapts to exercise training and therefore understand how to set realistic and practical goals. Knowledge is power, and the more you know about what to expect in an exercise program and the obstacles to progress, the better you will be able to make consistent improvements in your fitness. These principles are as follows:

- *Principle of individual differences*—We are all unique and have differences in how our body responds, even to the same stimuli.

- *Principle of overcompensation*—Muscles will respond to heavy resistance (stress) by growing stronger, larger, and more skillful.

- *Principle of progressive resistance*—This consists of overload and progression and is the combination of two principles:

  o *Principle of overload*—A greater-than-normal stress is required in order for the body to adapt; in order to increase strength and fitness, the demands (e.g., load, duration, total volume) must gradually increase.

  o *Principle of progression*—There is an optimal level of overload that will lead to progress in fitness. Too little will not cause improvements, and too much will likely lead to injury.

- *Principle of adaptation*—Your body will adjust to increasing physical demands (by getting stronger, fitter, more flexible, and so on).

- *Principle of reversibility*—Your body grows stronger with use and weaker with disuse (use it or lose it). This principle is the opposite of adaptation and is also called the *detraining principle*.

- *Principle of specificity*—You get better at a specific skill by practicing it. Your exercise selections should match your goals.

## ENERGY SYSTEMS

Kettlebell programs should be designed with exercises and volume that are complementary to both the energy systems and the motor patterns used in the sport. There are three primary energy systems that your body uses to produce energy:

- The *aerobic system,* also called the *oxidative system*, provides energy for activities that are sustained for more than 2 minutes. This system is aerobic.

- The *glycolytic system* provides energy for activities ranging from 30 seconds up to 2 minutes. It is also called the *lactic acid system*. This system is anaerobic.

- The *ATP-CP system* (short for adenosine triphosphate and creatine phosphate) provides an immediate energy source for activities that last 30 seconds or less. This system is anaerobic.

For the large majority of sports, especially team sports, the primary energy systems required are anaerobic. Exceptions include activities such as long-distance running, cross-country skiing, road cycling, long-distance swimming, and triathlons. Because of this, the cross-training programs selected should use more interval-based protocols rather than the LSD (long, slow, distance) protocols that were once a mainstay in many sport conditioning programs. At the same time, many sports that use predominantly anaerobic energy also require a solid base of aerobic conditioning. In tennis, hockey, wrestling, and other sports, plays and points are made via short, fast, explosive anaerobic efforts, yet because of the need to sustain effort throughout an entire game or match, aerobic energy is required to finish the game. Therefore, a mixture of anaerobic and aerobic exercise is appropriate for the majority of kettlebell sport-conditioning programs, as seen in the sample programs in this chapter.

Side by side with these exercise principles, a well-designed sport conditioning program should keep in mind the FITT acronym as we learned about in chapter 3:

- *Frequency:* How often should you train?

- *Intensity:* How much load should you use and what percentage of maximal effort should be given in a particular workout?

- *Time:* How long should the training session last?

- *Type:* What kind of exercise should you do to complement your sport—strength training, endurance training, power training, flexibility training, or a combination of these? Should your workouts be anaerobic, aerobic, or use a blend of energy systems?

A key point to keep in mind with GPP training for other sports, or cross-training, is that improvement in the sport itself is the only meaningful goal. GPP, or General Physical Preparation, is the foundation that provides a well-rounded base of general, unspecific fitness to enable a person to cope with the demands of a particular task, to include strength, flexibility, muscular endurance, aerobic endurance, speed and body composition. For an athlete, there is no value in simply working out; rather, the athlete works out in order to improve her strength and conditioning to be able to perform better in her sport. Working out just to work out would be detrimental to a competitive athlete, because it would take valuable energy that would be best used in the practice of the sport skill. In addition, the first rule for athletic cross-training is to not injure the athlete, that is, to keep her on the field of play. The last thing that should ever happen is for the athlete to injure herself in the weight room or gym! In line with this, most kettlebell cross-training sessions should be relatively short in duration to allow the athlete ample time to recover between sessions and save enough energy for practice and games.

# SAMPLE KETTLEBELL SPORT-CONDITIONING PROGRAMS

Now that you have an understanding of the basic exercise principles and energy systems involved, we provide some sample kettlebell programs for American football, basketball, boxing, golf, hockey, kickboxing, soccer, tennis, track and field, volleyball, and wrestling. Along with each program, we also briefly discuss the primary movement patterns and qualities employed in the sport.

Use the training templates in this chapter as starting points for developing your kettlebell sport-conditioning workouts, and let your understanding of exercise principles, energy systems, and movement patterns guide you in putting together your own effective cross-training programs.

**Figure 10.1** Kettlebell Program for American Football

American football is almost exclusively an anaerobic sport, using explosive linear and lateral movements lasting on average 10 seconds or less. Lower-body linear and lateral power and upper-body pushing strength are foundational for football athletes. Skills include jumping, throwing, catching, blocking, hitting, and kicking.

| | |
|---|---|
| **Warm-up** | 1. *Body-weight agility exercises (pg. 45):* 30 s each (skipping forward and backward, lateral shuffling, two-legged hop) |
| | 2. *Body-weight squat (pg. 97):* 30 s |
| | 3. *Push-ups:* 30 s |
| | 4. *Joint mobility exercises (pg. 46):* 30 s each (shoulder rolls, neck tilts, neck rotations, neck circles, hip circles, trunk twists, lateral bends, waist bends, figure-eight waist circles, spinal rolls, lateral rib openers, knee circles, ankle bounces) |
| | 5. *Dynamic mobility exercises (pg. 56):* 30 s each (arm twirls, chest hollow and expand, vertical chest opener, dynamic clapping, bootstrappers, leg swings) |
| **Main session** | Perform all sets for a given exercise before moving to the next. Follow the rest guidelines given for each exercise. |
| | 1. *Double swing (pg. 105):* 10 reps with light kettlebells, 10 reps with moderate-weight kettlebells, 10 reps with heavy kettlebells; rest 15 s between sets |
| | 2. *Double clean and jerk (pg. 161):* 10 reps with moderate-weight kettlebells, 5 reps with heavy kettlebells for 3 sets; rest 1 min between sets |
| | 3. *Double snatch (pg. 150):* 3 sets of 5 reps with heavy kettlebells; rest 1 min between sets |
| | 4. *Double front squat (pg. 112):* 3 sets of 10 reps with heavy kettlebells; rest 1 min between sets |
| | 5. *Single-leg kettlebell deadlift (pg. 102):* 3 sets of 5 reps on each leg with heavy kettlebells; rest 1 min between sets |
| | 6. *Double swing (pg. 105):* 10 reps for 3 sets with heavy kettlebells; rest 1 min between sets |
| **Cool-down** | *Stretch:* 1 min each (behind-the-back shoulder stretch, pg. 62; shoulder stretch, pg. 62; neck flexion stretch, pg. 63; lateral neck stretch, pg. 64; standing knee-to-chest stretch, pg. 64; standing quadriceps stretch, pg. 65; standing hamstrings stretch, pg. 65; knee-to-chest stretch, pg. 67; child's pose, pg. 68) |

## Figure 10.2 Kettlebell Program for Basketball

Basketball requires a strong aerobic base for the constant running it involves; however, the jumping is anaerobic and requires explosive leg power. Leg power and endurance, lateral agility, shoulder endurance, core stability, and dynamic mobility are necessary for basketball athletes.

| | |
|---|---|
| **Warm-up** | 1. *Around-the-body pass (pg. 77):* 1 min each direction with a light kettlebell<br><br>2. *Single swing (pg. 82):* 1 min each hand with light kettlebell<br><br>3. *Figure-eight between-the-legs pass (pg. 79):* 1 min each direction with a light kettlebell |
| **Main session** | Perform the following circuit for 3 rounds, resting 1 min between each round:<br><br>1. *Get-up* (pg. 136): 5 reps each side with a light kettlebell<br><br>2. *Single press (pg. 90):* 5 reps each arm with a light kettlebell<br><br>3. *Double windmill (pg. 134):* 5 reps on each side with two light kettlebells<br><br>4. *Push press (pg. 92):* 10 reps each arm with a moderate-weight kettlebell<br><br>5. *Single clean (pg. 84):* 10 reps each arm with a moderate-weight kettlebell<br><br>6. *Goblet squat (pg. 97):* 30 s with a moderate-weight kettlebell<br><br>7. *Kettlebell deadlift (pg. 81):* 15 reps with two moderate-weight kettlebells<br><br>8. *Kettlebell jump squat (pg. 121):* 15 reps with a light kettlebell |
| **Cool-down** | *Stretch:* 1 min each (behind-the-back shoulder stretch, pg. 62; shoulder stretch, pg. 62; triceps pulls, pg. 63; neck flexion stretch, pg. 63; lateral neck stretch, pg. 64; standing knee-to-chest stretch, pg. 64; standing quadriceps stretch, pg. 65; standing hamstrings stretch, pg. 64; calf stretch, pg. 66; spinal extension, pg. 67; spinal flexion, pg. 66; child's pose, pg. 68) |

## Figure 10.3  Kettlebell Program for Boxing

Boxing is primarily anaerobic due to the powerful strikes involved, but it also requires a solid base of aerobic development in order to excel over the 12 rounds of a professional fight. Conditioning requirements are great: lower-body endurance and agility, shoulder and triceps endurance, a stable core and neck, and wrist and forearm stability. Movements include twisting, lunging, rotation, and extension.

| | |
|---|---|
| **Warm-up** | 1. *Body-weight squat (pg. 97):* 1 min |
| | 2. *Shadowboxing (pg. 45):* 1 min |
| | 3. *Skipping (pg. 45):* 1 min |
| | 4. *Joint mobility exercises (pg. 46):* 20 s each (finger flexion and extension, interlocked wrist rolls, forearm flexion and extension, elbow circles, shoulder rolls, neck tilts, neck rotations, neck circles, hip circles, trunk twists, lateral bends, waist bends, figure-eight waist circles, spinal rolls, lateral rib openers, knee circles, ankle bounces) |
| | 5. *Dynamic mobility exercises (pg. 56):* 30 s each (arm twirls, chest hollow and expand, vertical chest opener, dynamic clapping) |
| **Main session** | Perform the following circuit for 3 rounds with 1 min rest between each round. |
| | 1. *Bottoms-up clean (pg. 142):* 5 reps with each hand with a light kettlebell, rest 30 s, 5 reps with each hand with a moderate-weight kettlebell |
| | 2. *Double jerk (pg. 158):* 1 min with two light kettlebells |
| | 3. *Goblet squat (pg. 97):* 1 min with a light kettlebell |
| | 4. *Renegade rows (pg. 128):* 10 reps with two moderate-weight kettlebells |
| | 5. *Bottoms-up press (pg. 144):* 5 reps per hand with a moderate-weight kettlebell, rest 1 min, repeat |
| | 6. *Bottoms-up push-up (pg. 164):* 15 reps |
| | 7. *Goblet squat (pg. 97):* 1 min with a moderate-weight kettlebell |
| | 8. *One-arm jerk (pg. 115):* 90 s each hand with a moderate-weight kettlebell |
| | 9. *Single swing (pg. 82):* 90 s each hand with a moderate-weight kettlebell |
| **Cool-down** | *Stretch:* 1 min each (behind-the-back shoulder stretch, pg. 62; shoulder stretch, pg. 62; triceps pulls, pg. 63; neck flexion stretch, pg. 63; lateral neck stretch, pg. 64; standing knee-to-chest stretch, pg. 64; standing quadriceps stretch, pg. 65; standing hamstrings stretch, pg. 64; spinal extension, pg. 67; spinal flexion, pg. 66; child's pose, pg. 68) |

## Figure 10.4 Kettlebell Program for Golf

Golf is primarily anaerobic. A golf swing lasts less than 2 seconds and so relies upon the ATP-CP system. There is a heavy rotational component to the driving, chipping, and putting motions. There is also an aerobic component during the walking from hole to hole, unless of course a golf cart is used. In addition, shoulder girdle mobility, torso flexibility for rotational torque, a solid core for midline stability, and steady wrists for accurate shots are all advised and should be considered in the program.

| | |
|---|---|
| **Warm-up** | 1. *Joint mobility exercises (pg. 46):* 20 s each for a total of 5 min (elbow circles, shoulder rolls, neck tilts, neck rotations, hip circles, trunk twists, lateral bends, waist bends, figure-eight waist circles, lateral rib openers, knee circles, ankle bounces) |
| | 2. *Dynamic mobility exercises (pg. 56):* 20 s each for a total of 5 min (arm twirls, chest hollow and expand, vertical chest opener, dynamic clapping, leg swings) |
| **Main session** | Perform the following circuit with little or no rest between exercises and rest 1 min between each completed circuit, working up to 3 rounds. |
| | 1. *Halo (pg. 78):* 10 reps each direction with a light kettlebell |
| | 2. *Double swing (pg. 105):* 15 reps with moderate-weight kettlebells |
| | 3. *High windmill (pg. 133):* 5 reps each side with a light kettlebell |
| | 4. *Bottoms-up clean (pg. 142):* 5 reps each hand with a moderate-weight kettlebell |
| | 5. *Single press (pg. 90):* 5 reps each arm with a moderate-weight kettlebell |
| | 6. *Goblet squat (pg. 97):* 10 reps with a moderate-weight kettlebell |
| | 7. *Russian twist (pg. 139):* 20 reps with a light-weight kettlebell |
| | 8. *Single swing (pg. 82):* 10 reps each hand with a moderate-weight kettlebell |
| **Cool-down** | *Stretch:* 30 s each side (behind-the-back shoulder stretch, pg. 62; shoulder stretch, pg. 62; triceps pulls, pg. 63; standing knee-to-chest stretch, pg. 64; standing quadriceps stretch, pg. 65; standing hamstrings stretch, pg. 64; calf stretch, pg. 66) |

**Figure 10.5** Kettlebell Program for Hockey

Hockey uses a fair mix of anaerobic and aerobic energy, and it becomes more aerobic as the game progresses due to the continuous skating involved. The shots on goal and save attempts by the goalie are examples of short-duration bursts that use anaerobic energy. Lateral movement, hip-dominant power, core stability, and single-leg strength and balance are some of the most important qualities for hockey players.

| | |
|---|---|
| **Warm-up** | 1. *Body-weight squat (pg. 97):* 25 s |
| | 2. *Skipping rope (pg. 45):* 1 min |
| | 3. *Joint mobility exercises (pg. 46):* 20 s each (finger flexion and extension, interlocked wrist rolls, forearm flexion and extension, elbow circles, shoulder rolls, neck tilts, neck rotations, neck circles, hip circles, trunk twists, lateral bends, waist bends, figure-eight waist circles, spinal rolls, lateral rib openers, knee circles, ankle bounces) |
| | 4. *Dynamic mobility exercises (pg. 56):* 30 s each (arm twirls, chest hollow and expand, vertical chest opener, dynamic clapping, bootstrappers, leg swings) |
| **Main session** | Perform the following circuit for 3 rounds and rest 1 min between each round, working up to 5 rounds. |
| | 1. *Single swing (pg. 82):* 10 reps each hand with a light kettlebell, rest 30 s, 10 reps each hand with a moderate-weight kettlebell, rest 45 s, 10 reps each hand with a heavy kettlebell |
| | 2. *Bottoms-up clean (pg. 142):* 5 reps each hand with a heavy kettlebell |
| | 3. *One-arm jerk (pg. 115):* 10 reps each arm with a moderate-weight kettlebell, rest 1 min, 10 reps each arm with a heavy kettlebell |
| | 4. *Double alternating clean (pg. 148):* 20 reps with two moderate-weight kettlebells |
| | 5. *One-arm contralateral single-leg kettlebell deadlift (pg. 103):* 8 reps each leg with a moderate-weight kettlebell |
| | 6. *Double swing (pg. 105):* 30 s with a heavy kettlebell |
| **Cool-down** | *Stretch:* 1 min each (behind-the-back shoulder stretch, pg. 62; shoulder stretch, pg. 62; triceps pulls, pg. 63; neck flexion stretch, pg. 63; lateral neck stretch, pg. 64; standing knee-to-chest stretch, pg. 64; standing quadriceps stretch, pg. 65; standing hamstrings stretch, pg. 64; calf stretch, pg. 66; spinal extension, pg. 67; spinal flexion, pg. 66; child's pose, pg. 68) |

## Figure 10.6 Kettlebell Program for Kickboxing

Kickboxing uses similar movement patterns and energy demands as boxing. In addition, it requires strong hip flexors and quadriceps for kicking.

| | |
|---|---|
| **Warm-up** | 1. *Easy jog for 5 min* |
| | 2. *Joint rotations (pg. 46)*: 20 sec each (shoulder rolls, neck tilts, neck rotations, neck circles, hip circles, trunk twists, lateral bends, waist bends, figure-eight waist circles, knee circles, ankle bounces) |
| | 3. *Dynamic mobility exercises (pg. 56)*: 30 sec each (arm twirls, chest hollow and expand, vertical chest opener, dynamic clapping, bootstrappers, leg swings) |
| **Main session** | Move from one exercise to the next with no more than 1 min rest between exercises. |
| | 1. *Single swing (pg. 82):* 1 min each hand with a light kettlebell |
| | 2. *Double windmill (pg. 134):* 10 reps each side with a light kettlebell |
| | 3. *Goblet squat (pg. 97):* 1 min with a light kettlebell |
| | 4. *Double clean and jerk (pg. 161):* 1 min with two light kettlebells |
| | 5. *Goblet squat (pg. 97):* 1 min with a moderate-weight kettlebell |
| | 6. *Single-leg kettlebell deadlift (pg. 102):* 10 reps each leg with two moderate-weight kettlebells |
| | 7. *Double clean and jerk (pg. 161):* 1 min with two moderate-weight kettlebells |
| | 8. *Goblet squat (pg. 97):* 1 min with a heavy kettlebell |
| | 9. *Russian twist (pg. 139):* 30 reps with a light kettlebell |
| | 10. *Kettlebell jump squat (pg. 121):* 20 reps with a light kettlebell |
| | 11. *Double windmill (pg. 134):* 10 reps each side with two moderate kettlebells |
| | 12. *Kettlebell jump squat (pg. 121):* 15 reps with a moderate-weight kettlebell |
| | 13. *Double swing (pg. 105):* 1 min with a moderate-weight kettlebell, rest 1 min, 1 min with a heavy kettlebell |
| **Cool-down** | *Stretch:* 1 min each (behind-the-back shoulder stretch, pg. 62; shoulder stretch, pg. 62; triceps pulls, pg. 63; neck flexion stretch, pg. 63; lateral neck stretch, pg. 64; standing knee-to-chest stretch, pg. 64; standing quadriceps stretch, pg. 65; standing hamstrings stretch, pg. 64; spinal extension, pg. 67; spinal flexion, pg. 66; child's pose, pg. 68) |

## Figure 10.7 Kettlebell Program for Soccer

Soccer has a strong aerobic base because of the prolonged running involved, but it also uses quick anaerobic bursts. Lower-body agility and joint integrity, upper-body agility and strength, a stable neck, and core stability are important movement qualities for soccer athletes.

| | |
|---|---|
| **Warm-up** | 1. *Easy jog for 5 min* |
| | 2. *Joint mobility exercises (pg. 46):* 20 s each (shoulder rolls, neck tilts, neck rotations, neck circles, hip circles, trunk twists, lateral bends, waist bends, figure-eight waist circles, knee circles, ankle bounces) |
| | 3. *Dynamic mobility exercises (pg. 56):* 30 s each (arm twirls, chest hollow and expand, vertical chest opener, dynamic clapping, bootstrappers, leg swings) |
| **Main session** | Soccer involves continuous movement for prolonged periods. Go through the following exercises with as little rest as possible between exercises. |
| | 1. *Single swing (pg. 82):* 1 min each arm with a light kettlebell |
| | 2. *Get-up (pg. 136):* 5 reps each arm with a light kettlebell, 3 reps each arm with a moderate-weight kettlebell |
| | 3. *Goblet squat (pg. 97):* 1 min with a light kettlebell, rest 30 s, 30 s with a moderate-weight kettlebell |
| | 4. *Single press (pg. 90):* max reps in 1 min each hand with a light kettlebell |
| | 5. *One-arm contralateral single-leg kettlebell deadlift (pg. 103):* 2 sets of 5 reps with a moderate-weight kettlebell |
| | 6. *Double clean (pg. 108):* 30 s with two light kettlebells, rest 1 min, 30 s with two moderate-weight kettlebells |
| | 7. *Kettlebell jump squat (pg. 121):* 3 sets of 15 reps with a light kettlebell; rest 30 s between sets |
| | 8. *Single swing (pg. 82):* 1 min each hand with a light kettlebell, rest 1 min, 1 min each hand with a moderate-weight kettlebell |
| **Cool-down** | *Stretch:* 1 min each position (standing knee-to-chest stretch, pg. 64; standing quadriceps stretch, pg. 65; standing hamstrings stretch, pg. 64; calf stretch, pg. 66; spinal extension, pg. 67; spinal flexion, pg. 66; child's pose, pg. 68) |

## Figure 10.8 Kettlebell Program for Tennis

Tennis uses a mixture of anaerobic and aerobic energy systems and therefore athletes must have a well-rounded conditioning program. The longer a given set and match last, the greater the aerobic involvement. The primary system, however, is the anaerobic, which is used in the lateral movements and in making various shots. Primary movement patterns and qualities include forward, backward, and lateral lunging; core stability; leg endurance; and arm and shoulder strength and stability.

| | |
|---|---|
| **Warm-up** | 1. *Easy jog for 3 min* |
| | 2. *Joint mobility exercises (pg. 46)*: 20 s each for a total of 5 min (finger flexion and extension, interlocked wrist rolls, forearm flexion and extension, elbow circles, shoulder rolls, neck tilts, neck rotations, hip circles, trunk twists, lateral bends, waist bends, figure-eight waist circles, lateral rib openers, knee circles, ankle bounces) |
| | 3. *Dynamic mobility exercises (pg. 56)*: 20 s each for a total of 3 min (arm twirls, chest hollow and expand, vertical chest opener, dynamic clapping, leg swings) |
| **Main session** | Perform the following circuit with little or no rest between exercises and rest 1 min between each completed circuit, working up to 2 rounds. |
| | 1. *Around-the-body pass (pg. 77)*: 30 s each direction with a light kettlebell |
| | 2. *Overhead hold (pg. 126)*: 30 s each hand with a light kettlebell |
| | 3. *Bottoms-up clean (pg. 142)*: 5 reps each hand with a light kettlebell, 5 reps each hand with a moderate-weight kettlebell |
| | 4. *Figure-eight between-the-legs pass (pg. 79)*: 30 s each direction with a light kettlebell |
| | 5. *Single clean (pg. 84)*: 30 s each hand with a light kettlebell, rest 30 s, 30 s each hand with a moderate-weight kettlebell |
| | 6. *Push press (pg. 92)*: 30 s each hand with a light kettlebell, rest 30 s, 30 s each hand with a moderate-weight kettlebell |
| | 7. *Single-leg kettlebell deadlift (pg. 102)*: 5 reps each leg with two light kettlebells |
| | 8. *Snatch (pg. 94)*: 1 min each hand with a light kettlebell |
| | 9. *Single-leg kettlebell deadlift (pg. 102)*: 5 reps each leg with two moderate-weight kettlebells |
| | 10. *Kettlebell jump squat (pg. 121)*: 3 sets of 10 reps with a light kettlebell; rest 30 s between sets |
| | 11. *Russian twist (pg. 139)*: 30 reps with a light kettlebell |
| | 12. *Single swing (pg. 82)*: 30 s each hand with a moderate-weight kettlebell, 30 s with a heavy kettlebell |
| **Cool-down** | *Stretch*: 30 s each (behind-the-back shoulder stretch, pg. 62; shoulder stretch, pg. 62; triceps pulls, pg. 63; standing knee-to-chest stretch, pg. 64; standing quadriceps stretch, pg. 65; standing hamstrings stretch, pg. 64; calf stretch, pg. 66; child's pose, pg. 68) |

## Figure 10.9  Kettlebell Program for Track and Field: Middle-Distance Runners

Track and field is an extremely diverse category of sport. Some events are anaerobic, such as sprinting, jumping, and throwing events, and some are aerobic, such as the middle-distance events. Of all track and field athletes, the decathlete has to have the broadest base of skills and energy systems because he has to perform at a high level in 10 events that incorporate sprinting, jumping, middle-distance running, and throwing. Middle-distance running involves distances of 800 meters up to about 3,000 meters or 2 miles. It uses primarily the aerobic system for energy, meaning there is a high-oxygen uptake. Middle-distance runners need a good finishing kick, which is an all-out anaerobic sprint, in the last part of the race. As such, the majority of conditioning involves developing the aerobic system, with some supplemental strength needed for anaerobic power.

| | |
|---|---|
| **Warm-up** | 1. *Easy jog for 8 min* |
| | 2. *Joint mobility exercises (pg. 46):* 30 s each (shoulder rolls, neck tilts, neck rotations, neck circles, hip circles, trunk twists, lateral bends, waist bends, figure-eight waist circles, spinal rolls, lateral rib openers, knee circles, ankle bounces) |
| | 3. *Dynamic mobility exercises (pg. 56):* 30 s each (arm twirls, chest hollow and expand, vertical chest opener, dynamic clapping, bootstrappers, leg swings) |
| **Main session** | Perform the following circuit for 2 rounds and rest 1 min between each round, working up to 4 rounds. |
| | 1. *Rack hold (pg. 126):* 1 min with two light kettlebells |
| | 2. *Single swing (pg. 82):* 1 min per hand with a light kettlebell |
| | 3. *Windmill (pg. 130):* 10 reps each side with a light kettlebell |
| | 4. *Double jerk (pg. 158):* 1 min with two light kettlebells |
| | 5. *Two-arm single-leg kettlebell deadlift (pg. 102):* 10 reps each leg with two light kettlebells |
| | 6. *Goblet squat (pg. 97):* 1 min with a light kettlebell |
| | 7. *Russian twist (pg. 139):* 30 twists with a light kettlebell |
| **Cool-down** | *Stretch:* 1 min each (behind-the-back shoulder stretch, pg. 62; shoulder stretch, pg. 62; triceps pulls, pg. 63; neck flexion stretch, pg. 63; lateral neck stretch, pg. 64; standing knee-to-chest stretch, pg. 64; standing quadriceps stretch, pg. 65; standing hamstrings stretch, pg. 64; calf stretch, pg. 66; spinal extension, pg. 67; spinal flexion, pg. 66; child's pose, pg. 68) |

## Figure 10.10 Kettlebell Program for Track and Field: Sprinters and Jumpers

Track and field is an extremely diverse category of sport. Some events are anaerobic, such as sprinting, jumping, and throwing events, and some are aerobic, such as the middle-distance events. Of all track and field athletes, the decathlete has to have the broadest base of skills and energy systems because she has to perform at a high level in 10 events that incorporate sprinting, jumping, middle-distance running, and throwing. Sprinters and jumpers use fast-twitch muscle fibers and anaerobic energy. Their events are high intensity and short duration.

| | |
|---|---|
| **Warm-up** | 1. *Easy jog for 5 min*<br>2. *Joint mobility exercises (pg. 46):* 30 s each (shoulder rolls, neck tilts, neck rotations, neck circles, hip circles, trunk twists, lateral bends, waist bends, figure-eight waist circles, spinal rolls, lateral rib openers, knee circles, ankle bounces)<br>3. *Dynamic mobility exercises (pg. 56):* 30 s each (arm twirls, chest hollow and expand, vertical chest opener, dynamic clapping, bootstrappers, leg swings) |
| **Main session** | Perform the following circuit for 2 rounds and rest 30 s between each round, working up to 5 rounds.<br>1. *Rack hold (pg. 126):* 1 min with two light kettlebells<br>2. *Double swing (pg. 105):* 30 s with a light kettlebell<br>3. *Goblet squat (pg. 97):* 30 s with a light kettlebell<br>4. *Double swing (pg. 105):* 30 s with moderate-weight kettlebells<br>5. *Double jerk (pg. 158):* 30 s with two moderate-weight kettlebells<br>6. *Goblet squat (pg. 97):* 30 s with a moderate-weight kettlebell<br>7. *One-arm contralateral single-leg kettlebell deadlift (pg. 103):* 1 set of 8 reps each leg with a moderate-weight kettlebell<br>8. *Single clean (pg. 84):* 30 s each hand with a moderate-weight kettlebell<br>9. *Kettlebell jump squat (pg. 121):* 20 reps with a moderate-weight kettlebell<br>10. *One-arm clean and jerk (pg. 118):* 30 s each hand with a heavy kettlebell<br>11. *Double swing (pg. 105):* 30 s with a heavy kettlebell |
| **Cool-down** | *Stretch:* 1 min each (behind-the-back shoulder stretch, pg. 62; shoulder stretch, pg. 62; triceps pulls, pg. 63; neck flexion stretch, pg. 63; lateral neck stretch, pg. 64; standing knee-to-chest stretch, pg. 64; standing quadriceps stretch, pg. 65; standing hamstrings stretch, pg. 64; calf stretch, pg. 66; spinal extension, pg. 67; spinal flexion, pg. 66; child's pose, pg. 68) |

## Figure 10.11 Kettlebell Program for Track and Field: Throwers

Track and field is an extremely diverse category of sport. Some events are anaerobic, such as sprinting, jumping, and throwing events, and some are aerobic, such as the middle-distance events. Of all track and field athletes, the decathlete has to have the broadest base of skills and energy systems because he has to perform at a high level in 10 events that incorporate sprinting, jumping, middle-distance running, and throwing. Throwing events require a combined effort of upper- and lower-body strength and are performed in fast, explosive bursts. This high-power exertion depends upon the anaerobic energy systems, and training mimics the quick, high-intensity outputs.

| | |
|---|---|
| **Warm-up** | 1. *Around-the-body pass (pg. 77):* 30 s each direction with a light kettlebell |
| | 2. *Figure-eight between-the-legs pass (pg. 79):* 30 s each direction with a light kettlebell |
| | 3. *Single swing (pg. 82):* 1 min each hand with a light kettlebell |
| **Main session** | Move from one exercise to the next with no more than 30 s rest between each set, keeping the heart rate high. |
| | 1. *Get-up (pg. 136):* 5 reps each side with a light kettlebell, 3 reps each side with a moderate-weight kettlebell, 3 reps each side with a heavy kettlebell |
| | 2. *Double windmill (pg. 134):* 2 sets of 5 reps each side with heavy kettlebells |
| | 3. *Bottoms-up clean (pg. 142):* 5 reps each hand with a heavy kettlebell |
| | 4. *Snatch (pg. 102):* 5 sets of 5 reps each hand with a heavy kettlebell; rest 30 s between sets |
| | 5. *One-arm jerk (pg. 115):* 3 sets of 10 reps each hand with a heavy kettlebell; rest 30 s between sets |
| | 6. *Double swing (pg. 105):* 30 s with heavy kettlebells, rest 30 s, repeat for 30 s |
| | 7. *Farmer's carry (pg. 123):* two heavy kettlebells for maximal time |
| **Cool-down** | *Stretch:* 1 min each (behind-the-back shoulder stretch, pg. 62; shoulder stretch, pg. 62; triceps pulls, pg. 63; neck flexion stretch, pg. 63; lateral neck stretch, pg. 64; standing knee-to-chest stretch, pg. 64; standing quadriceps stretch, pg. 65; standing hamstrings stretch, pg. 64; calf stretch, pg. 66; spinal extension, pg. 67; spinal flexion, pg. 66; child's pose, pg. 68) |

## Figure 10.12 Kettlebell Program for Volleyball

Volleyball is mostly anaerobic because of the lunging, squatting, and jumping and lateral movements involved. It also requires shoulder girdle stability for the extensive overhead movements. As in most sports, a good aerobic base is required to sustain performance throughout the duration of a match.

| | |
|---|---|
| **Warm-up** | 1. *Body-weight agility exercises (pg. 45):* 1 min each (lateral shuffles, forward and backward skipping) |
| | 2. *Joint mobility exercises (pg. 46):* 20 s each (elbow circles, shoulder rolls, neck tilts, neck rotations, neck circles, hip circles, trunk twists, lateral bends, waist bends, figure-eight waist circles, spinal rolls, lateral rib openers, knee circles, ankle bounces) |
| | 3. *Dynamic mobility exercises (pg. 56):* 30 s each (arm twirls, chest hollow and expand, vertical chest opener, dynamic clapping, leg swings) |
| **Main session** | Perform the following circuit for 2 rounds and rest 1 min between rounds, working up to 4 rounds. |
| | 1. *Halo (pg. 78):* 10 reps each direction with a light kettlebell |
| | 2. *High windmill (pg. 133):* 5 reps each side with a light kettlebell |
| | 3. *Double clean and jerk (pg. 161):* 15 reps with two moderate kettlebells |
| | 4. *Snatch (pg. 94):* 20 reps each hand with a light kettlebell |
| | 5. *Kettlebell jump squat (pg. 121):* 15 reps with a light kettlebell |
| | 6. *Double swing (pg. 105):* 15 reps with two moderate-weight kettlebells |
| **Cool-down** | *Stretch:* 1 min each (behind-the-back shoulder stretch, pg. 62; shoulder stretch, pg. 62; triceps pulls, pg. 63; neck flexion stretch, pg. 63; lateral neck stretch, pg. 64; standing knee-to-chest stretch, pg. 64; standing quadriceps stretch, pg. 65; standing hamstrings stretch, pg. 64; calf stretch, pg. 66; spinal extension, pg. 67; spinal flexion, pg. 66; child's pose, pg. 68) |

## Figure 10.13  Kettlebell Program for Wrestling

Wrestling uses all three energy systems to near maximal levels, so well-rounded conditioning is needed. Throws, takedowns, and counters rely upon the ATP system; mat control and clinching use the glycolytic system; and surviving a prolonged match uses the aerobic system. Structurally, a wrestler needs a strong grip and strong shoulders as well as back and leg power and endurance.

| | |
|---|---|
| **Warm-up** | 1. *Easy jog for 5 min* |
| | 2. *Joint mobility exercises (pg. 46):* 20 s each (finger flexion and extension, interlocked wrist rolls, forearm flexion and extension, elbow circles, shoulder rolls, neck tilts, neck rotations, neck circles, hip circles, trunk twists, lateral bends, waist bends, figure-eight waist circles, spinal rolls, lateral rib openers, knee circles, ankle bounces) |
| | 3. *Dynamic mobility exercises (pg. 56):* 30 s each (arm twirls, chest hollow and expand, vertical chest opener, dynamic clapping, bootstrappers, leg swings) |
| **Main session** | Perform the following exercises as directed with 1 min rest between each exercises. |
| | 1. *Get-up (pg. 136):* 2 sets of 3 reps each side with a moderate-weight kettlebell |
| | 2. *Bottoms-up clean (pg. 142):* 5 reps each hand with a moderate-weight kettlebell, rest 30 s, 5 reps each hand with a heavy kettlebell |
| | 3. *Double clean (pg. 108):* 3 sets of 10 reps with two moderate-weight kettlebells; rest 30 s between sets |
| | 4. *Double jerk (pg. 158):* 3 sets of 10 reps with two moderate-weight kettlebells; rest 30 s between sets |
| | 5. *Kettlebell deadlift (pg. 81):* 3 sets of 20 reps with two heavy kettlebells |
| | 6. *Kettlebell jump squat (pg. 121):* 15 reps with a moderate-weight kettlebell, rest 1 min, 15 reps with a heavy kettlebell, rest 1 min, 15 reps with a moderate-weight kettlebell |
| | 7. *Double swing (pg. 105):* 1 min with heavy kettlebells |
| | 8. *Farmer's carry (pg. 123):* two heavy kettlebells for maximal time |
| **Cool-down** | *Stretch:* 1 min each (behind-the-back shoulder stretch, pg. 62; shoulder stretch, pg. 62; triceps pulls, pg. 63; neck flexion stretch, pg. 63; lateral neck stretch, pg. 64; standing knee-to-chest stretch, pg. 64; standing quadriceps stretch, pg. 65; standing hamstrings stretch, pg. 64; spinal extension, pg. 67; spinal flexion, pg. 66; child's pose, pg. 68) |

# Appendix

## Nutrition and Hydration

Eating for caloric value and eating for health and performance are fundamentally different. Additionally, there does not seem to be one type of eating plan or diet that is universally successful or agreed upon by nutritional experts, and bookstores are filled with hundreds of diet books. Which one is the best?

Choosing the best diet for you is a process of self-discovery and experimentation; however, one thing that we can depend upon is a logical approach to nutrition. If something makes sense to you and it feels good and provides good results, you can reasonably assume that it is a good food or a good way to eat. If you feel healthy and strong and you perform well, stick with the balance of foods in type, amount, and combinations that gives you good results. But if you feel sluggish or have health problems, carefully consider what you are eating and try to become more educated about what is healthy for your body.

This is not a book on nutrition, but I can tell you what makes me feel great! Here are some of the nutritional tips that I share as part of my philosophy of healthy eating. You may choose to go with some of these ideas and forgo others, or you may combine some ideas with others until you find a formula that works for you and provides the health that you desire. Nutrition is a crucial part of our lives, and a healthy nutritional approach will help you to recover faster after workouts and perform better during them.

When it comes to nutrition for kettlebell training, one of the first things you need to consider is preworkout nutrition. My advice is to eat before kettlebell training if you are hungry, but not too much and not too soon before. It is a good idea to have a small amount of easily digestible food in your stomach, but do not overeat. It is better to eat nothing than to eat too

much. As a general rule of thumb, try to allow at least 1 hour for digestion before training and eat foods that will give you some energy but are not too heavy to digest easily.

Some of these ideas may interest you and you will decide to study them in greater depth. Again, there is no universal eating plan that is ideal for everyone, but if you have information about nutrition, you have a better chance to create the eating plan that provides you with energy and vitality. As Bruce Lee once said, "Absorb what is useful."

### Acidic and Alkaline Foods

One approach to eating pays close attention to the alkaline and acidic content of foods. This philosophy of eating considers that there are certain foods that are more acidic and others are more alkaline. Because health requires an optimal pH balance, adherents of this approach focus on increasing intake of more alkaline foods and reducing intake of highly acidic foods. Foods that are highly acidic include caffeine, carbonation, alcohol, red meat, fried food, processed food, dairy, and grains. Foods that are alkaline include green and herbal teas, lemon water, olives and olive oil, almonds, peas, green beans, sweet potatoes, asparagus, broccoli, onions, lemons, limes, grapefruit, orange, watermelon, mangos, and papayas.

### Caffeine

Some studies support the intake of coffee and other caffeinated foods while other studies advise against it. Keep in mind that caffeine stimulates the central nervous system, so if you do enjoy coffee or other forms of caffeine, it is a good idea to moderate your intake. Do not live on coffee and donuts! In some cases, a bit of caffeine can enhance performance because it can wake you up and make you feel more alert; just don't consume so much as to make yourself nervous or jittery. If you enjoy coffee, try to avoid adding sugar to it.

## Food Combining

Food combining looks at which foods should be eaten together and which should be eaten alone. It takes into account the different rates of digestion for different categories of food, including meat, dairy, vegetables, starches, and fruits. By learning how to combine foods properly and when to eat them, you can eliminate bloating, gas, constipation, and other digestive problems.

## Gluten

A lot of recent research has focused on the adverse health consequences of diets high in gluten-containing foods, which in the modern world means the large majority of most people's diets. Gluten is contained in grains, which are used in breads, cereals, pastas, pastries, and thousands of prepared foods. If it comes from a box, a bag, or a can, it most likely has gluten in it. Most commercial meats come from animals that were fed grains, so even these provide unhealthy gluten. If you care about your health and vitality, considering eating only grass-fed meats and wild fish. If you wish to learn about the adverse effects of gluten and how to live a gluten-free lifestyle, check out *The Paleo Solution*, the *New York Times* bestseller by Robb Wolf.

## Hydration

I always recommend water as the best thing to drink, especially clean, filtered water. Many people struggle with weight gain, and consuming additional calories via juice and other sweet drinks is not a good return on investment because they add calories without increasing satiety. You can't go wrong with drinking water—it has no calories and is vital to a myriad of body processes.

## Juice

Most nutritional experts will tell you that processed juices, especially fruit juices, contain too much sucrose and consuming them elevates blood sugar and insulin levels. I agree that processed juices, most of which are from concentrate and are even sweeter than the actual fruit juice, should be avoided. Even freshly squeezed fruit juices have a lot of sugar and should be consumed in moderation. However, vegetable juices, especially the powerful kale juice, are extremely nourishing and provide a host of antioxidant and immune-boosting benefits. Consider getting a juicer and having some fresh green juice first thing in the morning. In lieu of fresh vegetable juices, most well-stocked supplement stores carry high-quality green foods powder, which is made from freeze-dried juiced vegetables and provides potent nutrition.

## Meat

There are differences of opinion regarding the healthiness of eating meat. There are arguments supporting veganism and vegetarianism, and there are arguments supporting omnivore diets (eating animals and plants). I personally subscribe to a more Paleolithic type of eating, which focuses on lean animal protein and seasonal vegetables and fruits as dietary staples, the way our hunter–gatherer ancestors ate. It is worthwhile to consider eating only grass-fed meats instead of the grain-fed meats that are more common in American supermarkets.

## Processed Food

If it comes in a box, can, or plastic container, it is highly processed and should be avoided when possible. Opt for whole, natural, unprocessed foods whenever you can. Exceptions include frozen fruits and vegetables and dried grains such as brown rice, which tend to have every bit as much nutrition as the fresh versions.

## Raw Food

Rawists are people who eat almost exclusively uncooked, unprocessed foods. I personally enjoy steamed vegetables with butter on occasion, but I try to mix in at least some raw foods every day, such as celery, an apple, or green leafy veggies.

### Sugar

Although our body does need sugar for basic hormonal processes, we should try to get our sugar from naturally occurring sources such as fruits, which provide a slower release of blood insulin because they also contain fiber. As much as you can, stay away from sucrose- and fructose-filled items such as candies, cakes, sodas, canned or bottled fruit juices, and products containing high-fructose corn syrup. These items cause a fast insulin spike that can lead to health conditions that are less than ideal.

### Super Foods

Many so-called super foods have high nutritional value and immune-boosting functions and can be easily integrated into your diet. Examples include bee pollen, royal jelly, maca, cacao and MSM (methylsulfonylmethane). Although these foods are very nutritious, they are also very strong. There is no such thing as a perfect food, so if you decide to integrate some super foods into your diet, try them in small doses first. Some people are more sensitive than others and super foods may be too stimulating for them.

### Supplements

This is a topic that is difficult to cover in a short space, but my general recommendation is that you should not focus too much on supplementation until your eating is dialed in. Without a strong foundation of food-based nutrition, supplementation, which can be quite expensive, most likely will be a waste of money. To keep things simple, consider a high-quality fish oil, particularly of the omega-3 variety, and a high-quality multivitamin and mineral supplement. The rest of your nutritional needs should be met through healthy foods.

Nutrition is an important part of overall fitness, health, and wellness. Pay attention to what you eat and learn as much as you can about the types and combinations of foods that make you feel healthy. When you are eating the right foods, you will look, feel, and perform better not only in your kettlebell workouts but in your daily activities as well.

# Glossary

**acceleration pull**—The rapid change in velocity of the kettlebells as they are pulled vertically to the chest (in the clean) or overhead (in the snatch).

**adaptation**—The body's ability to adjust to increased physical demands; the physiological changes that occur as the result of training.

**adjustable kettlebells**—Kettlebells that you can load and unload to make them heavier or lighter. The most common types are plate-loaded and shot-loaded kettlebells.

**aerobic**—Literally meaning "with air," this is the cardio-respiratory component of exercise. It is performed at low to moderate intensities and relies upon oxygen for sustainable energy.

**agility**—Nimbleness, or the ability to move your body with control.

**amateur**—In girevoy sport, male competitors who compete with 24-kilogram (53 lb) kettlebells and female competitors who compete with 12-kilogram (26 lb) kettlebells.

**anabolic**—Muscle-building properties of exercise and nutrition. Occurs during the release of growth-producing hormones.

**anaerobic**—Literally meaning "without air," in this type of exercise oxygen is used more quickly than the body is able to replenish it, and the body uses carbohydrate without oxygen as fuel to produce energy, creating lactic acid as a by-product.

**anatomical breathing**—Also called *matching breathing* because the breath acts in coordination with the body action (i.e., exhaling on compression and inhaling on expansion). This method of breathing is more suitable for endurance and work capacity because it helps the athlete manage her heart rate.

**anterior**—The front of the body.

**anterior chain**—The abdominal muscles, hip flexors, and deep muscles along the spine and quadriceps working together to form a sort of corset.

**asymmetries**—Imbalances or unevenness between the right and left halves of the body; also can refer to imbalances in movement between one side and the other. A leg that is significantly shorter than the other leg is an example of an asymmetry.

**backswing**—The kettlebell moves behind you and between the legs; the opposite of the forward swing.

**ballistic**—Kettlebell lifts for power development that use acceleration and a fast velocity; also called the *fast lifts*. Ballistic literally means "to throw" and involves a release component.

**base of support**—The area within an outline of all ground contact points; generally refers to the area within the outline of the feet while standing. The center of mass must reside within the base of support in order to maintain stability and equilibrium.

**biathlon**—Two-sport competition in kettlebell sport consisting of the double jerk and one-arm snatch, each performed for up to 10 minutes for as many repetitions as possible in 1 set of each lift; also called *classic*.

**bilateral deficiency**—The limitation of the strength and endurance from the weaker or nondominant arm; also called *bilateral deficit*.

**body composition**—The overall proportion of body fat and lean or fat-free mass in the body.

**bottoms-up position**—Any position in which the bottom of the kettlebell is higher than the handle. This position makes the exercise more difficult.

**bump**—Also called the *send-off*, this is the second phase of the kettlebell jerk, following the half squat and preceding the undersquat, in which the knees, hips, ankles, and torso are all maximally extended in order to bump or push the kettlebells up without use of the arms.

**calisthenics**—Exercises consisting of simple movements, generally using only the weight of the body for resistance and no equipment; can include movements such as bending, jumping, swinging, twisting, and kicking.

**candidate master of sport (CMS)**—An expert level of ranking in girevoy sport, earned in competition by performing a requisite number of repetitions in either the biathlon (jerk and snatch) or long cycle.

**cardiorespiratory conditioning**—The enhancement of heart and circulatory function produced by regular vigorous aerobic exercise.

**catabolic**—Muscle-wasting or depleting properties of exercise and nutrition; the opposite of anabolic.

**center of mass**—The point at which all body mass is equally balanced or equally distributed in all directions; when the position of the body changes, the location of the center of mass changes. Also called *center of gravity*.

**classical lifts**—Foundational exercises that introduce the mechanical standards and principles that are used throughout all remaining kettlebell exercises.

These include the swing, clean, press, push press, snatch, and jerk.

**clean**—Lifting one or two kettlebells to the chest into the rack position and then dropping the kettlebells into the backswing.

**clean and jerk**—A kettlebell lift that is performed in three phases: Clean kettlebells to chest, jerk kettlebells overhead, and drop kettlebells into backswing position. These three movements are repeated continuously throughout the set. Also called the *long cycle*.

**coefficient winner**—In girevoy sport, the pound-for-pound winner of a given competition, which is determined by an algorithm taking into account total repetitions and the body weight of the lifters.

**combined center of mass**—The collective mass of the implement (kettlebell) and the center of gravity of the body as they reside vertically over the base of support.

**competition**—In girevoy sport, a contest in which one lifter tries to outperform another lifter by performing more repetitions of a lift or lifts.

**competition kettlebell**—The international standard kettlebell as used in kettlebell sport competitions. Competition kettlebells are of a uniform height, weight, diameter, and handle circumference.

**competition lifts**—In girevoy sport, the classical lifts for competition: the jerk, snatch, and long cycle.

**concentric**—The phase of a movement in which the muscle shortens as it contracts.

**contralateral**—Using the opposite arm and leg; the upper and lower body working in opposition.

**cool-down**—The final phase of a complete kettlebell training session, which allows time for the body and mind to return to their normal state by reducing the excitation caused by the main phase of the training session and helps to shorten the recovery period needed before the next workout is performed.

**core**—The musculature of the lumbo-pelvic-hip complex and transversus abdominis—the abdominal, gluteal, and lower-back muscles, the psoas muscle of the hips, and the multifidus of the spine—that collectively work to stabilize the trunk, including the spine and pelvis, and support posture.

**cortisol**—A hormone made in the adrenal glands; stress prompts the body to produce it.

**crush grip**—A strong, handshake-type grip where the kettlebell or other implement is squeezed firmly with the palm and fingers.

**cycle**—A movement that relies upon inertia and is repeated numerous times, each movement the same as the previous, such as the kettlebell clean or snatch.

**cyclical exercise**—Repetitive movement against resistance, such as repetition kettlebell lifting, running, bicycling, or swimming. The same movements are repeated one after the other for an extended period of time and are aerobic in nature.

**deflection**—Hyperextension of the trunk during kettlebell lifts. The trunk leans back in order to reduce the arc of the dropping kettlebell, thereby reducing the accelerative forces and slowing the kettlebell.

**duration**—How long a given set or workout lasts; also called *time*.

**dynamic**—Fast, intense, vigorous movement.

**dynamic mobility**—Performing movements in all directions while gently increasing range of motion and speed until reaching maximum range of motion.

**dynamic stability**—The ability of the body, when disturbed from its original position, to resist being unbalanced and to return to its original state.

**dynamic stretching**—Improves the range of motion at a joint with accompanying movement; consists of simple movements that require large ranges of motion.

**eccentric**—The phase of a movement in which the muscle elongates as it contracts.

**endurance**—The body's ability to exert itself while getting energy from the aerobic system during exercise.

**energy systems**—The body has three ways to produce energy for movement during exercise: the aerobic system, also called the *oxidative system*, which provides energy for activities that last over 2 minutes; the glycolytic system, also called the *lactic acid system*, which is an anaerobic system that provides energy for activities lasting from 30 seconds up to 2 minutes; and the ATP-CP system, an anaerobic system that provides energy for activities lasting 30 seconds or less.

**exercise selection**—Choosing exercises for a program.

**fantasy events or lifts**—In kettlebell sport, nontraditional lifts that are just for fun and are not typically competed.

**farmer's hold or carry**—Holding one or two kettlebells in the low hang position, with arms by the sides and a kettlebell gripped in one or both hands, usually held for time (hold) or distance (carry) to train grip strength and endurance.

**feats of strength**—Demonstrations of great strength that involve lifting heavy weights, such as barbells, barrels, anvils, stones, people, or large animals; performing hand-balancing and other gymnastics; bending nails, spikes, and horseshoes; breaking chains; tearing decks of cards and phone books; pulling trains; and in general showing extreme strength in unusual angles of movement. Kettlebells were often components of such strength exhibitions by professional strongmen and were once a popular feature in the circuses of the 19th and early 20th centuries.

**final phase**—The last phase of a workout, which includes the cool-down and allows the body and mind time to return to their normal state.

**FITT principle**—An acronym standing for frequency, intensity, type, and time, four variables used to guide, manipulate, and vary workouts.

**fixation**—When the kettlebells are held overhead with arms fully straightened with biceps next to the ears and legs fully extended. This is the top or finish position for all overhead lifts (e.g., snatch, press, push press, jerk, long cycle).

**fixed-load kettlebell**—A kettlebell with a permanent, nonchanging load, typically made of steel or cast iron.

**flexibility**—The ability of the joints or muscles to move through the full range of motion; lengthening or stretching the muscles.

**flights**—In girevoy sport, a row of competitors all lifting at the same time; the order, arrangement, and schedule of the lifts.

**force**—Mass times acceleration; the strength exerted upon an object.

**frequency**—How often you exercise in days per week or per month.

**frontal plane**—A vertical plane that divides the body into front and back sections; also called *coronal plane*.

**functional fitness training**—Exercise that addresses the body as a whole system in order to train the movements and motor patterns that result in effective movement. Functional fitness programs focus on performance rather than aesthetics.

**general adaptation principle (GAS)**—See *principle of adaptation*.

**general assistance exercises**—Conditioning exercises to develop general physical attributes (e.g., strength, endurance, mobility, flexibility).

**general fitness training**—In contrast to sport-specific training, these exercises are aimed toward the broad goals of overall health and well-being and may be used to promote weight loss, increase tone, or build muscle.

**general physical preparation (GPP)**—Provides a well-rounded base of general fitness to enable a person to cope with the demands of a particular task. Includes strength, flexibility, muscular endurance, aerobic endurance, speed, and body composition.

**general warm-up**—The first part of a warm-up contained within the preparation phase of a workout for the purpose of warming up the large muscle groups of the body; includes a pulse-raiser (aerobic activity) and joint rotations.

**girevoy sport**—Also called *kettlebell sport*, this is a Russian national sport in which the *girya* (kettlebell) is used either in single or double form to accumulate as many repetitions as possible in 10 minutes in order to compare one lifter with the next in a sporting framework. Athletes compete against others within the same weight category.

**girya**—The Russian term for a kettlebell; the literal translation is "handleball."

**glucose**—A simple sugar that provides the body with its primary source of energy and comes from digesting carbohydrate that the body converts to energy.

**group competitions**—In power juggling, teams of men, women, or mixed pairs compete against other teams.

**half squat (or first dip)**—The initial part of the kettlebell jerk, which involves a rapid, slight flexion of the knees; precedes the send-off phase of the jerk.

**hand insertion**—Placement of the hand deep inside the handle of the kettlebell such that the inside of the handle rests between the forefinger and thumb at approximately a 45-degree downward angle.

**hand switch**—Changing hands during a kettlebell set.

**hang position**— See *farmer's hold or carry*.

**heart rate training zones**—The various percentages of maximal heart rate, reflecting various levels of exercise intensity, including the warm-up training zone or healthy heart zone, fitness or fat-burning zone, endurance or aerobic training zone, performance or anaerobic training zone, and maximal effort zone.

**HIIT**—An acronym for high-intensity interval training.

**hook position**—Holding one or two kettlebells with flexed fingers in the hang position and in the forward swing and backswing (in the swing, clean, snatch, and long cycle).

**hypertrophy**—An increase in muscle size as a result of resistance training.

**inertia**—The resistance of any physical object to a change in its state of motion or rest, or the tendency of an object to resist any change in its motion. Newton describes inertia in his first law of motion.

**instinctive training**—Putting together a training program based on what you feel like doing. There is no particular structure to instinctive training programs.

**intensity**—The percentage of maximal effort used in a given rep, set, or workout. Can be measured as a percentage of 1 repetition max (1RM) or subjectively as a rating of perceived exertion (RPE).

**interval**—The period of rest between high-intensity training sets.

**ipsilateral**—The same side; using the same-side arm and leg.

**isometric holds**—Also called *static holds*; refers to holding the load in one place without movement.

**isometric strength**—Also called *static strength*; refers to muscle action in which the length of the muscle does not change and there is no visible movement at the joint.

**jerk**—A kettlebell exercise using one or two kettlebells, performed with five phases of motion—half squat, bump (or send-off), undersquat, lockout (of knees), and fixation overhead.

**joint rotations**—The second part of a general warm-up, following the gentle pulse-raiser, in which all the joints are loosened and lubricated so that they move smoothly and with relative ease; also called *joint mobility*.

**juniors**—In girevoy sport competition, competitors under 18 years of age; typically junior males compete with 24-kilogram (53 lb) kettlebells and junior females compete with 12-kilogram (26 lb) kettlebells.

**kinetic chain**—The body as a series of interconnected links that form a system of levers composed of the joints, muscles, bones, nerves, and connective tissues working together to produce effective movement; also called a *movement chain*.

**limit strength**—The amount of musculoskeletal force you can generate for a single maximal effort; also called *maximal strength*.

**load**—The amount of weight being lifted.

**lockout**—When the elbows are fully extended with the kettlebells overhead.

**long cycle**—See *clean and jerk.*

**long slow distance (LSD)**—The conventional method for developing aerobic capacity, consisting of prolonged distance and duration of low- to moderate-intensity cyclical aerobic exercise, such as running, cycling, or swimming.

**low hang position**—See *farmer's hold or carry.*

**macrocycle**—Annual or semiannual training period; the entire length of a training cycle.

**main phase**—In a kettlebell workout, the main phase is the workout or training and includes acquiring skills (learning), mastering the kettlebell exercises, and practicing and progressing in those exercises. The main phase follows the preparation or warm-up phase.

**marathon**—In kettlebell lifting, an event in which the lifter repeats a particular lift as many times as possible in an allotted time period without putting the kettlebell down, typically 30 minutes, 1 hour, or longer.

**master of sport (MS)**—A high ranking in girevoy sport, earned in competition by performing a requisite number of repetitions in either the biathlon (jerk and snatch) or the long cycle.

**master of sport international class (MSIC)**—The highest level or ranking in girevoy sport, earned in competition by performing a requisite number of repetitions in either the biathlon (jerk and snatch) or the long cycle.

**masters**—In girevoy sport competition, male competitors over 40 years of age and female competitors over 35 years of age; typically masters males compete with 24-kilogram (53 lb) kettlebells and masters females compete with 12-kilogram (26 lb) kettlebells.

**maximal heart rate (MHR)**—The fastest rate the heart will beat in 1 minute; typically determined by the layman's formula of 220 − age = MHR.

**maximal strength**—See *limit strength.*

**mesocycle**—The monthly training period of a macrocycle.

**method**—The approaches used to achieve the goals of a kettlebell training program, including the exercises, sets, reps, load, frequency, and rest periods.

**microcycle**—The weekly or biweekly training period of a macrocycle.

**midpoint**—The phase between the concentric and eccentric phases of a rep; also called *fixation.*

**mixed pairs**—In power juggling competitions, teams of males and females.

**mobility**—Actively moving the joints through a full range of motion with the intention of maintaining or possibly even restoring movement capabilities in those joints.

**modality**—The means used to acquire your training goals, including the equipment and programs selected.

**mode**—A method or way of achieving your training goals.

**movement**—The act of changing place, position, or posture.

**movement patterns**—How the body moves through space; the typical ranges of motion and positions the body moves in during exercise and daily activities.

**muscular endurance**—The ability to perform many repetitions of an exercise or movement.

**overstretching**—Stretching the body or muscles to the point of strain or injury.

**overtraining**—A physical condition that occurs when the volume and intensity of exercise exceed the capacity to recover, resulting in a decrease in progress.

**paradoxical breathing**—When the breath is opposite of the body action, such as inhaling as the body is compressing and exhaling as the body is extending. Used while lifting maximal or near-maximal loads and appropriate for deconditioned people due to the thoracic pressure and spinal stability it provides.

**pause**—Stopping while performing a lift with kettlebells in rack, fixation, or low hang positions; also called a *static hold.*

**periodization**—The organized incorporation of specific training phases during a period of time, generally annually or semiannually; consists of the macrocycle, mesocycles, and microcycles.

**plateau**—A state of little or no change during the training process; when progress stalls.

**platforms**—In girevoy sport, the lifting areas where the athletes stand, which are not less than 2 by 2 meters and should be flat and not slippery; the distance between each platform must not be less than 1.5 meters.

**plyometrics**—Exercises involving repeated rapid stretching and contracting of muscles to increase muscle power; also called *jump training.*

**posterior chain**—The muscles of the rear side of the body, including the glutes, hamstrings, calves, and lower-back muscles.

**power**—The ability to exert maximal force in minimum time; the speed with which you can perform a lift. Muscular power incorporates speed with the movement and equals the force generated times velocity.

**power juggling**—A competitive sport in which performers demonstrate a routine and are graded on particular elements that are scored by the judges; points are awarded on such factors as uniform and music that coordinate with the artistic nature of the routine, grace, confidence, expression, and beauty. Men use 16-kilogram (35 lb) kettlebells and women use 8-kilogram (18 lb) kettlebells in power juggling competitions or demonstrations.

**preparation phase**—In a kettlebell training session, the first part of the workout in which you prepare your mind and body for the hard work to follow; consists of the warm-up.

**press**—A kettlebell exercise in which one or two kettlebells are cleaned to the chest and then pushed overhead into fixation using the upper-body muscles only and no leg drive.

**principle of adaptation**—Describes the body's short-term and long-term reactions to stress, including the physical stress of exercise; the body will adjust to increasing physical demands. Also called *general adaptation principle (GAS).*

**principle of individual differences**—Every person is unique in how his body responds to various stimuli.

**principle of overcompensation**—Muscles will respond to heavy resistance by growing stronger, larger, and more skillful.

**principle of overload**—Stress that is greater than normal is required in order for the body to adapt.

**principle of progression**—There is an optimal level of overload that will lead to progress in fitness.

**principle of progressive resistance**—An overlying principle that consists of the combination of two principles: overload and progression.

**principle of reversibility**—The opposite of adaptation; also called *detraining* or the *use and disuse principle.* The body grows stronger with use and weaker with disuse—use it or lose it.

**principle of specificity**—You get better at a specific skill by practicing that skill. The technical terms is *specific adaptation to imposed demands (SAID).*

**principle of use and disuse**—See *principle of reversibility.*

**professional**—In girevoy sport, male competitors who compete with 32-kilogram (71 lb) kettlebells and female competitors who compete with 16- to 24-kilogram (35-53 lb) kettlebells.

**program**—A planned training schedule to follow in order to achieve training goals.

**program design**—The details of a training schedule, including the sets, reps, duration, frequency, intensity, and rest periods.

**prone**—Lying facedown on the floor or bench.

**proprioception**—Your awareness of your body; how you are oriented or how your body moves through space.

**protocol**—The details and procedures of a training program.

**pulse-raiser**—Performed at the beginning of the general warm-up, pulse-raisers are any light aerobic activities that circulate blood and oxygen to supply the muscles with more energy to use.

**quadruple extension**—The complete extension of four areas of the body: ankles, knees, hips, and trunk.

**rack position**—One or two kettlebells are resting on the chest and sitting on the forearms between the forearm and shoulder. The ideal position is with elbows resting on the ilium of the pelvis, with knees fully extended and the kettlebells aligned vertically over the base of support.

**rank or ranking**—A level of achievement in kettlebell sport based on accomplishing a certain number of repetitions with a particular weight.

**rating of perceived exertion (RPE)**—A subjective way to gauge the intensity of effort in a given rep, set, or workout. Most RPE scales are from 1 to 10, with 1 being extremely easy, 5 being moderately challenging, and 10 being maximal effort.

**reciprocal inhibition**—The muscles on opposite sides of a joint work in opposition.

**recovery**—A phase of training in which you take some time off from kettlebell training to allow the body to recharge, heal, and regain motivation; usually follows completion of a competition or accomplishment of a training goal.

**relay**—In girevoy sport competition, a team event in which lifters from one club or one nation form a team to compete against other clubs or nations; each lifter lifts for up to 3 minutes and the highest cumulative score wins. The most common relay lifts are the double jerk and long cycle.

**repetitions (reps)**—The number of times a weight is lifted during a training set.

**rest period**—The time off between training sets, sessions, or cycles.

**rhythmic**—Kettlebell movements that are performed at regular and repeated patterns.

**sagittal plane**—A vertical plane that passes from front to rear, dividing the body into right and left halves.

**send-off**—See *bump.*

**seniors**—In girevoy sport competition, competitors over 55 years of age; typically senior males compete with 16-kilogram (35 lb) kettlebells and senior females compete with 8-kilogram (18 lb) kettlebells.

**set**—The repetitions done with a kettlebell without putting it down. Exercises can be done in single or multiple sets.

**SMART goals**—Acronym standing for specific, measurable, attainable, relevant, and timely goals. These five words tell us about the nature of goals and how to create and then realize them in your kettlebell training programs.

**snatch**—A kettlebell exercise performed in six phases of motion—inertia, acceleration pull, hand insertion, fixation, drop (amortization), and backswing. The kettlebell is swung above the head and the arm is fully extended as the kettlebell reaches overhead.

**special assistance exercises**—Individual components of the classical lifts or specific exercises that are similar in movement to the main exercises; used to teach technique refinement and correct technical mistakes.

**speed**—The tempo or repetitions per minute of the kettlebell lift. Speed is the most direct method of increasing power output of an exercise. The terms *speed*, *tempo*, and *pacing* are used interchangeably.

**sport-specific warm-up**—Performed during the preparation phase of a training session; involves exercises and drills that mimic the main activity to follow but are performed at a low intensity and can be viewed as the transition between the warm-up and main phase.

**sport-specific training**—Specialized physical preparation for a specific sport.

**stability**—The ability to maintain equilibrium or resume your original upright position.

**static holds**—See *isometric holds.*

**static strength**—See *isometric strength.*

**static stretching**—Flexibility training that involves stretching to the furthest tolerable position of the muscle length without pain and then holding that position for 10 seconds up to 3 minutes or longer with no bouncing or jerking movements.

**strength**—The ability of a muscle or muscle group to generate force against an external resistance; typically described by how much weight you can lift in a given exercise.

**stress hormones**—Chemicals that are released by the body in stressful situations that the body interprets as danger, such as intense exercise. Cortisol is the primary stress hormone related to intense exercise.

**stretch–shortening cycle**—An active stretch (eccentric contraction) of a muscle followed by an immediate shortening (concentric contraction) of that same muscle.

**suitcase deadlift**—Lifting kettlebells or dumbbells from the floor with the load placed to the side of the body, as if lifting a suitcase by the handle.

**supine**—Lying faceup on the floor or bench.

**swing**—The first kettlebell exercise that teaches the principle of inertia. Like a pendulum, a swing moves the kettlebell forward and up and then back and down.

**Tabata protocol**—A high-intensity, short-duration anaerobic training method developed by Dr. Izumi Tabata that shows favorable increases in both aerobic and anaerobic work capacity in the test subjects and is a popular form of fitness training.

**tempo**—The number of reps per unit of time, also called *speed* or *pace*, and usually measured in RPM (reps per minute); tempo is the time it takes to do a set, and also the time it takes to do a single rep. In kettlebell lifting tempo is used as a measure of rpm, although in some bodybuilding and strength training protocols tempo measures the time it takes to do each phase of a rep (e.g., concentric, midpoint, eccentric).

**thoracolumbar fascia**—Connective tissue that serves as a bridge between the glutes on one side and the lats on the opposite side and helps to stabilize the spine.

**time**—The duration of a given set or workout.

**tonnage or total tonnage**—The total amount of load lifted (work done) in a period of time (e.g., session, week, month); calculated as sets × reps × load lifted.

**tools**—The training equipment used in an exercise program; kettlebells, dumbbells, and sandbags are examples of training tools.

**transverse plane**—An imaginary plane that divides the body into upper and lower parts (also called the *horizontal plane*, *axial plane*, or *transaxial plane*).

**trunk extension**—Leaning the trunk backward; in many kettlebell movements, trunk extension is referred to as *deflection* of the trunk.

**trunk flexion**—Bending the trunk forward or laterally.

**type**—The kind of exercise you do in your training, such as strength training, endurance training, power training, flexibility training, and so on.

**undersquat (or second dip)**—A rapid movement following the send-off (bump) of the kettlebells from the chest in which the lifter drops under the kettlebells the same time as fully extending the elbows.

**unilateral training**—Training one side of the body at a time, such as single-arm training or training while standing on one leg.

**valgus collapse**—Collapsing of the knees toward the midline, putting unnatural stress on the medial ligaments of the knees.

**vestibular system**—The inner ears house a system called the *vestibular apparatus*, which provides information about the position of the head in relation to gravity and movements of the head.

**visual system**—A component of the body's balance mechanism, in the visual system the eyes receive information about the environment and how it relates to the body's postures and positions.

**volume**—The total amount of work done during a specified length of time.

**warm-up**—Included in the preparation phase of a workout to get your body and mind ready for the main phase of the training; includes such variables as increasing blood flow to the muscles, increasing heart rate and circulation, increasing muscle temperature and raising core body temperature, increasing concentration, and reducing anxiety.

**weight class**—In girevoy sport, this is the division a lifter competes in based upon body weight. Kettlebell sport lifters compete against other lifters in the same weight class.

**work capacity**—The ability to generate a high workload and to recover sufficiently; the ability to resist fatigue while training. Work capacity involves a coordination of the cardiovascular, metabolic, and nervous systems and is a mixture of capacity, power, and efficiency.

**youth division**—In girevoy sport, a competition category for children under junior level; competition weights may range from 4 kilograms (9 lb) up to 16 kilograms (35 lb) depending upon the age and level of the lifter.

# About the Author

**Steve Cotter** draws from a diverse background as a champion athlete and cutting-edge trainer in developing some of the most exciting programs in strength and conditioning today. He continues to research and implement the most effective training methods in kettlebell training, martial arts, qigong, strength and conditioning, athletics, and the human performance fields.

Cotter shares his years of experience as a martial artist, world-class athlete, and fitness coach in designing and supervising programs for those who take their training seriously. He is the founder and director of the International Kettlebell and Fitness Federation (IKFF) and an international lecturer and teacher in more

than 40 countries. He consults with numerous professional sport teams, including the NFL's San Francisco 49ers and San Diego Chargers; Major League Baseball's Texas Rangers, Seattle Mariners, and Los Angeles Dodgers; and the NHL's Anaheim Ducks. He is a subject matter expert to the U.S. Navy SEALs, a strength and conditioning trainer for the United States Marines, and a certified strength and conditioning specialist (CSCS) through the National Strength and Conditioning Association (NSCA).

Cotter is also the creator of both the authoritative Encyclopedia of Kettlebell Lifting DVD series and the Full KOntact Kettlebells System and best-selling DVD series.

You'll find other outstanding strength training resources at

# www.HumanKinetics.com/strengthtraining

In the U.S. call 1-800-747-4457

Australia 08 8372 0999 • Canada 1-800-465-7301
Europe +44 (0) 113 255 5665 • New Zealand 0800 222 062

 **HUMAN KINETICS**
*The Premier Publisher for Sports & Fitness*
P.O. Box 5076 • Champaign, IL 61825-5076 USA

 **eBook**
available at
HumanKinetics.com